Traveling Light

—

A LOVE WORTH GIVING

—

IT'S NOT ABOUT ME

THOMAS NELSON
Since 1798

NASHVILLE DALLAS MEXICO CITY RIO DE JANEIRO BEIJING

Published in Nashville, Tennessee, by Thomas Nelson. Thomas Nelson is a trademark of Thomas Nelson, Inc.

Thomas Nelson, Inc., titles may be purchased in bulk for educational, business, fund-raising, or sales promotional use. For information, please e-mail SpecialMarkets@ThomasNelson.com.

ISBN 978-0-8499-2046-2

Printed in the United States of America

07 08 09 10 11 QW 5 4 3 2 1

Contents

Traveling Light

A Love Worth Giving

It's Not About Me

TRAVELING LIGHT

Releasing the Burdens
You Were Never Intended to Bear

Traveling Light

Published in Nashville, Tennessee, by Thomas Nelson. Thomas Nelson is a trademark of Thomas Nelson, Inc.

Thomas Nelson, Inc. titles may be purchased in bulk for educational, business, fund-raising, or sales promotional use. For information, please e-mail SpecialMarkets@ThomasNelson.com.

Library of Congress Cataloging-in-Publication Data

Lucado, Max.
Traveling light / by Max Lucado.
p. cm.
Includes bibliographical references.
ISBN-10: 0-8499-1345-4 (tp)
ISBN-13: 978-0-8499-1345-7 (tp)
ISBN-10: 0-8499-1297-0 (hc)
ISBN-13: 978-0-8499-1297-9 (hc)
1. Christian life—Meditations. I. Title.

BV4501.3 .L86 2001
242—dc21

2001026267

Printed in the United States of America

To my dear friend Joey Paul,
celebrating thirty years of words at Word,
sharing the Word

Acknowledgments

Here are well-deserved pats on some sturdy backs:

To Liz Heaney and Karen Hill—my editors and my assistant, midwives of the manuscript. Sorry I groaned so much.

To Steve and Cheryl Green—my representative and my friends. Because of you, contracts are read, and bills are paid, and this old boy sleeps well at night.

To Greg Pruett—Bible translator and Hebrew student. Thanks for the great insights.

To Eugene Peterson—Bible translator, author, and hero to many. Thanks for letting me use the title. And, much more, thanks for sharing your heart.

To Steve Halliday—study guide author par excellence.

To my friends at Thomas Nelson. Once again, you're the best.

To Laura Kendall and Carol Bartley—the great sleuths of the English language. Thanks for making me look smart.

To Jenna, Andrea, and Sara—my delightful daughters. I couldn't be prouder.

To Denalyn—my wife of two decades. Before you were born, where did poets go for inspiration?

To you—the reader. May the real Author speak to you.

And, most of all, to you, Jesus. The only reason we can release a burden is because you are there to take it. All the applause is yours.

1

The Luggage of Life

I've never been one to travel light.

I've tried. Believe me, I've tried. But ever since I stuck three fingers in the air and took the Boy Scout pledge to be prepared, I've been determined to be exactly that—prepared.

Prepared for a bar mitzvah, baby dedication, or costume party. Prepared to parachute behind enemy lines or enter a cricket tournament. And if, perchance, the Dalai Lama might be on my flight and invite me to dine in Tibet, I carry snowshoes. One has to be prepared.

I don't know how to travel light.

Fact is, there's a lot about travel I don't know. I don't know how to interpret the restrictions of a supersaver seat—*half price if you leave on Wednesdays during duck-hunting season and return when the moon is full in a nonelection year.* I don't know why they don't build the whole plane out of the same metal they use to build the little black box. I don't know how to escape the airplane toilet without sacrificing one of my extremities to the jaws of the folding door. And I don't know what to say to guys like the taxi driver in Rio who learned I was an American and asked me if I knew his cousin Eddie who lives in the U.S.

There's a lot about traveling I don't know.

I don't know why we men would rather floss a crocodile than ask for directions. I don't know why vacation slides aren't used to treat insomnia, and I don't know when I'll learn not to eat food whose names I can't pronounce.

But most of all, I don't know how to travel light.

I don't know how to travel without granola bars, sodas, and rain gear. I don't know how to travel without flashlights and a generator and a global tracking system. I don't know how to travel without an ice chest of wieners. What if I stumble upon a backyard barbecue? To bring nothing to the party would be rude.

Every travel-catalog company in the world has my credit-card number. I've got an iron that doubles as a paperweight, a hair dryer the size of a coach's whistle, a Swiss Army knife that expands into a pup tent, and a pair of pants that inflate upon impact. (On one flight my wife, Denalyn, gave me a swat on the leg, and I couldn't get out of my seat.)

I don't know how to travel light. But I need to learn. Denalyn refuses to give birth to any more children even though the airlines allow each passenger three checked bags and two carry-ons.

I need to learn to travel light.

You're wondering why I can't. *Loosen up!* you're thinking. *You can't enjoy a journey carrying so much stuff. Why don't you just drop all that luggage?*

Funny you should ask. I'd like to inquire the same of you. Haven't you been known to pick up a few bags?

Odds are, you did this morning. Somewhere between the first step on the floor and the last step out the door, you grabbed some luggage. You stepped over to the baggage carousel and loaded up. Don't remember doing so? That's because you did it without thinking. Don't remember seeing a baggage terminal? That's because the carousel is not the one in the airport; it's the one in the mind. And the bags we grab are not made of leather; they're made of burdens.

The suitcase of guilt. A sack of discontent. You drape a duffel bag of weariness on one shoulder and a hanging bag of grief on the other. Add on a backpack of doubt, an overnight bag of loneliness, and a trunk of fear. Pretty soon you're pulling more stuff than a skycap. No wonder you're so tired at the end of the day. Lugging luggage is exhausting.

What you were saying to me, God is saying to you, "Set that stuff down! You're carrying burdens you don't need to bear."

"Come to me," he invites, "all of you who are weary and carry heavy burdens, and I will give you rest" (Matt. 11:28 NLT).

If we let him, God will lighten our loads . . . but how do we let him? May I invite an old friend to show us? The Twenty-third Psalm.

> The LORD is my shepherd;
> I shall not want.
> He makes me to lie down in green pastures;
> He leads me beside the still waters.
> He restores my soul;
> He leads me in the paths of righteousness
> For His name's sake.
>
> Yea, though I walk through the valley of the shadow of death,
> I will fear no evil;
> For You are with me;
> Your rod and Your staff, they comfort me.
>
> You prepare a table before me in the presence of my enemies;
> You anoint my head with oil.
> My cup runs over.
> Surely goodness and mercy shall follow me
> All the days of my life;
> And I will dwell in the house of the LORD
> Forever. (NKJV)

Do more beloved words exist? Framed and hung in hospital halls, scratched on prison walls, quoted by the young, and whispered by the dying. In these lines sailors have found a harbor, the frightened have found a father, and strugglers have found a friend.

And because the passage is so deeply loved, it is widely known. Can you find ears on which these words have never fallen? Set to music in a hundred songs, translated into a thousand tongues, domiciled in a million hearts.

One of those hearts might be yours. What kinship do you feel with these words? Where do the verses transport you? To a fireside? Bedside? Graveside?

Hardly a week passes that I don't turn to them. This passage is to the minister what balm is to the physician. I recently applied them to the heart of a dear friend. Summoned to his house with the words "The doctors aren't giving him more than a few days," I looked at him and understood. Face pale. Lips stretched and parched. Skin draping between bones like old umbrella cloth between spokes. The cancer had taken so much: his appetite, his strength, his days. But the cancer hadn't touched his faith. Pulling a chair to his bed and squeezing his hand, I whispered, "Bill, 'The Lord is my shepherd; I shall not want.'" He rolled his head toward me as if to welcome the words.

"He makes me to lie down in green pastures; He leads me beside the still waters. He restores my soul; He leads me in the paths of righteousness for His name's sake."

Reaching the fourth verse, fearful that he might not hear, I leaned forward until I was a couple of inches from his ear and said, "Though I walk through the valley of the shadow of death, I will fear no evil; for You are with me; Your rod and Your staff, they comfort me."

He didn't open his eyes, but he arched his brows. He didn't speak, but his thin fingers curled around mine, and I wondered if the Lord was helping him set down some luggage, the fear of dying.

Do you have some luggage of your own? Do you think God might use David's psalm to lighten your load? *Traveling light means trusting God with the burdens you were never intended to bear.*

Why don't you try traveling light? Try it for the sake of those you love. Have you ever considered the impact that excess baggage has on relationships? We've made this point at our church by virtue of a drama. A wedding is reenacted in which we hear the thoughts of the bride and groom. The groom enters, laden with luggage. A bag dangles from every appendage. And each bag is labeled: guilt, anger, arrogance, insecurities. This fellow is loaded. As he stands at the altar, the audience hears him thinking, *Finally, a woman who will help me carry all my burdens. She's so strong, so stable, so . . .*

As his thoughts continue, hers begin. She enters, wearing a wedding gown but, like her fiancé, covered with luggage. Pulling a hanging bag, shouldering a carry-on, hauling a makeup kit, paper sack—everything you could imagine and everything labeled. She has her own bags: prejudice, loneliness, disappointments. And her expectations? Listen to what she is thinking: *Just a few more minutes and I've got me a man. No more counselors. No more group sessions. So long, discouragement and worry. I won't be seeing you anymore. He's going to fix me.*

Finally they stand at the altar, lost in a mountain of luggage. They smile their way through the ceremony, but when given the invitation to kiss each other, they can't. How do you embrace someone if your arms are full of bags?

For the sake of those you love, learn to set them down.

And, for the sake of the God you serve, do the same. He wants to use you, you know. But how can he if you are exhausted? This truth came home to me yesterday afternoon on a run. Preparing for a jog, I couldn't decide what to wear. The sun was out, but the wind was chilly. The sky was clear, but the forecast said rain. Jacket or sweatshirt? The Boy Scout within me prevailed. I wore both.

I grabbed my Walkman but couldn't decide which tape to bring. A sermon or music? You guessed it, I took both. Needing to stay in touch with my kids, I carried a cell phone. So no one would steal my car, I pocketed my keys. As a precaution against thirst, I brought along some drink money in a pouch. I looked more like a pack mule than a runner! Within half a mile I was peeling off the jacket and hiding it in a bush. That kind of weight will slow you down.

What's true in jogging is true in faith. God has a great race for you to run. Under his care you will go where you've never been and serve in ways you've never dreamed. But you have to drop some stuff. How can you share grace if you are full of guilt? How can you offer comfort if you are disheartened? How can you lift someone else's load if your arms are full with your own?

For the sake of those you love, travel light.

For the sake of the God you serve, travel light.

For the sake of your own joy, travel light.

There are certain weights in life you simply cannot carry. Your Lord is asking you to set them down and trust him. He is the father at the baggage claim. When a dad sees his five-year-old son trying to drag the family trunk off the carousel, what does he say? The father will say to his son what God is saying to you.

"Set it down, child. I'll carry that one."

What do you say we take God up on his offer? We just might find ourselves traveling a little lighter.

By the way, I may have overstated my packing problems. (I don't usually take snowshoes.) But I can't overstate God's promise: "Unload all your worries onto him, since he is looking after you" (1 Pet. 5:7 JB).

2

The Middle C of Life

The Burden of a Lesser God

The Lord . . .

Psalm 23:1

I'm only five feet from an eagle. His wings are spread, and his talons are lifted above the branch. White feathers cap his head, and black eyes peer at me from both sides of a golden beak. He is so close I could touch him. So near I could stroke him. With only a lean and a stretch of my right arm, I could cover the eagle's crown with my hand.

But I don't. I don't reach. Why not? Am I afraid of him?

Hardly. He hasn't budged in two years. When I first opened the box, he impressed me. When I first set him on the shelf, I admired him. Man-made eagles are nice for a while, but you quickly get used to them.

David is concerned that you and I don't make the same mistake with God. His pen has scarcely touched papyrus, and he's urging us to avoid gods of our own making. With his very first words in this psalm, David sets out to deliver us from the burden of a lesser deity.

One might argue that he seeks to do nothing else. For though he will speak of green pastures, his thesis is not rest. He will describe death's somber valley, but this poem is not an ode to dying. He will tell of the Lord's forever house, but his theme is not heaven. Why did David write the Twenty-third Psalm? To build our trust in God . . . to remind us of who he is.

In this psalm David devotes one hundred and fifteen words to explaining the first two:[1] "The Lord." In the arena of unnecessary luggage, the psalmist begins with the weightiest: the refashioned god. One who looks nice but does little. God as . . .

A genie in a bottle. Convenient. Congenial. Need a parking place, date, field goal made or missed? All you do is rub the bottle and *poof*—it's yours. And, what's even better, this god goes back into the bottle after he's done.

A sweet grandpa. So soft hearted. So wise. So kind. But very, very, very old. Grandpas are great when they are awake, but they tend to doze off when you need them.

A busy dad. Leaves on Mondays, returns on Saturdays. Lots of road trips and business meetings. He'll show up on Sunday, however, so clean up and look spiritual. On Monday, be yourself again. He'll never know.

Ever held these views of God? If so, you know the problems they cause. A busy dad doesn't have time for your questions. A kind grandpa is too weak to carry your load. And if your god is a genie in a bottle, then you are greater than he is. He comes and goes at your command.

A god who looks nice but does little.

Reminds me of a briefcase I own. Though I'd like to fault the salesman, I can't. The purchase was my decision. But he certainly made it easy. I didn't need a new satchel. The one I had was fine. Scarred and scratched but fine. The paint was worn off the zippers, and the edges were scuffed, but the bag was fine.

Oh, but this new one, to use the words of the college-age boy in the leather store, was "really fine." Loaded with features: copper covers on the corners, smooth leather from Spain, and, most of all, an Italian name near the handle. The salesman gave his line and handed me the bag, and I bought them both.

I left the store with a briefcase that I have used maybe twice. What was I thinking? It carries so little. My old bag had no copper-covered corners, but it had a belly like a beluga. This new one reminds me of a high-fashion model: slim, stiff, and tight-lipped. A book and a newspaper, and this Italian satchel is *"fullisimo."*

The bag looks nice but does nothing.

Is that the kind of God you want? Is that the kind of God we have?

David's answer is a resounding no. "You want to know who God really is?" he asks. "Then read this." And he writes the name *Yahweh*. "Yahweh is my shepherd."

Though foreign to us, the name was rich to David. So rich, in fact, that David chose *Yahweh* over *El Shaddai* (God Almighty), *El Elyon* (God Most High), and *El Olam* (God the Everlasting). These and many other titles for God were at David's disposal. But when he considered all the options, David chose *Yahweh*.

Why *Yahweh?* Because *Yahweh* is God's name. You can call me preacher or writer or half-baked golfer—these are accurate descriptions, but these aren't my names. I might call you dad, mom, doctor, or student, and those terms may describe you, but they aren't your name. If you want to call me by my name, say *Max*. If I call you by your name, I say it. And if you want to call God by his name, say *Yahweh*.

God has told us his name. (How he must long to be close to us.)

Moses was the first to learn it. Seven centuries prior to David, the eighty-year-old shepherd was tending sheep when the bush began to blaze and his life began to change. Moses was told to return to Egypt and rescue the enslaved Hebrews. He raised more excuses than a kid at bedtime, but God trumped each one. Finally Moses asked,

> "When I go to the Israelites, I will say to them, 'The God of your fathers sent me to you.' What if the people say, 'What is his name?' What should I tell them?"
>
> Then God said to Moses, "I AM WHO I AM. When you go to the people of Israel, tell them, 'I AM sent me to you.'" (Exod. 3:13–14)

God would later remind Moses: "I am Yahweh. To Abraham and Isaac and Jacob I appeared as El Shaddai; I did not make myself known to them by my name Yahweh" (Exod. 6:2–3 JB).

The Israelites considered the name too holy to be spoken by human lips. Whenever they needed to say *Yahweh,* they substituted the word *Adonai,* which means "Lord." If the name needed to be written, the scribes would take a bath before they wrote it and destroy the pen afterward.[2]

God never gives a definition of the word *Yahweh,* and Moses never requests one. Many scholars wish he had, for the study of the name has raised some healthy discussions.

The name I AM sounds strikingly close to the Hebrew verb *to be—havah.* It's quite possibly a combination of the present tense form (I am) and the causative tense (I cause to be). *Yahweh,* then, seems to mean "I AM" and "I cause." God is the "One who is" and the "One who causes."

Why is that important? Because we need a big God. And if God is the "One who is," then he is an unchanging God.

Think about it. Do you know anyone who goes around saying, "I am"? Neither do I. When we say "I am," we always add another word. "I am *happy.*" "I am *sad.*" "I am *strong.*" "I am *Max.*" God, however, starkly states, "I AM" and adds nothing else.

"You are what?" we want to ask. "I AM," he replies. God needs no descriptive word because he never changes. God is what he is. He is what he has always been. His immutability motivated the psalmist to declare, "But thou art the same" (Ps. 102:27 KJV). The writer is saying, "You are the One who is. You never change."[3] Yahweh is an unchanging God.

He is also an uncaused God.

Though he creates, God was never created. Though he makes, he was never made. Though he causes, he was never caused. Hence the psalmist's proclamation: "Before the mountains were born or you brought forth the earth and the world, from everlasting to everlasting you are God" (Ps. 90:2 NIV).

God is Yahweh—an unchanging God, an uncaused God, and an ungoverned God.

You and I are governed. The weather determines what we wear. The terrain tells us how to travel. Gravity dictates our speed, and health determines our strength. We may challenge these forces and alter them slightly, but we never remove them.

God—our Shepherd—doesn't check the weather; he makes it. He doesn't defy gravity; he created it. He isn't affected by health; he has no body. Jesus said, "God is spirit" (John 4:24). Since he has no body, he has no limitations—equally active in Cambodia as he is in Connecticut. "Where can I go to get away from your Spirit?" asked David. "Where can I run from you? If I go up to the heavens, you are there. If I lie down in the grave, you are there" (Ps. 139:7–8).

Unchanging. Uncaused. Ungoverned. These are only a fraction of God's qualities, but aren't they enough to give you a glimpse of your Father? Don't we need this kind of shepherd? Don't we need an unchanging shepherd?

When Lloyd Douglas, author of *The Robe* and other novels, attended college, he lived in a boardinghouse. A retired, wheelchair-bound music professor resided on the first floor. Each morning Douglas would stick his head in the door of the teacher's apartment and ask the same question, "Well, what's the good news?" The old man would pick up his tuning fork, tap it on the side of the wheelchair, and say, "That's middle C! It was middle C yesterday; it will be middle C tomorrow; it will be middle C a thousand years from now. The tenor upstairs sings flat. The piano across the hall is out of tune, but, my friend, that is middle C."[4]

You and I need a middle C. Haven't you had enough change in your life? Relationships change. Health changes. The weather changes. But the Yahweh who ruled the earth last night is the same Yahweh who rules it today. Same convictions. Same plan. Same mood. Same love. He never changes. You can no more alter God than a pebble can alter the rhythm of the Pacific. Yahweh is our middle C. A still point in a turning world. Don't we need a still point? Don't we need an unchanging shepherd?

We equally need an uncaused shepherd. No one breathed life into Yahweh. No one sired him. No one gave birth to him. No one caused him. No act brought him forth.

And since no act brought him forth, no act can take him out. Does he fear an earthquake? Does he tremble at a tornado? Hardly. Yahweh sleeps through storms and calms the winds with a word. Cancer does not trouble him, and cemeteries do not disturb him. He was here before they came. He'll be here after they are gone. He is uncaused.

And he is ungoverned. Counselors can comfort you *in* the storm, but you need a God who can *still* the storm. Friends can hold your hand at your deathbed, but you need a Yahweh who has defeated the grave. Philosophers can debate the meaning of life, but you need a Lord who can declare the meaning of life.

You need a Yahweh.

You don't need what Dorothy found. Remember her discovery in *The Wonderful Wizard of Oz*? She and her trio followed the yellow-brick road only to discover that the wizard was a wimp! Nothing but smoke and mirrors and tin-drum thunder. Is that the kind of god you need?

You don't need to carry the burden of a lesser god . . . a god on a shelf, a god in a box, or a god in a bottle. No, you need a God who can place 100 billion stars in our galaxy and 100 billion galaxies in the universe. You need a God who can shape two fists of flesh into 75 to 100 billion nerve cells, each with as many as 10,000 connections to other nerve cells, place it in a skull, and call it a brain.[5]

And you need a God who, while so mind-numbingly mighty, can come in the soft of night and touch you with the tenderness of an April snow.

You need a Yahweh.

And, according to David, you have one. He is your shepherd.

3

I'll Do It My Way

The Burden of Self-Reliance

The LORD *is my shepherd.*

PSALM 23:1 NKJV

ou say you can swing a club like Tiger Woods? That's saying a lot.

You hope to score touchdowns like Joe Montana? You'll have to work hard.

And you, young lady? You aspire to be the next Mia Hamm? Good for you.

And me? Well, actually there is one fellow who's caught my attention. He reminds me of me. You've probably never heard of him. Did you see the British Open in '99? Yeah, the one in Carnoustie, Scotland? Remember the player who had a seven-stroke lead with one hole to go?

That's right, the Frenchman. Jean Van de Velde. He was six strokes and 480 yards away from a major championship, a wad of cash, and a place in history. All he needed to do was score a six on a par four.

I could shoot a six on a par four. My mother could make a six on a par four. This guy could shoot a six with a waffle iron and a banana. Tell the trophy engraver to warm up the pen and practice his *V*s. He'll need two to write "Jean Van de Velde."

Granted the hole was not easy. Bisected three times by a "wee burn," the Scottish term for a marshy creek. No sweat. Hit three short shots . . . putt three times if you have to. Just take a six, win the hole, and smile for the cameras. Besides it's windy, and the "wee burn" is wee deep. Don't flirt with it.

Oh, but the French love to flirt. Van de Velde pulls out his driver, and somewhere in Des Moines an armchair duffer who'd been lured to sleep by the seven-stroke lead opens one eye. *He's holding a driver?*

Van de Velde's caddie was a thirty-year-old Parisian named Christopher with untidy English and a paintbrush on his chin and bleached hair under his hat. "I think he and I—we want too much show," he later confessed.

Van de Velde pushes his drive halfway to the Eiffel Tower. Now he has 240 yards to the green with nothing but deep grass and heartache in between. Surely he will hit a short shot back in the fairway.

Logic says, "Don't go for the green."

Golf 101 says, "Don't go for the green."

Every Scot in the gallery says, "Aye, laddie. Don't go for the green."

Van de Velde says, "I'm going for the green."

He pulls out a two iron, and the armchair golfer in Des Moines opens the other eye. *A two iron!? Maybe if you're teed up on the beach, trying to hit into the Caribbean!* The spectators are silent. Most out of respect. A few in prayer. Van de Velde's two iron becomes a FORE! iron. *Whack. Clang. Plop.* The ball caroms off the bleachers and disappears into marsh tall enough to hide a lawn gnome.

His lie would've made Pinocchio's nose grow. The next shot lands in the water and the next in the sand. Tally the damage, and you've got four strokes plus a penalty. He's lying five and not on the green. So much for winning the hole. By now he's praying for a seven and a tie. To the great relief of the civilized world, Van de Velde makes the seven. You've got to wonder if he ever recovered from the "wee burn." He lost the play-off.

Golf, like nylon running shorts, reveals a lot about a person. What the eighteenth hole revealed about Van de Velde reminds me of me.

I've done the same thing. The same blasted thing. All he needed was a five iron, but he had to go and pull out the driver. Or, in my case:

All I needed to do was apologize, but I had to argue.

All I needed to do was listen, but I had to open my big mouth.

All I needed to do was be patient, but I had to take control.

All I had to do was give it to God, but I tried to fix it myself.

Why don't I leave the driver in the bag? I know how Christopher the caddie would answer: "I think he and I and Max—we want too much show."

Too much stubbornness. Too much independence. Too much self-reliance.

I don't need advice—*Whack.*

I can handle this myself—*Clang.*

I don't need a shepherd, thank you—*Plop.*

Can you relate? Are Jean and I the only ones to make an anthem out of Sinatra's song "I Did It My Way"? Are we the only two dragging around the cast-iron chest of self-reliance? I don't think so.

We humans want to do things our way. Forget the easy way. Forget the common way. Forget the best way. Forget God's way. We want to do things *our* way.

And, according to the Bible, that's precisely our problem. "We all have wandered away like sheep; each of us has gone his own way" (Isa. 53:6).

You wouldn't think sheep would be obstinate. Of all God's animals, the sheep is the least able to take care of himself.

Sheep are dumb! Have you ever met a sheep trainer? Ever seen sheep tricks? Know anyone who has taught his sheep to roll over? Ever witnessed a circus sideshow featuring "Mazadon and his jumping sheep"? No. Sheep are just too dumb.

And defenseless. They have no fangs or claws. They can't bite you or outrun you. That's why you never see sheep as team mascots. We've heard of the St. Louis Rams and the Chicago Bulls and the Seattle

Seahawks, but the New York Lambs? Who wants to be a lamb? You couldn't even stir up a decent yell for the cheerleaders.

> We are the sheep.
> We don't make a peep.
> Victory is yours to keep.
> But count us if you want to sleep.

What's more, sheep are dirty. A cat can clean itself. So can a dog. We see a bird in a birdbath or a bear in a river. But sheep? They get dirty and stay that way.

Couldn't David have thought of a better metaphor? Surely he could have. After all, he outran Saul and outgunned Goliath. Why didn't he choose something other than sheep?

How about:

"The Lord is my commander in chief, and I am his warrior." There. We like that better. A warrior gets a uniform and a weapon, maybe even a medal.

Or, "The Lord is my inspiration, and I am his singer." We are in God's choir; what a flattering assignment.

Or, "The Lord is my king, and I am his ambassador." Who wouldn't like to be a spokesperson for God?

Everyone stops when the ambassador speaks. Everyone listens when God's minstrel sings. Everyone applauds when God's warrior passes.

But who notices when God's sheep show up? Who notices when the sheep sing or speak or act? Only one person notices. The shepherd. And that is precisely David's point.

When David, who was a warrior, minstrel, and ambassador for God, searched for an illustration of God, he remembered his days as a shepherd. He remembered how he lavished attention on the sheep day and night. How he slept with them and watched over them.

And the way he cared for the sheep reminded him of the way God cares for us. David rejoiced to say, "The LORD is my shepherd," and in so doing he proudly implied, "I am his sheep."

Still uncomfortable with being considered a sheep? Will you humor me and take a simple quiz? See if you succeed in self-reliance. Raise your hand if any of the following describe you.

You can control your moods. You're never grumpy or sullen. You can't relate to Jekyll and Hyde. You're always upbeat and upright. Does that describe you? No? Well, let's try another.

You are at peace with everyone. Every relationship as sweet as fudge. Even your old flames speak highly of you. Love all and are loved by all. Is that you? If not, how about this description?

You have no fears. Call you the Teflon toughie. Wall Street plummets—no problem. Heart condition discovered—yawn. World War III starts—what's for dinner? Does this describe you?

You need no forgiveness. Never made a mistake. As square as a game of checkers. As clean as grandma's kitchen. Never cheated, never lied, never lied about cheating. Is that you? No?

Let's evaluate this. You can't control your moods. A few of your relationships are shaky. You have fears and faults. Hmmm. Do you really want to hang on to your chest of self-reliance? Sounds to me as if you could use a shepherd. Otherwise, you might end up with a Twenty-third Psalm like this:

> I am my own shepherd. I am always in need.
> I stumble from mall to mall and shrink to shrink, seeking relief but never finding it.
> I creep through the valley of the shadow of death and fall apart.

I fear everything from pesticides to power lines, and I'm starting to act like my mother.

I go down to the weekly staff meeting and am surrounded by enemies. I go home, and even my goldfish scowls at me.

I anoint my headache with extra-strength Tylenol.

My Jack Daniel's runneth over.

Surely misery and misfortune will follow me, and I will live in self-doubt for the rest of my lonely life.

Why is it that the ones who most need a shepherd resist him so?

Ah, now there is a question for the Van de Veldes of life. Scripture says, "Do it God's way." Experience says, "Do it God's way." Every Scot in heaven begs, "Aye, laddie, do it God's way."

And, every so often, we do. And when we do, when we follow the lead of *Notre Dieu* and keep the driver in the bag, somehow the ball stays in the fairway.

Yes, Van de Velde reminds me of me.

After losing the play-off hole, he kept his composure for the crowds. But once he sat in the scorer's tent, he buried his face in his hands. "Next time I'll hit zee wedge," he sobbed. "You'll say I'm a coward, but next time I'll hit zee wedge."

You and me both, Jean.[1]

4

The Prison of Want

The Burden of Discontent

The LORD is my shepherd; I shall not want.

PSALM 23:1 NKJV

Come with me to the most populated prison in the world. The facility has more inmates than bunks. More prisoners than plates. More residents than resources.

Come with me to the world's most oppressive prison. Just ask the inmates; they will tell you. They are overworked and underfed. Their walls are bare and bunks are hard.

No prison is so populated, no prison so oppressive, and, what's more, no prison is so permanent. Most inmates never leave. They never escape. They never get released. They serve a life sentence in this overcrowded, underprovisioned facility.

The name of the prison? You'll see it over the entrance. Rainbowed over the gate are four cast-iron letters that spell out its name:

W-A-N-T

The prison of want. You've seen her prisoners. They are "in want." They want something. They want something bigger. Nicer. Faster. Thinner. They want.

They don't want much, mind you. They want just one thing. One new job. One new car. One new house. One new spouse. They don't want much. They want just one.

And when they have "one," they will be happy. And they are right—

they will be happy. When they have "one," they will leave the prison. But then it happens. The new-car smell passes. The new job gets old. The neighbors buy a larger television set. The new spouse has bad habits. The sizzle fizzles, and before you know it, another ex-con breaks parole and returns to jail.

Are you in prison? You are if you feel better when you have more and worse when you have less. You are if joy is one delivery away, one transfer away, one award away, or one makeover away. If your happiness comes from something you deposit, drive, drink, or digest, then face it—you are in prison, the prison of want.

That's the bad news. The good news is, you have a visitor. And your visitor has a message that can get you paroled. Make your way to the receiving room. Take your seat in the chair, and look across the table at the psalmist David. He motions for you to lean forward. "I have a secret to tell you," he whispers, "the secret of satisfaction. 'The LORD is my shepherd; I shall not want'" (Ps. 23:1 NKJV).

David has found the pasture where discontent goes to die. It's as if he is saying, "What I have in God is greater than what I don't have in life."

You think you and I could learn to say the same?

Think for just a moment about the things you own. Think about the house you have, the car you drive, the money you've saved. Think about the jewelry you've inherited and the stocks you've traded and the clothes you've purchased. Envision all your stuff, and let me remind you of two biblical truths.

Your stuff isn't yours. Ask any coroner. Ask any embalmer. Ask any funeral-home director. No one takes anything with him. When one of the wealthiest men in history, John D. Rockefeller, died, his accountant was asked, "How much did John D. leave?" The accountant's reply? "All of it."[1]

"Naked a man comes from his mother's womb, and as he comes, so he departs. He takes nothing from his labor that he can carry in his hand" (Eccles. 5:15 NIV).

All that stuff—it's not yours. And you know what else about all that stuff? *It's not you.* Who you are has nothing to do with the clothes you wear or the car you drive. Jesus said, "Life is not defined by what you have, even when you have a lot" (Luke 12:15 MSG). Heaven does not know you as the fellow with the nice suit or the woman with the big house or the kid with the new bike. Heaven knows your heart. "The LORD does not look at the things man looks at. Man looks at the outward appearance, but the LORD looks at the heart" (1 Sam. 16:7 NIV). When God thinks of you, he may see your compassion, your devotion, your tenderness or quick mind, but he doesn't think of your things.

And when you think of you, you shouldn't either. Define yourself by your stuff, and you'll feel good when you have a lot and bad when you don't. Contentment comes when we can honestly say with Paul: "I have learned to be satisfied with the things I have. . . . I know how to live when I am poor, and I know how to live when I have plenty" (Phil. 4:11–12).

Doug McKnight could say those words. At the age of thirty-two he was diagnosed with multiple sclerosis. Over the next sixteen years it would cost him his career, his mobility, and eventually his life. Because of MS, he couldn't feed himself or walk; he battled depression and fear. But through it all, Doug never lost his sense of gratitude. Evidence of this was seen in his prayer list. Friends in his congregation asked him to compile a list of requests so they could intercede for him. His response included eighteen blessings for which to be grateful and six concerns for which to be prayerful. His blessings outweighed his needs by three times. Doug McKnight had learned to be content.[2]

So had the leper on the island of Tobago. A short-term missionary met her on a mission trip. On the final day, he was leading worship in a leper colony. He asked if anyone had a favorite song. When he did, a woman turned around, and he saw the most disfigured face he'd ever seen. She had no ears and no nose. Her lips were gone. But she raised a fingerless hand and asked, "Could we sing 'Count Your Many Blessings'?"

The missionary started the song but couldn't finish. Someone later commented, "I suppose you'll never be able to sing the song again." He answered, "No, I'll sing it again. Just never in the same way."[3]

Are you hoping that a change in circumstances will bring a change in your attitude? If so, you are in prison, and you need to learn a secret of traveling light. *What you have in your Shepherd is greater than what you don't have in life.*

May I meddle for a moment? What is the one thing separating you from joy? How do you fill in this blank: "I will be happy when ________________"? When I am healed. When I am promoted. When I am married. When I am single. When I am rich. How would you finish that statement?

Now, with your answer firmly in mind, answer this. If your ship never comes in, if your dream never comes true, if the situation never changes, could you be happy? If not, then you are sleeping in the cold cell of discontent. You are in prison. And you need to know what you have in your Shepherd.

You have a God who hears you, the power of love behind you, the Holy Spirit within you, and all of heaven ahead of you. If you have the Shepherd, you have grace for every sin, direction for every turn, a candle for every corner, and an anchor for every storm. You have everything you need.

And who can take it from you? Can leukemia infect your salvation? Can bankruptcy impoverish your prayers? A tornado might take your earthly house, but will it touch your heavenly home?

And look at your position. Why clamor for prestige and power? Are you not already privileged to be part of the greatest work in history?

According to Russ Blowers, we are. He is a minister in Indianapolis. Knowing he would be asked about his profession at a Rotary Club meeting, he resolved to say more than "I'm a preacher."

Instead he explained, "Hi, I'm Russ Blowers. I'm with a global enterprise. We have branches in every country in the world. We have representatives in nearly every parliament and boardroom on earth. We're into motivation and behavior alteration. We run hospitals, feeding stations, crisis-pregnancy centers, universities, publishing houses, and nursing homes. We care for our clients from birth to death. We are into life insurance and fire insurance. We perform spiritual heart transplants. Our original Organizer owns all the real estate on earth plus an assortment of galaxies and constellations. He knows everything and lives everywhere. Our product is free for the asking. (There's not enough money to buy it.) Our CEO was born in a hick town, worked as a carpenter, didn't own a home, was misunderstood by his family and hated by his enemies, walked on water, was condemned to death without a trial, and arose from the dead. I talk with him every day."[4]

If you can say the same, don't you have reason to be content?

A man once went to a minister for counseling. He was in the midst of a financial collapse. "I've lost everything," he bemoaned.

"Oh, I'm so sorry to hear that you've lost your faith."

"No," the man corrected him, "I haven't lost my faith."

"Well, then I'm sad to hear that you've lost your character."

"I didn't say that," he corrected. "I still have my character."

"I'm so sorry to hear that you've lost your salvation."

"That's not what I said," the man objected. "I haven't lost my salvation."

"You have your faith, your character, your salvation. Seems to me," the minister observed, "that you've lost none of the things that really matter."

We haven't either. You and I could pray like the Puritan. He sat down to a meal of bread and water. He bowed his head and declared, "All this and Jesus too?"

Can't we be equally content? Paul says that "godliness with contentment is great gain" (1 Tim. 6:6 NIV). When we surrender to God the cumbersome sack of discontent, we don't just give up something; we gain something. God replaces it with a lightweight, tailor-made, sorrow-resistant attaché of gratitude.

What will you gain with contentment? You may gain your marriage. You may gain precious hours with your children. You may gain your self-respect. You may gain joy. You may gain the faith to say, "The LORD is my shepherd; I shall not want."

Try saying it slowly. "The LORD is my shepherd; I shall not want."

Again, "The LORD is my shepherd; I shall not want."

Again, "The LORD is my shepherd; I shall not want."

Shhhhhhh. Did you hear something? I think I did. I'm not sure . . . but I think I heard the opening of a jail door.

5

I Will Give You Rest

The Burden of Weariness

He makes me to lie down in green pastures.

PSALM 23:2 NKJV

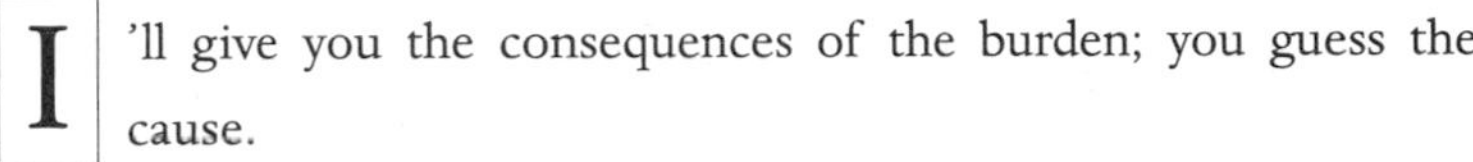

I'll give you the consequences of the burden; you guess the cause.

- It afflicts 70 million Americans and is faulted for 38,000 deaths each year.
- The condition annually costs the U.S. $70 billion worth of productivity.
- Teenagers suffer from it. Studies show that 64 percent of teens blame it for poor school performance.
- Middle agers face it. Researchers say the most severe cases occur between ages thirty and forty.
- Senior citizens are afflicted by it. One study suggests that the condition impacts 50 percent of the over-sixty-five population.
- Treatments involve everything from mouth guards to herbal teas to medication.[1]

Any idea what's being described?

Chemical abuse? Divorce? Long sermons? None of those answers are correct, though the last one was a good hunch. The answer may surprise you. Insomnia. America can't get to sleep.

For most of my life I secretly snickered at the thought of sleep difficulties. My problem was not in going to sleep. My problem was staying awake. But a few years ago I went to bed one night, closed my eyes, and nothing happened. I didn't fall asleep. Rather than slow to a halt, my mind kicked into high gear. A thousand and one obligations rushed at me. Midnight passed, and I was still awake. I drank some milk, returned to bed. I was still awake. I woke up Denalyn, using the blue ribbon of dumb questions, "Are you awake?" She told me to quit thinking about things. So I did. I quit thinking about things and started thinking about people. But as I thought of people, I thought of what those people were doing. They were sleeping. That made me mad and kept me awake. Finally, somewhere in the early hours of the morning, having been initiated into the fraternity of 70 million sleepless Americans, I dozed off.

I don't snicker at the thought of sleep difficulties anymore. Nor do I question the inclusion of the verse about rest in the Twenty-third Psalm.

People with too much work and too little sleep step over to the baggage claim of life and grab the duffel bag of weariness. You don't carry this one. You don't hoist it onto your shoulder and stride down the street. You drag it as you would a stubborn St. Bernard. Weariness wearies.

Why are we so tired? Have you read a newspaper lately? We long to have the life of Huck and Tom on the Mississippi, but look at us riding the white waters of the Rio Grande. Forks in the river. Rocks in the water. Heart attacks, betrayal, credit-card debt, and custody battles. Huck and Tom didn't have to face these kinds of things. We do, however, and they keep us awake. And since we can't sleep, we have a second problem.

Our bodies are tired. Think about it. If 70 million Americans aren't sleeping enough, what does that mean? That means one-third of our country is dozing off at work, napping through class, or sleeping at the wheel. (Fifteen hundred road deaths per year are blamed on heavy-eyed truckdrivers.) Some even snooze while reading Lucado books.

(Hard to fathom, I know.) Thirty tons of aspirins, sleeping pills, and tranquilizers are consumed every day![2] The energy gauge on the dashboard of our forehead says empty.

Were we to invite an alien to solve our problem, he'd suggest a simple solution—everybody go to sleep. We'd laugh at him. He doesn't understand the way we work. Literally. He doesn't understand *the way* we work. We work hard. There is money to be made. Degrees to be earned. Ladders to be climbed. In our book, busyness is next to godliness. We idolize Thomas Edison, who claimed he could live on fifteen-minute naps. Somehow we forget to mention Albert Einstein, who averaged eleven hours of sleep a night.[3] In 1910 Americans slept nine hours a night; today we sleep seven and are proud of it. And we are tired because of it. Our minds are tired. Our bodies are tired. But much more important, our souls are tired.

We are eternal creatures, and we ask eternal questions: Where did I come from? Where am I going? What is the meaning of life? What is right? What is wrong? Is there life after death? These are the primal questions of the soul. And left unanswered, such questions will steal our rest.

Only one other living creature has as much trouble resting as we do. Not dogs. They doze. Not bears. They hibernate. Cats invented the catnap, and the sloths slumber twenty hours a day. (So that's what I was rooming with my sophomore year in college.) Most animals know how to rest. There is one exception. These creatures are woolly, simpleminded, and slow. No, not husbands on Saturday—sheep! Sheep can't sleep.

For sheep to sleep, everything must be just right. No predators. No tension in the flock. No bugs in the air. No hunger in the belly.[4] Everything has to be just so.

Unfortunately, sheep cannot find safe pasture, nor can they spray insecticide, deal with the frictions, or find food. They need help. They need a shepherd to "lead them" and help them "lie down in green pastures." Without a shepherd, they can't rest.

Without a shepherd, neither can we.

In the second verse of the Twenty-third Psalm, David the poet becomes David the artist. His quill becomes a brush, his parchment a canvas, and his words paint a picture. A flock of sheep on folded legs, encircling a shepherd. Bellies nestled deep in the long shoots of grass. A still pond on one side, the watching shepherd on the other. "He makes me to lie down in green pastures; He leads me beside the still waters" (Ps. 23:2 NKJV).

Note the two pronouns preceding the two verbs. *He* makes me . . . *He* leads me . . .

Who is the active one? Who is in charge? The shepherd. The shepherd selects the trail and prepares the pasture. The sheep's job—our job—is to watch the shepherd. With our eyes on our Shepherd, we'll be able to get some sleep. "You will keep him in perfect peace, whose mind is stayed on You" (Isa. 26:3 NKJV).

May I show you something? Flip to the back of this book, and look at an empty page. When you look at it, what do you see? What you see is a white piece of paper. Now place a dot in the center of the sheet. Look at it again. Now what do you see? You see the dot, don't you? And isn't that our problem? We let the dark marks eclipse the white space.

We see the waves of the water rather than the Savior walking through them. We focus on our paltry provisions rather than on the One who can feed five thousand hungry people. We concentrate on the dark Fridays of crucifixion and miss the bright Sundays of resurrection.

Change your focus and relax.

And while you are at it, change your schedule and rest!

The other day my wife met a friend at a restaurant for coffee. The two entered the parking lot at the same time. When Denalyn stepped out of her car, she saw her friend waving her over. Denalyn thought she was saying something, but she couldn't hear a word. A jack-hammer was pounding pavement only a few feet away. She walked toward her friend, who, as it turned out, was just saying hello, and the two entered the restaurant.

When it came time to leave, my wife couldn't find her keys. She looked in her purse, on the floor, in her friend's car. Finally when she went to her car, there they were. Not only were the keys in the ignition, the car was running. It had been running the entire time she and her friend were in the café.

Denalyn blames the oversight on the noise. "Everything was so loud, I forgot to turn it off."

The world gets that way. Life can get so loud we forget to shut it down. Maybe that's why God made such a big deal about rest in the Ten Commandments.

Since you did so well on the dot exercise, let me give you another. Of the ten declarations carved in the tablets, which one occupies the most space? Murder? Adultery? Stealing? You'd think so. Certainly each is worthy of ample coverage. But curiously, these commands are tributes to brevity. God needed only five English words to condemn adultery and four to denounce thievery and murder.

But when he came to the topic of rest, one sentence would not suffice.

> Remember the Sabbath day, to keep it holy. Six days you shall labor and do all your work, but the seventh day is the Sabbath of the LORD your God. In it you shall do no work: you, nor your son, nor your daughter, nor your manservant, nor your maidservant, nor your cattle, nor your stranger who is within your gates. For in six days the LORD made the heavens and the earth, the sea, and all that is in them, and rested the

> seventh day. Therefore the LORD blessed the Sabbath day and hallowed it. (Exod. 20:8–11 NKJV)

God knows us so well. He can see the store owner reading this verse and thinking, "Somebody needs to work that day. If I can't, my son will." So God says, *Nor your son.* "Then my daughter will." *Nor your daughter.* "Then maybe an employee." *Nor them.* "I guess I'll have to send my cow to run the store, or maybe I'll find some stranger to help me." *No,* God says. *One day of the week you will say no to work and yes to worship. You will slow and sit down and lie down and rest.*

Still we object. "But . . . but . . . but . . . who is going to run the store?" "What about my grades?" "I've got my sales quota." We offer up one reason after another, but God silences them all with a poignant reminder: "In six days the LORD made the heavens and the earth, the sea, and all that is in them, and rested the seventh day." God's message is plain: "If creation didn't crash when I rested, it won't crash when you do."

Repeat these words after me: It is not my job to run the world.

A century ago Charles Spurgeon gave this advice to his preaching students:

> Even beasts of burden must be turned out to grass occasionally; the very sea pauses at ebb and flood; earth keeps the Sabbath of the wintry months; and man, even when exalted to God's ambassador, must rest or faint, must trim his lamp or let it burn low; must recruit his vigor or grow prematurely old. . . . In the long run we shall do more by sometimes doing less.[5]

The bow cannot always be bent without fear of breaking. For a field to bear fruit, it must occasionally lie fallow. And for you to be healthy, you must rest. Slow down, and God will heal you. He will bring rest to your mind, to your body, and most of all to your soul. He will lead you to green pastures.

Green pastures were not the natural terrain of Judea. The hills around Bethlehem where David kept his flock were not lush and green. Even today they are white and parched. Any green pasture in Judea is the work of some shepherd. He has cleared the rough, rocky land. Stumps have been torn out, and brush has been burned. Irrigation. Cultivation. Such are the work of a shepherd.

Hence, when David says, "He makes me to lie down in green pastures," he is saying, "My shepherd makes me lie down in his finished work." With his own pierced hands, Jesus created a pasture for the soul. He tore out the thorny underbrush of condemnation. He pried loose the huge boulders of sin. In their place he planted seeds of grace and dug ponds of mercy.

And he invites us to rest there. Can you imagine the satisfaction in the heart of the shepherd when, with work completed, he sees his sheep rest in the tender grass?

Can you imagine the satisfaction in the heart of God when we do the same? His pasture is his gift to us. This is not a pasture that you have made. Nor is it a pasture that you deserve. It is a gift of God. "For it is by grace you have been saved, through faith—and this not from yourselves, it is the gift of God" (Eph. 2:8 NIV).

In a world rocky with human failure, there is a land lush with divine mercy. Your Shepherd invites you there. He wants you to lie down. Nestle deeply until you are hidden, buried, in the tall shoots of his love, and there you will find rest.

6

Whaddifs and Howells

The Burden of Worry

He leads me beside the still waters.

PSALM 23:2 NKJV

Your ten-year-old is worried. So anxious he can't eat. So worried he can't sleep. "What's wrong?" you inquire. He shakes his head and moans, "I don't even have a pension plan."

Or your four-year-old is crying in bed. "What's wrong, sweetheart?" She whimpers, "I'll never pass college chemistry."

Your eight-year-old's face is stress-struck. "I'll be a rotten parent. What if I set a poor example for my kids?"

How would you respond to such statements? Besides calling a child psychologist, your response would be emphatic: "You're too young to worry about those things. When the time comes, you'll know what to do."

Fortunately, most kids don't have such thoughts.

Unfortunately, we adults have more than our share. Worry is the burlap bag of burdens. It's overflowing with "whaddifs" and "howells." "Whaddif it rains at my wedding?" "Howell I know when to discipline my kids?" "Whaddif I marry a guy who snores?" "Howell we pay our baby's tuition?" "Whaddif, after all my dieting, they learn that lettuce is fattening and chocolate isn't?"

The burlap bag of worry. Cumbersome. Chunky. Unattractive. Scratchy. Hard to get a handle on. Irritating to carry and impossible to give away. No one wants your worries.

The truth be told, you don't want them either. No one has to remind you of the high cost of anxiety. (But I will anyway.) Worry divides the mind. The biblical word for *worry (merimnao)* is a compound of two Greek words, *merizo* ("to divide") and *nous* ("the mind"). Anxiety splits our energy between today's priorities and tomorrow's problems. Part of our mind is on the now; the rest is on the not yet. The result is half-minded living.

That's not the only result. Worrying is not a disease, but it causes diseases. It has been connected to high blood pressure, heart trouble, blindness, migraine headaches, thyroid malfunctions, and a host of stomach disorders.

Anxiety is an expensive habit. Of course, it might be worth the cost if it worked. But it doesn't. Our frets are futile. Jesus said, "You cannot add any time to your life by worrying about it" (Matt. 6:27). Worry has never brightened a day, solved a problem, or cured a disease.

How can a person deal with anxiety? You might try what one fellow did. He worried so much that he decided to hire someone to do his worrying for him. He found a man who agreed to be his hired worrier for a salary of $200,000 per year. After the man accepted the job, his first question to his boss was, "Where are you going to get $200,000 per year?" To which the man responded, "That's your worry."

Sadly, worrying is one job you can't farm out, but you can overcome it. There is no better place to begin than in verse two of the shepherd's psalm.

"He leads me beside the still waters," David declares. And, in case we missed the point, he repeats the phrase in the next verse: "He leads me in the paths of righteousness."

"He leads me." God isn't behind me, yelling, "Go!" He is ahead of me, bidding, "Come!" He is in front, clearing the path, cutting the brush, showing the way. Just before the curve, he says, "Turn here."

Prior to the rise, he motions, "Step up here." Standing next to the rocks, he warns, "Watch your step here."

He leads us. He tells us what we need to know when we need to know it. As a New Testament writer would affirm: "We will find grace to help us *when we need it*" (Heb. 4:16 NLT, emphasis mine).

Listen to a different translation: "Let us therefore boldly approach the throne of our gracious God, where we may receive mercy and in his grace find *timely help*" (Heb. 4:16 NEB, emphasis mine).

God's help is timely. He helps us the same way a father gives plane tickets to his family. When I travel with my kids, I carry all our tickets in my satchel. When the moment comes to board the plane, I stand between the attendant and the child. As each daughter passes, I place a ticket in her hand. She, in turn, gives the ticket to the attendant. Each one receives the ticket in the nick of time.

What I do for my daughters God does for you. He places himself between you and the need. And at the right time, he gives you the ticket. Wasn't this the promise he gave his disciples? "When you are arrested and judged, don't worry ahead of time about what you should say. Say whatever *is given you to say at that time,* because it will not really be you speaking; it will be the Holy Spirit" (Mark 13:11, emphasis mine).

Isn't this the message God gave the children of Israel? He promised to supply them with manna each day. But he told them to collect only one day's supply at a time. Those who disobeyed and collected enough for two days found themselves with rotten manna. The only exception to the rule was the day prior to the Sabbath. On Friday they could gather twice as much. Otherwise, God would give them what they needed, in their time of need.

God leads us. God will do the right thing at the right time. And what a difference that makes.

Since I know his provision is timely, I can enjoy the present.

"Give your entire attention to what God is doing right now, and don't get worked up about what may or may not happen tomorrow. God will help you deal with whatever hard things come up when the time comes" (Matt. 6:34 MSG).

That last phrase is worthy of your highlighter: "when the time comes."

"I don't know what I'll do if my husband dies." You will, *when the time comes.*

"When my children leave the house, I don't think I can take it." It won't be easy, but strength will arrive *when the time comes.*

"I could never lead a church. There is too much I don't know." You may be right. Or you may be wanting to know everything too soon. Could it be that God will reveal answers to you *when the time comes?*

The key is this: Meet today's problems with today's strength. Don't start tackling tomorrow's problems until tomorrow. You do not have tomorrow's strength yet. You simply have enough for today.

More than eighty years ago a great Canadian man of medicine, Sir William Osler, delivered a speech to the students of Yale University entitled "A Way of Life." In the message he related an event that occurred while he was aboard an ocean liner.

One day while he was visiting with the ship's captain, a loud, piercing alarm sounded, followed by strange grinding and crashing sounds below the deck. "Those are our watertight compartments closing," the captain explained. "It's an important part of our safety drill. In case of real trouble, water leaking into one compartment would not affect the rest of the ship. Even if we should collide with an iceberg, as did the *Titanic,* water rushing in will fill only that particular ruptured compartment. The ship, however, will still remain afloat."

When he spoke to the students at Yale, Osler remembered the captain's description of the boat:

> Each one of you is certainly a much more marvelous organization than that great liner and bound on a far longer voyage. What I urge is that you learn to master your life by living each day in a day-tight compartment and this will certainly ensure your safety throughout your entire journey of life. Touch a button and hear, at every level of your life, the iron doors shutting out the Past—the dead yesterdays. Touch another and shut off, with a metal curtain, the Future—the unborn tomorrows. Then you are safe—safe for today.
>
> Think not of the amount to be accomplished, the difficulties to be overcome, but set earnestly at the little task near your elbow, letting that be sufficient for the day; for surely our plain duty is not to see what lies dimly at a distance but to do what lies clearly at hand.[1]

Jesus made the same point in fewer words: "So don't worry about tomorrow, because tomorrow will have its own worries. Each day has enough trouble of its own" (Matt. 6:34).

Easy to say. Not always easy to do, right? We are so prone to worry. Just last night I was worrying in my sleep. I dreamed that I was diagnosed with ALS, a degenerative muscle disease, which took the life of my father. I awakened from the dream and, right there in the middle of the night, began to worry. Then Jesus' words came to my mind, "Don't worry about tomorrow." And for once, I decided not to. I dropped the burlap sack. After all, why let tomorrow's imaginary problem rob tonight's rest? Can I prevent the disease by staying awake? Will I postpone the affliction by thinking about it? Of course not. So I did the most spiritual thing I could have done. I went back to sleep.

Why don't you do the same? God is leading you. Leave tomorrow's problems until tomorrow.

Arthur Hays Sulzberger was the publisher of the *New York Times* during the Second World War. Because of the world conflict, he found it almost impossible to sleep. He was never able to banish worries from his mind until he adopted as his motto these five words—"one step enough for me"—taken from the hymn "Lead Kindly Light."[2]

> Lead, kindly Light . . .
> Keep Thou my feet; I do not ask to see
> The distant scene; one step enough for me.

God isn't going to let you see the distant scene either. So you might as well quit looking for it. He promises a lamp unto our feet, not a crystal ball into the future.[3] We do not need to know what will happen tomorrow. We only need to know he leads us and "we will find grace to help us when we need it" (Heb. 4:16 NLT).

7

It's a Jungle Out There

The Burden of Hopelessness

He restores my soul.

Psalm 23:3 NKJV

I wonder if you could imagine yourself in a jungle. A dense jungle. A dark jungle. Your friends convinced you it was time for a once-in-a-lifetime trip, and here you are. You paid the fare. You crossed the ocean. You hired the guide and joined the group. And you ventured where you had never ventured before—into the thick, strange world of the jungle.

Sound interesting? Let's take it a step farther. Imagine that you are in the jungle, lost and alone. You paused to lace your boot, and when you looked up, no one was near. You took a chance and went to the right; now you're wondering if the others went to the left. (Or did you go left and they go right?)

Whatever, you are alone. And you have been alone for, well, you don't know how long it has been. Your watch was attached to your pack, and your pack is on the shoulder of the nice guy from New Jersey who volunteered to hold it while you tied your boots. You didn't intend for him to walk off with it. But he did. And here you are, stuck in the middle of nowhere.

You have a problem. First, you were not made for this place. Drop you in the center of avenues and buildings, and you could sniff your way home. But here in sky-blocking foliage? Here in trail-hiding thickets? You are out of your element. You weren't made for this jungle.

What's worse, you aren't equipped. You have no machete. No knife.

No matches. No flares. No food. You aren't equipped, but now you are trapped—and you haven't a clue how to get out.

Sound like fun to you? Me either. Before moving on, let's pause and ask how you would feel. Given such circumstances, what emotions would surface? With what thoughts would you wrestle?

Fear? Of course you would.

Anxiety? To say the least.

Anger? I could understand that. (You'd like to get your hands on those folks who convinced you to take this trip.)

But most of all, what about hopelessness? No idea where to turn. No hunch what to do. Who could blame you for sitting on a log (better check for snakes first), burying your face in your hands, and thinking, *I'll never get out of here.* You have no direction, no equipment, no hope.

Can you freeze frame that emotion for a moment? Can you sense, for just a second, how it feels to be out of your element? Out of solutions? Out of ideas and energy? Can you imagine, just for a moment, how it feels to be out of hope?

If you can, you can relate to many people in this world.

For many people, life is—well, life is a jungle. Not a jungle of trees and beasts. Would that it were so simple. Would that our jungles could be cut with a machete or our adversaries trapped in a cage. But our jungles are comprised of the thicker thickets of failing health, broken hearts, and empty wallets. Our forests are framed with hospital walls and divorce courts. We don't hear the screeching of birds or the roaring of lions, but we do hear the complaints of neighbors and the demands of bosses. Our predators are our creditors, and the brush that surrounds us is the rush that exhausts us.

It's a jungle out there.

And for some, even for many, hope is in short supply. Hopelessness is an odd bag. Unlike the others, it isn't full. It is empty, and its emptiness creates the burden. Unzip the top and examine all the pockets. Turn it upside down and shake it hard. The bag of hopelessness is painfully empty.

Not a very pretty picture, is it? Let's see if we can brighten it up. We've imagined the emotions of being lost; you think we can do the same with being rescued? What would it take to restore your hope? What would you need to reenergize your journey?

Though the answers are abundant, three come quickly to mind.

The first would be a person. Not just any person. You don't need someone equally confused. You need someone who knows the way out.

And from him you need some vision. You need someone to lift your spirits. You need someone to look you in the face and say, "This isn't the end. Don't give up. There is a better place than this. And I'll lead you there."

And, perhaps most important, you need direction. If you have only a person but no renewed vision, all you have is company. If he has a vision but no direction, you have a dreamer for company. But if you have a person with direction—who can take you from this place to the right place—ah, then you have one who can restore your hope.

Or, to use David's words, "He restores my soul."

Our Shepherd majors in restoring hope to the soul. Whether you are a lamb lost on a craggy ledge or a city slicker alone in a deep jungle, everything changes when your rescuer appears.

Your loneliness diminishes, because you have fellowship.

Your despair decreases, because you have vision.

Your confusion begins to lift, because you have direction.

Please note: You haven't left the jungle. The trees still eclipse the sky, and the thorns still cut the skin. Animals lurk and rodents scurry. The jungle is still a jungle. It hasn't changed, but you have. You have changed because you have hope. And you have hope because you have met someone who can lead you out.

Your Shepherd knows that you were not made for this place. He knows you are not equipped for this place. So he has come to guide you out.

He has come to restore your soul. He is the perfect one to do so.

He has the right vision. He reminds you that "you are like foreigners and strangers in this world" (1 Pet. 2:11). And he urges you to lift your eyes from the jungle around you to the heaven above you. "Don't shuffle along, eyes to the ground, absorbed with the things right in front of you. Look up, and be alert to what is going on around Christ. . . . See things from his perspective" (Col. 3:2 MSG).

David said it this way, "I lift up my eyes to the hills—where does my help come from? My help comes from the LORD, the Maker of heaven and earth. He will not let your foot slip—he who watches over you will not slumber. . . . The LORD watches over you . . . the sun will not harm you by day, nor the moon by night. The LORD will keep you from all harm—he will watch over your life" (Ps. 121:1–7 NIV).

God, your rescuer, has the right vision. He also has the right direction. He made the boldest claim in the history of man when he declared, "I am the way" (John 14:6). People wondered if the claim was accurate. He answered their questions by cutting a path through the underbrush of sin and death . . . and escaping alive. He's the only One who ever did. And he is the only One who can help you and me do the same.

He has the right vision: He has seen the homeland. He has the right directions: He has cut the path. But most of all, he is the right person, for he is our God. Who knows the jungle better than the One who made it? And who knows the pitfalls of the path better than the One who has walked it?

The story is told of a man on an African safari deep in the jungle. The guide before him had a machete and was whacking away the tall weeds and thick underbrush. The traveler, wearied and hot, asked in frustration, "Where are we? Do you know where you are taking me? Where is the path?!" The seasoned guide stopped and looked back at the man and replied, "I am the path."

We ask the same questions, don't we? We ask God, "Where are you taking me? Where is the path?" And he, like the guide, doesn't tell us. Oh, he may give us a hint or two, but that's all. If he did, would we understand? Would we comprehend our location? No, like the traveler, we are unacquainted with this jungle. So rather than give us an answer, Jesus gives us a far greater gift. He gives us himself.

Does he remove the jungle? No, the vegetation is still thick.

Does he purge the predators? No, danger still lurks.

Jesus doesn't give hope by changing the jungle; he restores our hope by giving us himself. And he has promised to stay until the very end. "I am with you always, to the very end of the age" (Matt. 28:20 NIV).

We need that reminder. We all need that reminder. For all of us need hope.

Some of you don't need it right now. Your jungle has become a meadow and your journey a delight. If such is the case, congratulations. But remember—we do not know what tomorrow holds. We do not know where this road will lead. You may be one turn from a cemetery, from a hospital bed, from an empty house. You may be a bend in the road from a jungle.

And though you don't need your hope restored today, you may tomorrow. And you need to know to whom to turn.

Or perhaps you do need hope today. You know you were not made for this place. You know you are not equipped. You want someone to lead you out.

If so, call out for your Shepherd. He knows your voice. And he's just waiting for your request.

8

A Heavenly Exchange

The Burden of Guilt

He leads me in the paths of righteousness for His name's sake.

PSALM 23:3 NKJV

A friend organized a Christmas cookie swap for our church office staff. The plan was simple. Price of admission was a tray of cookies. Your tray entitled you to pick cookies from the other trays. You could leave with as many cookies as you brought.

Sounds simple, if you know how to cook. But what if you can't? What if you can't tell a pan from a pot? What if, like me, you are culinarily challenged? What if you're as comfortable in an apron as a bodybuilder in a tutu? If such is the case, you've got a problem.

Such was the case, and I had a problem. I had no cookies to bring; hence I would have no place at the party. I would be left out, turned away, shunned, eschewed, and dismissed. (Are you feeling sorry for me yet?)

This was my plight.

And, forgive me for bringing it up, but your plight's even worse.

God is planning a party . . . a party to end all parties. Not a cookie party, but a feast. Not giggles and chitchat in the conference room, but wide-eyed wonder in the throne room of God.

Yes, the guestlist is impressive. Your question to Jonah about undergoing a gut check in a fish gut? You'll be able to ask him. But more impressive than the names of the guests is the nature of the guests. No egos, no power plays. Guilt, shame, and sorrow will be checked at the gate. Disease, death, and depression will be the Black Plagues of a distant past. What we now see daily, there we will never see.

And what we now see vaguely, there we will see clearly. We will see God. Not by faith. Not through the eyes of Moses or Abraham or David. Not via Scripture or sunsets or summer rains. We will see not God's work or words, but we will see him! For he is not the host of the party; he is the party. His goodness is the banquet. His voice is the music. His radiance is the light, and his love is the endless topic of discussion.

There is only one hitch. The price of admission is somewhat steep. In order to come to the party, you need to be righteous. Not good. Not decent. Not a taxpayer or churchgoer.

Citizens of heaven are righteous. R-i-g-h-t.

All of us *occasionally* do what is right. A few *predominantly* do what is right. But do any of us *always* do what is right? According to Paul we don't. "There is none righteous, no, not one" (Rom. 3:10 NKJV).

Paul is adamant about this. He goes on to say, "No one anywhere has kept on doing what is right; not one" (Rom. 3:12 TLB).

Some may beg to differ. "I'm not perfect, Max, but I'm better than most folks. I've led a good life. I don't break the rules. I don't break hearts. I help people. I like people. Compared to others, I think I could say I'm a righteous person."

I used to try that one on my mother. She'd tell me my room wasn't clean, and I'd ask her to go with me to my brother's room. His was always messier than mine. "See, my room is clean; just look at his."

Never worked. She'd walk me down the hall to her room. When it came to tidy rooms, my mom was righteous. Her closet was just right. Her bed was just right. Her bathroom was just right. Compared to hers, my room was, well, just wrong. She would show me her room and say, "This is what I mean by clean."

God does the same. He points to himself and says, "This is what I mean by righteousness."

Righteousness is who God is.

"Our God and Savior Jesus Christ does what is right" (2 Pet. 1:1).

"God is a righteous judge" (Ps. 7:11 NIV).

"The LORD is righteous, he loves justice" (Ps. 11:7 NIV).

God's righteousness "endures forever" (Ps. 112:3 NIV) and "reaches to the skies" (Ps. 71:19 NIV).

Isaiah described God as "a righteous God and a Savior" (Isa. 45:21 NIV).

On the eve of his death, Jesus began his prayer with the words "Righteous Father" (John 17:25 NIV).

Get the point? God is righteous. His decrees are righteous (Rom. 1:32). His judgment is righteous (Rom. 2:5). His requirements are righteous (Rom. 8:4). His acts are righteous (Dan. 9:16). Daniel declared, "Our God is right in everything he does" (Dan. 9:14).

God is never wrong. He has never rendered a wrong decision, experienced the wrong attitude, taken the wrong path, said the wrong thing, or acted the wrong way. He is never too late or too early, too loud or too soft, too fast or too slow. He has always been and always will be right. He is righteous.

When it comes to righteousness, God runs the table without so much as a bank shot. And when it comes to righteousness, we don't know which end of the cue stick to hold. Hence, our plight.

Will God, who is righteous, spend eternity with those who are not? Would Harvard admit a third-grade dropout? If it did, the act might be benevolent, but it wouldn't be right. If God accepted the unrighteous, the invitation would be even nicer, but would he be right? Would he be right to overlook our sins? Lower his standards? No. He wouldn't be right. And if God is anything, he is right.

He told Isaiah that righteousness would be his plumb line, the standard by which his house is measured (Isa. 28:17). If we are unrighteous, then, we are left in the hallway with no cookies. Or to use Paul's analogy, "we're sinners, every one of us, in the same sinking boat with everybody else" (Rom. 3:19 MSG). Then what are we to do?

Carry a load of guilt? Many do. So many do.

What if our spiritual baggage were visible? Suppose the luggage in our hearts was literal luggage on the street. You know what you'd see most of all? Suitcases of guilt. Bags bulging with binges, blowups, and compromises. Look around you. The fellow in the gray-flannel suit? He's dragging a decade of regrets. The kid with the baggy jeans and nose ring? He'd give anything to retract the words he said to his mother. But he can't. So he tows them along. The woman in the business suit? Looks as if she could run for senator? She'd rather run for help, but she can't run at all. Not hauling that carpetbag of cagmag everywhere she goes.

Listen. The weight of weariness pulls you down. Self-reliance misleads you. Disappointments discourage you. Anxiety plagues you. But guilt? Guilt consumes you.

So what do we do? Our Lord is right, and we are wrong. His party is for the guiltless, and we are anything but. What do we do?

I can tell you what I did. I confessed my need. Remember my cookie dilemma? This is the e-mail I sent to the whole staff. "I can't cook, so I can't be at the party."

Did any of the assistants have mercy on me? No.

Did any of the staff have mercy on me? No.

Did any of the Supreme Court justices have mercy upon me? No.

But a saintly sister in the church did have mercy on me. How she heard of my problem, I do not know. Perhaps my name found its way on an emergency prayer list. But I do know this. Only moments before the celebration, I was given a gift, a plate of cookies, twelve circles of kindness.

And by virtue of that gift, I was privileged a place at the party.

Did I go? You bet your cookies I did. Like a prince carrying a crown on a pillow, I carried my gift into the room, set it on the table, and stood tall. And because some good soul heard my plea, I was given a place at the table.

And because God hears your plea, you'll be given the same. Only, he did more—oh, so much more—than bake cookies for you.

It was, at once, history's most beautiful and most horrible moment. Jesus stood in the tribunal of heaven. Sweeping a hand over all creation, he pleaded, "Punish me for their mistakes. See the murderer? Give me his penalty. The adulteress? I'll take her shame. The bigot, the liar, the thief? Do to me what you would do to them. Treat me as you would a sinner."

And God did. "For Christ died for sins once for all, the righteous for the unrighteous, to bring you to God" (1 Pet. 3:18 NIV).

Yes, righteousness is what God is, and, yes, righteousness is what we are not, and, yes, righteousness is what God requires. But "God has a way to make people right with him" (Rom. 3:21).

David said it like this: "He leads me in the paths of righteousness" (Ps. 23:3 NKJV).

The path of righteousness is a narrow, winding trail up a steep hill. At the top of the hill is a cross. At the base of the cross are bags. Countless bags full of innumerable sins. Calvary is the compost pile for guilt. Would you like to leave yours there as well?

One final thought about the Christmas cookie party. Did everyone know I didn't cook the cookies? If they didn't, I told them. I told them I was present by virtue of someone else's work. My only contribution was my own confession.

We'll be saying the same for eternity.

9

Get Over Yourself

The Burden of Arrogance

For His name's sake . . .

PSALM 23:3 NKJV

Humility is such an elusive virtue. Once you think you have it, you don't, or you wouldn't think you did. You've heard the story of the boy who received the "Most Humble" badge and had it taken away because he wore it?

Something similar happened to me just the other morning. I had retreated to a nearby town to work on this book. The village is a perfect hideaway; it is quaint, quiet, and has great food.

I'd gone to a café for breakfast when I noticed that people were staring at me. As I parked, two fellows turned and looked in my direction. A woman did a double take as I entered, and several patrons looked up as I passed. When I took my seat, the waitress gave me a menu but not before she'd given me a good study.

Why the attention? Couldn't be my fly; I was wearing sweats. After some thought I took the mature posture and assumed they recognized me from my book jackets. *Why, this must be a town of readers. And,* I shrugged to myself, *they know a good author when they see one.* My appreciation for the village only increased.

Giving a smile to the folks at the other tables, I set about to enjoy my meal. When I walked to the cash register, the heads turned again. *I'm sure Steinbeck had the same problem.* The woman who took my money started to say something but then paused. Overwhelmed, I guessed.

It was only when I stopped in the rest room that I saw the real reason for the attention—a ribbon of dried blood on my chin. My patch job on the shaving nick hadn't worked, and I was left with my own turkey wattle.

So much for feeling famous. They probably thought I was an escapee from a Texas prison.

Oh, the things God does to keep us humble. He does it for our own good, you know. Would you set a saddle on the back of your five-year-old? Would God let you be saddled with arrogance? No way.

This is one piece of luggage God hates. He doesn't dislike arrogance. He doesn't disapprove of arrogance. He's not unfavorably disposed toward arrogance. God hates arrogance. What a meal of maggots does for our stomach, human pride does for God's.

"I hate pride and arrogance" (Prov. 8:13 NIV).

"The LORD despises pride" (Prov. 16:5 NLT).

God says, "Do nothing out of . . . vain conceit" (Phil. 2:3 NIV). And, "Do not let arrogance come out of your mouth" (1 Sam. 2:3 NASB). And, in the same way that he gives grace to the humble, "God opposes the proud" (1 Pet. 5:5 NIV). As humility goes before honor, "pride goes . . . before a fall" (Prov. 16:18 NIV).

Ever wonder why churches are powerful in one generation but empty the next? Perhaps the answer is found in Proverbs 15:25: "The LORD will tear down the house of the proud" (NASB).

God hates arrogance. He hates arrogance because we haven't done anything to be arrogant about. Do art critics give awards to the canvas? Is there a Pulitzer for ink? Can you imagine a scalpel growing smug after a successful heart transplant? Of course not. They are only tools, so they get no credit for the accomplishments.

And the message of the Twenty-third Psalm is that we have nothing to be proud about either. We have rest, salvation, blessings, and a home in heaven—and we did nothing to earn any of it. Who did? Who did the work? The answer threads through the psalm like a silk thread through pearls.

"He makes me . . ."

"He leads me . . ."

"He restores my soul . . ."

"You are with me . . ."

"Your rod and Your staff . . . comfort me . . ."

"You prepare a table . . ."

"You anoint my head . . ."

We may be the canvas, the paper, or the scalpel, but we are not the ones who deserve the applause. And just to make sure we get the point, right smack-dab in the middle of the poem, David declares who does. The shepherd leads his sheep, not for our names' sake, but "for His name's sake."

Why does God have anything to do with us? *For his name's sake.* No other name on the marquee. No other name up in lights. No other name on the front page. This is all done for God's glory.

Why? What's the big deal? Does God have an ego problem?

No, but we do. We are about as responsible with applause as I was with the cake I won in the first grade. In the grand finale of the musical chairs competition, guess who had a seat? And guess what the little red-headed, freckle-faced boy won? A tender, moist coconut cake. And guess what the boy wanted to do that night in one sitting? Eat the whole thing! Not half of it. Not a piece of it. All of it! After all, I'd won it.

But you know what my folks did? They rationed the cake. They gave me only what I could handle. Knowing that today's binge is tomorrow's bellyache, they made sure I didn't get sick on my success.

God does the same. He takes the cake. He takes the credit, not because he needs it, but because he knows we can't handle it. We aren't content with a bite of adulation; we tend to swallow it all. It messes with our systems. The praise swells our heads and shrinks our brains, and pretty soon we start thinking we had something to do with our survival. Pretty soon we forget we were made out of dirt and rescued from sin.

Pretty soon we start praying like the fellow at the religious caucus: "God, I thank you that the world has people like me. The man on the corner needs welfare—I don't. The prostitute on the street has AIDS—I don't. The drunk at the bar needs alcohol—I don't. The gay caucus needs morality—I don't. I thank you that the world has people like me."

Fortunately, there was a man in the same meeting who had deflected all the applause. Too contrite even to look to the skies, he bowed and prayed, "God, have mercy on me, a sinner. Like my brother on welfare, I'm dependent on your grace. Like my sister with AIDS, I'm infected with mistakes. Like my friend who drinks, I need something to ease my pain. And as you love and give direction to the gay, grant some to me as well. Have mercy on me, a sinner."

After telling a story like that, Jesus said, "I tell you, when this man went home, he was right with God, but the Pharisee was not. All who make themselves great will be made humble, but all who make themselves humble will be made great" (Luke 18:14).

With the same intensity that he hates arrogance, God loves humility. The Jesus who said, "I am gentle and humble in heart" (Matt. 11:29 NASB) loves those who are gentle and humble in heart. "Though the LORD is supreme, he takes care of those who are humble" (Ps. 138:6). God says, "I live with people who are . . . humble" (Isa. 57:15). He also says, "To this one I will look, to him who is humble and contrite" (Isa. 66:2 NASB). And to the humble, God gives great treasures:

He gives honor: "Humility goes before honor" (Prov. 15:33 NRSV).

He gives wisdom: "With the humble is wisdom" (Prov. 11:2 NASB).

He gives direction: "He teaches the humble His way" (Ps. 25:9 NASB).

And most significantly, he gives grace: "God . . . gives grace to the humble" (1 Pet. 5:5).

And this reassurance: "He crowns the humble with salvation" (Ps. 149:4 NIV).

The mightiest of the saints were known for their humility. Though Moses had served as prince of Egypt and emancipator of the slaves, the Bible says, "Moses was . . . more humble than anyone else" (Num. 12:3 NIV).

The apostle Paul was saved through a personal visit from Jesus. He was carried into the heavens and had the ability to raise the dead. But when he introduced himself, he mentioned none of these. He simply said, "I, Paul, am God's slave" (Titus 1:1 MSG).

John the Baptist was a blood relative of Jesus and the first evangelist in history, but he is remembered in Scripture as the one who resolved, "He must increase, but I must decrease" (John 3:30 NKJV).

God loves humility. Could that be the reason he offers so many tips on cultivating it? May I, ahem, humbly articulate a few?

1. Assess yourself honestly. Humility isn't the same as low self-esteem. Being humble doesn't mean you think you have nothing to offer; it means you know exactly what you have to offer and no more. "Don't cherish exaggerated ideas of yourself or your importance, but try to have a sane estimate of your capabilities by the light of the faith that God has given to you" (Rom. 12:3 PHILLIPS).

2. Don't take success too seriously. Scripture gives this warning: "When your . . . silver and gold increase, . . . your heart will become proud" (Deut. 8:13–14). Counteract this pride with reminders of the brevity of life and the frailty of wealth.

Ponder your success and count your money in a cemetery, and remember that neither of the two is buried with you. "People come into this world with nothing, and when they die they leave with nothing" (Eccles. 5:15). I saw a reminder of this in a cemetery. Parked next to the entrance was a nice recreational boat with a For Sale sign. You had to wonder if the fisherman realized he couldn't take it with him.

3. *Celebrate the significance of others.* "In humility consider others better than yourselves" (Phil. 2:3 NIV). Columnist Rick Reilly gave this advice to rookie professional athletes: "Stop thumping your chest. The line blocked, the quarterback threw you a perfect spiral while getting his head knocked off, and the *good* receiver blew the double coverage. Get over yourself."[1]

The truth is, every touchdown in life is a team effort. Applaud your teammates. An elementary-age boy came home from the tryouts for the school play. "Mommy, Mommy," he announced, "I got a part. I've been chosen to sit in the audience and clap and cheer." When you have a chance to clap and cheer, do you take it? If you do, your head is starting to fit your hat size.

4. *Don't demand your own parking place.* This was the instruction of Jesus to his followers: "Go sit in a seat that is not important. When the host comes to you, he may say, 'Friend, move up here to a more important place.' Then all the other guests will respect you" (Luke 14:10).

Demanding respect is like chasing a butterfly. Chase it, and you'll never catch it. Sit still, and it may light on your shoulder. The French philosopher Blaise Pascal asked, "Do you wish people to speak well of you? Then never speak well of yourself."[2] Maybe that's why the Bible says, "Don't praise yourself. Let someone else do it" (Prov. 27:2).

5. *Never announce your success before it occurs.* Or as one of the kings of Israel said, "One who puts on his armor should not boast like one who takes it off" (1 Kings 20:11 NIV). Charles Spurgeon trained many young ministers. On one occasion a student stepped up to preach with great confidence but failed miserably. He came down, humbled and

meek. Spurgeon told him, "If you had gone up as you came down, you would have come down as you went up."[3] If humility precedes an event, then confidence may follow.

6. *Speak humbly.* "Let no arrogance come from your mouth" (1 Sam. 2:3 NKJV). Don't be cocky. People aren't impressed with your opinions. Take a tip from Benjamin Franklin.

> [I developed] the habit of expressing myself in terms of modest diffidence, never using when I advance any thing that may possibly be disputed, the words certainly, undoubtedly, or any others that give the air of positiveness to an opinion; but rather I say, I conceive or I apprehend a thing to be so or so. . . . This habit I believe has been a great advantage to me.[4]

It would be a great advantage to us as well.

One last thought to foster humility.

7. *Live at the foot of the cross.* Paul said, "The cross of our Lord Jesus Christ is my only reason for bragging" (Gal. 6:14). Do you feel a need for affirmation? Does your self-esteem need attention? You don't need to drop names or show off. You need only pause at the base of the cross and be reminded of this: The maker of the stars would rather die for you than live without you. And that is a fact. So if you need to brag, brag about that.

And check your chin occasionally.

10

I Will Lead You Home

The Burden of the Grave

Yea, though I walk through the valley of the shadow of death, I will fear no evil; for You are with me; Your rod and Your staff, they comfort me.

PSALM 23:4 NKJV

Summer in ancient Palestine. A woolly bunch of bobbing heads follow the shepherd out of the gate. The morning sun has scarcely crested the horizon, and he is already leading his flock. Like every other day, he guides them through the gate and out into the fields. But unlike most days, the shepherd will not return home tonight. He will not rest on his bed, and the sheep will not sleep in their fenced-in pasture. This is the day the shepherd takes the sheep to the high country. Today he leads his flock to the mountains.

He has no other choice. Springtime grazing has left his pasture bare, so he must seek new fields. With no companion other than his sheep and no desire other than their welfare, he leads them to the deep grass of the hillsides. The shepherd and his flock will be gone for weeks, perhaps months. They will stay well into the autumn, until the grass is gone and the chill is unbearable.

Not all shepherds make this journey. The trek is long. The path is dangerous. Poisonous plants can infect the flock. Wild animals can attack the flock. There are narrow trails and dark valleys. Some shepherds choose the security of the barren pasture below.

But the good shepherd doesn't. He knows the path. He has walked this trail many times. Besides, he is prepared. Staff in hand

and rod attached to his belt. With his staff he will nudge the flock; with his rod he will protect and lead the flock. He will lead them to the mountains.

David understood this annual pilgrimage. Before he led Israel, he led sheep. And could his time as a shepherd be the inspiration behind one of the greatest verses in the Bible? "Yea, though I walk through the valley of the shadow of death, I will fear no evil; for You are with me; Your rod and Your staff, they comfort me" (Ps. 23:4 NKJV).

For what the shepherd does with the flock, our Shepherd will do with us. He will lead us to the high country. When the pasture is bare down here, God will lead us up there. He will guide us through the gate, out of the flatlands, and up the path of the mountain.

As one shepherd writes:

> Every mountain has its valleys. Its sides are scarred by deep ravines and gulches and draws. And the best route to the top is always through these valleys.
>
> Any sheepman familiar with the high country knows this. He leads his flock gently, but persistently up the paths that wind through the dark valleys.[1]

Someday our Shepherd will do the same with us. He will take us to the mountain by way of the valley. He will guide us to his house through the valley of the shadow of death.

Many years ago when I lived in Miami, our church office received a call from a nearby funeral home. A man had identified the body of an indigent as his brother and wanted a memorial service. He didn't know any ministers in the area. Would we say a few words? The senior minister and I agreed. When we arrived, the brother of the deceased had selected a text from a Spanish Bible: "Yea, though I walk through the valley of the shadow of death, I will fear no evil; for You are with me; Your rod and Your staff, they comfort me" (Ps. 23:4 NKJV).

He needed assurance that, though his brother had lived alone, he did not die alone. And for that assurance, he turned to this verse. You've likely done the same.

If you've attended a memorial service, you've heard the words. If you've walked through a cemetery, you've read them. They're quoted at the gravesides of paupers, carved on the headstones of kings. Those who know nothing of the Bible know this part of the Bible. Those who quote no scripture can remember this scripture, the one about the valley and the shadow and the shepherd.

Why? Why are these words so treasured? Why is this verse so beloved? I can think of a couple of reasons. By virtue of this psalm, David grants us two important reminders that can help us surrender our fear of the grave.

We all have to face it. In a life marked by doctor appointments, dentist appointments, and school appointments, there is one appointment that none of us will miss, the appointment with death. "Everyone must die once, and after that be judged by God" (Heb. 9:27 TEV). Oh, how we'd like to change that verse. Just a word or two would suffice. "*Nearly* everyone must die . . ." or "*Everyone but me* must die . . ." or "*Everyone who forgets to eat right and take vitamins* must die . . ." But those are not God's words. In his plan everyone must die, even those who eat right and take their vitamins.

I could have gone all day without reminding you of that. We do our best to avoid the topic. One wise man, however, urges us to face it squarely: "We all must die, and everyone living should think about this" (Eccles. 7:2). Solomon isn't promoting a morbid obsession with death. He is reminding us to be honest about the inevitable.

Moses gave the same exhortation. In the only psalm attributed to his pen, he prayed, "Teach us how short our lives really are so that we may be wise" (Ps. 90:12).

The wise remember the brevity of life. Exercise may buy us a few more heartbeats. Medicine may grant us a few more breaths. But in the end, there is an end. And the best way to face life is to be honest about death.

David was. He may have slain Goliath, but he had no illusions about sidestepping the giant of death. And though his first reminder sobers us, his second reminder encourages us: *We don't have to face death alone.*

Don't miss the shift in David's vocabulary. Up to this point, you and I have been the audience and God has been the topic. "The LORD is my shepherd." "He makes me to lie down." "He leads me beside the still waters." "He restores my soul." "He leads me in the paths of righteousness." For the first three verses, David speaks to us and God listens.

But suddenly in verse four, David speaks to God and we listen. It's as if David's face, which was on us, now lifts toward God. His poem becomes a prayer. Rather than speak to us, he speaks to the Good Shepherd. "You are with me; Your rod and Your staff, they comfort me."

David's implied message is subtle but crucial. Don't face death without facing God. Don't even speak of death without speaking to God. He and he alone can guide you through the valley. Others may speculate or aspire, but only God knows the way to get you home. And only God is committed to getting you there safely.

Years after David wrote these words, another Bethlehem Shepherd would say: "There are many rooms in my Father's house; I would not tell you this if it were not true. I am going there to prepare a place for you. After I go and prepare a place for you, I will come back and take you to be with me so that you may be where I am" (John 14:2–3).

Note the promise of Jesus. "I will come back and take you to be with me." He pledges to take us home. He does not delegate this task. He may send missionaries to teach you, angels to protect you, teachers to guide you, singers to inspire you, and physicians to heal you, but he sends no one to take you. He reserves this job for himself. "I will come back and take you home." He is your personal Shepherd. And he is personally responsible to lead you home. And because he is present when any of his sheep dies, you can say what David said, "I will fear no evil."

When my daughters were younger, we enjoyed many fun afternoons in the swimming pool. Just like all of us, they had to overcome their fears in order to swim. One of the final fears they had to face was the fear of the deep. It's one thing to swim on the surface; it's another to plunge down to the bottom. I mean, who knows what kind of dragons and serpents dwell in the depths of an eight-foot pool? You and I know there is no evil to fear, but a six-year-old doesn't. A child feels the same way about the deep that you and I feel about death. We aren't sure what awaits us down there.

I didn't want my daughters to be afraid of the deep end, so with each I played Shamu the whale. My daughter would be the trainer. I would be Shamu. She would pinch her nose and put her arm around my neck, then down we would go. Deep, deep, deep until we could touch the bottom of the pool. Then up we would explode, breaking the surface. After several plunges they realized they had nothing to fear. They feared no evil. Why? Because I was with them.

And when God calls us into the deep valley of death, he will be with us. Dare we think that he would abandon us in the moment of death? Would a father force his child to swim the deep alone? Would the shepherd require his sheep to journey to the highlands alone? Of course not. Would God require his child to journey to eternity alone? Absolutely not! He is with you!

What God said to Moses, he says to you: "My Presence will go with you, and I will give you rest" (Exod. 33:14 NIV).

What God said to Jacob, he says to you: "I am with you and will watch over you wherever you go" (Gen. 28:15 NIV).

What God said to Joshua, he says to you: "As I was with Moses, so I will be with you; I will never leave you nor forsake you" (Josh. 1:5 NIV).

What God said to the nation of Israel, he says to you: "When you pass through the waters, I will be with you" (Isa. 43:2 NIV).

The Good Shepherd is with you. And because he is with you, you can say what David said: "I will fear no evil; for You are with me; Your rod and Your staff, they comfort me."

Years ago a chaplain in the French army used the Twenty-third Psalm to encourage soldiers before battle. He would urge them to repeat the opening clause of the psalm, ticking it off, one finger at a time. The little finger represented the word *the;* the ring finger represented the word *LORD;* the middle finger, *is;* the index finger, *my;* and the thumb, *shepherd*. Then he asked every soldier to write the words on the palm of his hand and to repeat the verse whenever he needed strength.

The chaplain placed special emphasis on the message of the index finger—*my*. He reminded the soldiers that God is a personal shepherd with a personal mission—to get them home safely.

Did the chaplain's words find their mark? In the life of one man they did. After a battle one of the young soldiers was found dead, his right hand clutching the index finger of the left. "The LORD is my shepherd . . ."[2]

I pray that your final hours will find you clutching the same hope.

11

When Mourning Comes

The Burden of Grief

Though I walk through the valley of the shadow of death . . .

PSALM 23:4 NKJV

Carlos Andres Baisdon-Niño lay down with his favorite Bible storybook. He began with the first chapter and turned every page until the end. When he finished, he blew his good-night kisses to Mami and Papi, to his three *"niñas,"* and then, as always, he blew one to Papa Dios. He closed his eyes, drifted off to sleep, and awoke in heaven.

Carlos was three years old.

When Tim and Betsa, his parents, and I met to plan the funeral, they wanted me to watch a video of Carlos. "You've got to see him dancing," Tim told me. One look and I could see why. What little Carlos did to the rhythm of a Latin song can't be described with words. He shook from top to bottom. His feet moved, his hands bounced, his head swayed. You got the impression that his heart rate had switched over to his native Colombian beat.

We laughed, the three of us did. And in the laughter, for just a moment, Carlos was with us. For just a moment there was no leukemia, syringes, blankets, or chemotherapy. There was no stone to carve or grave to dig. There was just Carlos. And Carlos was just dancing.

But then the video stopped, and so did the laughter. And this mom and dad resumed their slow walk through the valley of the shadow of death.

Are you passing through the same shadow? Is this book being held by the same hands that touched the cold face of a friend? And the eyes that fall upon this page, have they also fallen upon the breathless figure of a husband, wife, or child? Are you passing through the valley? If not, this chapter may seem unnecessary. Feel free to move on—it will be here when you need it.

If so, however, you know that the black bag of sorrow is hard to bear.

It's hard to bear because not everyone understands your grief. They did at first. They did at the funeral. They did at the graveside. But they don't now; they don't understand. Grief lingers.

As silently as a cloud slides between you and the afternoon sun, memories drift between you and joy, leaving you in a chilly shadow. No warning. No notice. Just a whiff of the cologne he wore or a verse of the song she loved, and you are saying good-bye all over again.

Why won't the sorrow leave you alone?

Because you buried more than a person. You buried some of yourself. Wasn't it John Donne who said, "Any man's death diminishes me"? It's as if the human race resides on a huge trampoline. The movements of one can be felt by all. And the closer the relationship, the more profound the exit. When someone you love dies, it affects you.

It affects your dreams.

Some years ago my wife and I served with other missionaries in Rio de Janeiro, Brazil. Our team consisted of several young couples who, by virtue of being far away from home, became very close. We rejoiced greatly when two of our team members, Marty and Angela, announced that she was pregnant with their first child.

The pregnancy was difficult, however, and the joy became concern. Angela was told to stay in bed, and we were urged to stay in prayer. We did. And the Lord answered our prayers, though not as we desired. The baby died in the womb.

I've never forgotten Marty's comment. "More than a baby died, Max. A dream died."

Why does grief linger? Because you are dealing with more than memories—you are dealing with unlived tomorrows. You're not just battling sorrow—you're battling disappointment. You're also battling anger.

It may be on the surface. It may subterranean. It may be a flame. It may be a blowtorch. But anger lives in sorrow's house. Anger at self. Anger at life. Anger at the military or the hospital or the highway system. But most of all, anger at God. Anger that takes the form of the three-letter question—why? Why him? Why her? Why now? Why us?

You and I both know I can't answer that question. Only God knows the reasons behind his actions. But here is a key truth on which we can stand.

Our God is a good God.

"You are good, LORD. The LORD is good and right" (Ps. 25:7–8).

"Taste and see that the LORD is good" (Ps. 34:8 NIV).

God is a good God. We must begin here. Though we don't understand his actions, we can trust his heart.

God does only what is good. But how can death be good? Some mourners don't ask this question. When the quantity of years has outstripped the quality of years, we don't ask how death can be good.

But the father of the dead teenager does. The thirty-year-old widow does. The parents of Carlos did. My friends in Rio did. How could death be good?

Part of the answer may be found in Isaiah 57:1–2: "Good people are taken away, but no one understands. Those who do right are being taken away from evil and are given peace. Those who live as God wants find rest in death."

Death is God's way of taking people away from evil. From what kind of evil? An extended disease? An addiction? A dark season of rebellion? We don't know. But we know that no person lives one day more or less than God intends. "All the days planned for me were written in your book before I was one day old" (Ps. 139:16).

But her days here were so few . . .

His life was so brief . . .

To us it seems that way. We speak of a short life, but compared to eternity, who has a long one? A person's days on earth may appear as a drop in the ocean. Yours and mine may seem like a thimbleful. But compared to the Pacific of eternity, even the years of Methuselah filled no more than a glass. James was not speaking just to the young when he said, "Your life is like a mist. You can see it for a short time, but then it goes away" (James 4:14).

In God's plan every life is long enough and every death is timely. And though you and I might wish for a longer life, God knows better.

And—this is important—though you and I may wish a longer life for our loved ones, they don't. Ironically, the first to accept God's decision of death is the one who dies.

While we are shaking heads in disbelief, they are lifting hands in worship. While we are mourning at a grave, they are marveling at heaven. While we are questioning God, they are praising God.

But, Max, what of those who die with no faith? My husband never prayed. My grandpa never worshiped. My mother never opened a Bible, much less her heart. What about the one who never believed?

How do we know he didn't?

Who among us is privy to a person's final thoughts? Who among us knows what transpires in those final moments? Are you sure no prayer was offered? Eternity can bend the proudest knees. Could a person stare into the yawning canyon of death without whispering a plea for mercy? And could our God, who is partial to the humble, resist it?

He couldn't on Calvary. The confession of the thief on the cross was both a first and final one. But Christ heard it. Christ received it. Maybe you never heard your loved one confess Christ, but who's to say Christ didn't?

We don't know the final thoughts of a dying soul, but we know this. We know our God is a good God. He is "not willing that any should perish but that all should come to repentance" (2 Pet. 3:9 NKJV). He wants your loved one in heaven more than you do. And he usually gets what he wants.

You know what else God wants? He wants you to face your sorrow. Denial and dismissal are not a part of God's grief therapy.

David faced his. When he learned of the death of Saul and Jonathan, David and the entire army tore their clothing, wept aloud, and fasted until sunset. His lament was intense and public. "May there be no dew or rain on the mountains of Gilboa," he mourned, "and may their fields produce no grain. . . . We loved Saul and Jonathan and enjoyed them while they lived. They are together even in death. They were faster than eagles. They were stronger than lions" (2 Sam. 1:21–23).

David not only sang this dirge, he "ordered that the people of Judah be taught this song" (v. 18). Death was not soft-pedaled or passed over. Face it, fight it, question it, or condemn it, but don't deny it. As his son Solomon explained, "There is . . . a time to mourn" (Eccles. 3:1, 4 NIV). Don't heed, but do forgive, those who urge you not to.

God will lead you *through,* not around, the valley of the shadow of death. And, by the way, aren't you glad it's just a shadow?

Dr. Donald Grey Barnhouse told of the occasion of his first wife's death. He and his children were driving home from the burial, overcome with grief. He searched for a word of comfort to offer but could think of nothing. Just then, a large moving van drove by. As it passed, the shadow of the truck swept over the car. An inspiration came to Dr. Barnhouse. He turned to his family and asked, "Children, would you rather be run over by a truck or by its shadow?"

The children said, "Well, of course, Dad, we'd rather be run over by the shadow. That can't hurt us at all."

Dr. Barnhouse explained, "Did you know that two thousand years ago the truck of death ran over the Lord Jesus . . . in order that only its shadow might run over us?"[1]

We face death, but thanks to Jesus, we only face its shadow. And thanks to Jesus, we believe that our loved ones are happy and that the little Carloses of the world are dancing as never before.

12

From Panic to Peace

The Burden of Fear

I will fear no evil.

Psalm 23:4 NKJV

It's the expression of Jesus that puzzles us. We've never seen his face like this.

Jesus smiling, yes.

Jesus weeping, absolutely.

Jesus stern, even that.

But Jesus anguished? Cheeks streaked with tears? Face flooded in sweat? Rivulets of blood dripping from his chin? You remember the night.

> Jesus left the city and went to the Mount of Olives, as he often did, and his followers went with him. When he reached the place, he said to them, "Pray for strength against temptation."
>
> Then Jesus went about a stone's throw away from them. He kneeled down and prayed, "Father, if you are willing, take away this cup of suffering. But do what you want, not what I want." Then an angel from heaven appeared to him to strengthen him. Being full of pain, Jesus prayed even harder. His sweat was like drops of blood falling to the ground. (Luke 22:39–44)

The Bible I carried as a child contained a picture of Jesus in the Garden of Gethsemane. His face was soft, hands calmly folded as he knelt beside a rock and prayed. Jesus seemed peaceful. One reading of the Gospels disrupts that image. Mark says, "Jesus fell to the ground" (Mark 14:35). Matthew tells us Jesus was "very sad and troubled . . . to the point of death" (Matt. 26:37–38). According to Luke, Jesus was "full of pain" (Luke 22:44).

Equipped with those passages, how would you paint this scene? Jesus flat on the ground? Face in the dirt? Extended hands gripping grass? Body rising and falling with sobs? Face as twisted as the olive trees that surround him?

What do we do with this image of Jesus?

Simple. We turn to it when we look the same. We read it when we feel the same; we read it when we feel afraid. For isn't it likely that fear is one of the emotions Jesus felt? One might even argue that fear was the primary emotion. He saw something in the future so fierce, so foreboding that he begged for a change of plans. "Father, if you are willing, take away this cup of suffering" (Luke 22:42).

What causes you to pray the same prayer? Boarding an airplane? Facing a crowd? Public speaking? Taking a job? Taking a spouse? Driving on a highway? The source of your fear may seem small to others. But to you, it freezes your feet, makes your heart pound, and brings blood to your face. That's what happened to Jesus.

He was so afraid that he bled. Doctors describe this condition as hematidrosis. Severe anxiety causes the release of chemicals that break down the capillaries in the sweat glands. When this occurs, sweat comes out tinged with blood.

Jesus was more than anxious; he was afraid. Fear is worry's big brother. If worry is a burlap bag, fear is a trunk of concrete. It wouldn't budge.

How remarkable that Jesus felt such fear. But how kind that he told us about it. We tend to do the opposite. Gloss over our fears. Cover them up. Keep our sweaty palms in our pockets, our nausea and dry mouths a secret. Not so with Jesus. We see no mask of strength. But we do hear a request for strength.

"Father, if you are willing, take away this cup of suffering." The first one to hear his fear is his Father. He could have gone to his mother. He could have confided in his disciples. He could have assembled a prayer meeting. All would have been appropriate, but none were his priority. He went first to his Father.

Oh, how we tend to go everywhere else. First to the bar, to the counselor, to the self-help book or the friend next door. Not Jesus. The first one to hear his fear was his Father in heaven.

A millennium earlier David was urging the fear-filled to do the same. "I will fear no evil." How could David make such a claim? Because he knew where to look. "You are with me; Your rod and Your staff, they comfort me."

Rather than turn to the other sheep, David turned to the Shepherd. Rather than stare at the problems, he stared at the rod and staff. Because he knew where to look, David was able to say, "I will fear no evil."

I know a fellow who has a fear of crowds. When encircled by large groups, his breath grows short, panic surfaces, and he begins to sweat like a sumo wrestler in a sauna. He received some help, curiously, from a golfing buddy.

The two were at a movie theatre, waiting their turn to enter, when fear struck again. The crowd closed in like a forest. He wanted out and out fast. His buddy told him to take a few deep breaths. Then he helped manage the crisis by reminding him of the golf course.

"When you are hitting your ball out of the rough, and you are surrounded by trees, what do you do?"

"I look for an opening."

"You don't stare at the trees?"

"Of course not. I find an opening and focus on hitting the ball through it."

"Do the same in the crowd. When you feel the panic, don't focus on the people; focus on the opening."

Good counsel in golf. Good counsel in life. Rather than focus on the fear, focus on the solution.

That's what Jesus did.

That's what David did.

And that's what the writer of Hebrews urges us to do. "Let us run with endurance the race that is set before us, looking unto Jesus, the author and finisher of our faith" (Heb. 12:1–2 NKJV).

The writer of Hebrews was not a golfer, but he could have been a jogger, for he speaks of a runner and a forerunner. The forerunner is Jesus, the "author and finisher of our faith." He is the author—that is to say he wrote the book on salvation. And he is the finisher—he not only charted the map, he blazed the trail. He is the forerunner, and we are the runners. And we runners are urged to keep our eyes on Jesus.

I'm a runner. More mornings than not I drag myself out of bed and onto the street. I don't run fast. And compared to marathoners, I don't run far. But I run. I run because I don't like cardiologists. Nothing personal, mind you. It's just that I come from a family that keeps them in business. One told my dad he needed to retire. Another opened the chests of both my mom and brother. I'd like to be the one family member who doesn't keep a heart surgeon's number on speed dial.

Since heart disease runs in our family, I run in our neighborhood. As the sun is rising, I am running. And as I am running, my body is groaning. It doesn't want to cooperate. My knee hurts. My hip is stiff. My ankles complain. Sometimes a passerby laughs at my legs, and my ego hurts.

Things hurt. And as things hurt, I've learned that I have three options. Go home. (Denalyn would laugh at me.) Meditate on my hurts until I start imagining I'm having chest pains. (Pleasant thought.) Or I can keep running and watch the sun come up. My trail has just enough easterly bend to give me a front-row seat for God's morning miracle. If I watch God's world go from dark to golden, guess what? The same happens to my attitude. The pain passes and the joints loosen, and before I know it, the run is half over and life ain't half bad. Everything improves as I fix my eyes on the sun.

Wasn't that the counsel of the Hebrew epistle—"looking unto Jesus"? What was the focus of David? "You are with me; Your rod and Your staff, they comfort me."

How did Jesus endure the terror of the crucifixion? He went first to the Father with his fears. He modeled the words of Psalm 56:3: "When I am afraid, I put my trust in you" (NLT).

Do the same with yours. Don't avoid life's Gardens of Gethsemane. Enter them. Just don't enter them alone. And while there, be honest. Pounding the ground is permitted. Tears are allowed. And if you sweat blood, you won't be the first. Do what Jesus did; open your heart.

And be specific. Jesus was. "Take *this* cup," he prayed. Give God the number of the flight. Tell him the length of the speech. Share the details of the job transfer. He has plenty of time. He also has plenty of compassion.

He doesn't think your fears are foolish or silly. He won't tell you to "buck up" or "get tough." He's been where you are. He knows how you feel.

And he knows what you need. That's why we punctuate our prayers as Jesus did. "If you are willing . . ."

Was God willing? Yes and no. He didn't take away the cross, but he took the fear. God didn't still the storm, but he calmed the sailor.

Who's to say he won't do the same for you?

"Do not be anxious about anything, but in everything, by prayer and petition, with thanksgiving, present your requests to God" (Phil. 4:6 NIV).

Don't measure the size of the mountain; talk to the One who can move it. Instead of carrying the world on your shoulders, talk to the One who holds the universe on his. Hope is a look away.

Now, what were you looking at?

13

Silent Nights and Solitary Days

The Burden of Loneliness

You are with me.

PSALM 23:4 NKJV

A friend of mine worked at a pharmacy while attending the University of Texas. Steve's primary job was to deliver supplies to nursing homes in the Austin area. An additional task, however, involved a short trip next door.

Every four days he shouldered a large jug of water and carried it fifty or so feet to a building behind the pharmacy. The customer was an older woman, perhaps in her seventies, who lived alone in a dark, sparse, and tarnished apartment. A single light bulb hung from the ceiling. The wallpaper was stained and peeling. The shades were drawn, and the room was shadowy. Steve would deliver the jug, receive the payment, thank the woman, and leave.

Over the weeks he grew puzzled by her purchase. He learned that the woman had no other source of water. She would rely on his delivery for four days of washing, bathing, and drinking. Odd choice. Municipal water was cheaper. The city would have charged her twelve to fifteen dollars a month; her expense at the pharmacy added up to fifty dollars a month. Why didn't she choose the less expensive source?

The answer was in the delivery system. Yes, the city water cost less. But the city sent only the water; they didn't send a person. She preferred to pay more and see a human being than pay less and see no one.

Could anyone be that lonely?

It seems that David was. Some of his psalms have the feel of a lone oak on a winter prairie.

He wrote:

> Turn to me and be gracious to me,
>   for I am lonely and afflicted. (Ps. 25:16 NIV)

> I'm tired of all this—so tired. My bed
>   has been floating forty days and nights
> On the flood of my tears.
>   My mattress is soaked, soggy with tears.
> The sockets of my eyes are black holes;
>   Nearly blind, I squint and grope. (Ps. 6:6–7 MSG)

David knew what it feels like to be lonely . . . betrayed.

> When they were sick, I dressed in black;
>   instead of eating, I prayed.
> My prayers were like lead in my gut,
>   like I'd lost my best friend, my brother.
> I paced, distraught as a motherless child,
>   hunched and heavyhearted.

> But when I was down
>   they threw a party!
> All the nameless riffraff of the town came
>   chanting insults about me.
> Like barbarians desecrating a shrine,
>   they destroyed my reputation.

> YAHWEH, how long are you going
> to stand there doing nothing? (Ps. 35:13–17 MSG)

David knew the feeling of loneliness.

He knew it in his family. He was one of eight sons of Jesse. But when Samuel the prophet asked to see Jesse's boys, David was overlooked. The prophet counted and asked if there wasn't another child somewhere. Jesse snapped his fingers as if he'd forgotten his keys. "I still have the youngest son. He is out taking care of the sheep" (1 Sam. 16:11).

Jesse's term for "youngest son" was not complimentary. He literally said, "I still have the runt." Some of you were the runt in your family. The runt is the one the others have to put up with and keep an eye on. And on this day the runt was left out. How would you feel if a family meeting was called and your name wasn't?

Things didn't improve when he changed households.

His inclusion in the royal family was King Saul's idea. His exclusion was Saul's idea as well. Had David not ducked, he would have been pinned to the wall by the spear of the jealous king. But David did duck, and David did run. For ten years he ran. Into the wilderness he ran. Sleeping in caves, surviving on wild animals. He was hated and hunted like a jackal.

David was no stranger to loneliness.

You aren't either. By now you've learned that you don't have to be alone to feel lonely. Two thousand years ago 250 million people populated the earth. Now there are more than 5 billion. If loneliness could be cured by the presence of people, then surely there would be less loneliness today. But loneliness lingers.

Very early in my ministry I offered this Sunday morning prayer: "Thank you, Lord, for all our friends. We have so many we can't spend time with them all." After the service a successful businessman corrected me, "You may have more friends than you can see. Not me. I have none." A person can be surrounded by a church and still be lonely.

Loneliness is not the absence of faces. It is the absence of intimacy. Loneliness doesn't come from being alone; it comes from feeling alone. Feeling as if you are

facing death alone,

facing disease alone,

facing the future alone.

Whether it strikes you in your bed at night or on your drive to the hospital, in the silence of an empty house or the noise of a crowded bar, loneliness is when you think, *I feel so alone. Does anyone care?*

Bags of loneliness show up everywhere. They litter the floors of boardrooms and clubs. We drag them into parties and usually drag them back out. You'll spot them near the desk of the overworker, beside the table of the overeater, and on the nightstand of the one-night stand. We'll try anything to unload our loneliness. This is one bag we want to drop quickly.

But should we? Should we be so quick to drop it? Rather than turn from loneliness, what if we turned toward it? Could it be that loneliness is not a curse but a gift? A gift from God?

Wait a minute, Max. That can't be. Loneliness heavies my heart. Loneliness leaves me empty and depressed. Loneliness is anything but a gift.

You may be right, but work with me for a moment. I wonder if loneliness is God's way of getting our attention.

Here's what I mean. Suppose you borrow a friend's car. His radio doesn't work, but his CD player does. You rummage through his collection, looking for your style of music—let's say, country-western. But you find nothing. He has nothing but his style of music—let's say, classical.

It's a long trip. And you can talk to yourself for only so long. So eventually you reach for a CD. You'd prefer some steel guitar, but you're stuck with soaring tenors. Initially it's tolerable. At least it fills the air. But eventually it's enjoyable. Your heart picks up the pattern of the kettledrums, your head rolls with the cellos, and you even catch yourself attempting a little Italian aria. "Hey, this isn't so bad."

Now, let me ask you. Would you have made this discovery on your own? No. What led to it? What caused you to hear music you'd never heard before? Simple. You had no other choice, no other option. You had nowhere else to go. Finally, when the silence was too loud, you took a chance on a song you'd never heard.

Oh, how God wants you to hear his music.

He has a rhythm that will race your heart and lyrics that will stir your tears. You want to journey to the stars? He can take you there. You want to lie down in peace? His music can soothe your soul.

But first, he's got to get rid of that country-western stuff. (Forgive me, Nashville. Only an example.)

And so he begins tossing the CDs. A friend turns away. The job goes bad. Your spouse doesn't understand. The church is dull. One by one he removes the options until all you have left is God.

He would do that? Absolutely. "The Lord disciplines those he loves" (Heb. 12:6). If he must silence every voice, he will. He wants you to hear his music. He wants you to discover what David discovered and to be able to say what David said.

"You are with me."

Yes, you, Lord, are in heaven. Yes, you rule the universe. Yes, you sit upon the stars and make your home in the deep. But yes, yes, yes, you are with me.

The Lord is with me. The Creator is with me. Yahweh is with me.

Moses proclaimed it: "What great nation has a god as near to them as the LORD our God is near to us" (Deut. 4:7 NLT).

Paul announced it: "He is not far from each one of us" (Acts 17:27 NIV).

And David discovered it: "You are with me."

Somewhere in the pasture, wilderness, or palace, David discovered that God meant business when he said:

"I will not leave you" (Gen. 28:15).

"I will . . . not forsake My people" (1 Kings 6:13 NKJV).

"The LORD will not abandon His people" (Ps. 94:14 NASB).

"God . . . will never leave you nor forsake you" (Deut. 31:6 NIV).

The discovery of David is indeed the message of Scripture—*the Lord is with us.* And, since the Lord is near, everything is different. Everything!

You may be facing death, but you aren't facing death alone; the Lord is with you. You may be facing unemployment, but you aren't facing unemployment alone; the Lord is with you. You may be facing marital struggles, but you aren't facing them alone; the Lord is with you. You may be facing debt, but you aren't facing debt alone; the Lord is with you.

Underline these words: You are not alone.

Your family may turn against you, but God won't. Your friends may betray you, but God won't. You may feel alone in the wilderness, but you are not. He is with you. And because he is, everything is different. *You* are different.

God changes your *n* into a *v*. You go from *lonely* to *lovely.*

When you know God loves you, you won't be desperate for the love of others.

You'll no longer be a hungry shopper at the market. Have you ever gone to the grocery on an empty stomach? You're a sitting duck. You buy everything you don't need. Doesn't matter if it is good for you—you just want to fill your tummy. When you're lonely, you do the same in life, pulling stuff off the shelf, not because you need it, but because you are hungry for love.

Why do we do it? Because we fear facing life alone. For fear of not fitting in, we take the drugs. For fear of standing out, we wear the clothes. For fear of appearing small, we go into debt and buy the house. For fear of going unnoticed, we dress to seduce or to impress. For fear of sleeping alone, we sleep with anyone. For fear of not being loved, we search for love in all the wrong places.

But all that changes when we discover God's perfect love. And "perfect love casts out fear" (1 John 4:18 NKJV).

Loneliness. Could it be one of God's finest gifts? If a season of solitude is his way to teach you to hear his song, don't you think it's worth it?

So do I.

14

The Crowing Rooster and Me

The Burden of Shame

You prepare a table before me in the presence of my enemies.

PSALM 23:5 NKJV

See the fellow in the shadows? That's Peter. Peter the apostle. Peter the impetuous. Peter the passionate. He once walked on water. Stepped right out of the boat onto the lake. He'll soon preach to thousands. Fearless before friends and foes alike. But tonight the one who stepped on the water has hurried into hiding. The one who will speak with power is weeping in pain.

Not sniffling or whimpering, but weeping. Bawling. Bearded face buried in thick hands. His howl echoing in the Jerusalem night. What hurts more? The fact that he did it? Or the fact that he swore he never would?

"Lord, I am ready to go with you to prison and even to die with you!" he pledged only hours earlier. "But Jesus said, 'Peter, before the rooster crows this day, you will say three times that you don't know me'" (Luke 22:33–34).

Denying Christ on the night of his betrayal was bad enough, but did he have to boast that he wouldn't? And one denial was pitiful, but three? Three denials were horrific, but did he have to curse? "Peter began to place a curse on himself and swear, 'I don't know the man'" (Matt. 26:74).

And now, awash in a whirlpool of sorrow, Peter is hiding. Peter is weeping. And soon Peter will be fishing.

We wonder why he goes fishing. We know why he goes to Galilee.

He had been told that the risen Christ would meet the disciples there. The arranged meeting place is not the sea, however, but a mountain (Matt. 28:16). If the followers were to meet Jesus on a mountain, what are they doing in a boat? No one told them to fish, but that's what they did. "Simon Peter said, 'I am going out to fish.' The others said, 'We will go with you'" (John 21:3). Besides, didn't Peter quit fishing? Two years earlier, when Jesus called him to fish for men, didn't he drop his net and follow? We haven't seen him fish since. We never see him fish again. Why is he fishing now? Especially now! Jesus has risen from the dead. Peter has seen the empty tomb. Who could fish at a time like this?

Were they hungry? Perhaps that's the sum of it. Maybe the expedition was born out of growling stomachs.

Or then again, maybe it was born out of a broken heart.

You see, Peter could not deny his denial. The empty tomb did not erase the crowing rooster. Christ had returned, but Peter wondered, he must have wondered, "After what I did, would he return for someone like me?"

We've wondered the same. Is Peter the only person to do the very thing he swore he'd never do?

"Infidelity is behind me!"

"From now on, I'm going to bridle my tongue."

"No more shady deals. I've learned my lesson."

Oh, the volume of our boasting. And, oh, the heartbreak of our shame.

Rather than resist the flirting, we return it.

Rather than ignore the gossip, we share it.

Rather than stick to the truth, we shade it.

And the rooster crows, and conviction pierces, and Peter has a partner in the shadows. We weep as Peter wept, and we do what Peter did. We go fishing. We go back to our old lives. We return to our pre-Jesus practices. We do what comes naturally, rather than what comes spiritually. And we question whether Jesus has a place for folks like us.

Jesus answers that question. He answers it for you and me and all who tend to "Peter out" on Christ. His answer came on the shore of the sea in a gift to Peter. You know what Jesus did? Split the waters? Turn the boat to gold and the nets to silver? No, Jesus did something much more meaningful. He invited Peter to breakfast. Jesus prepared a meal.

Of course, the breakfast was one special moment among several that morning. There was the great catch of fish and the recognition of Jesus. The plunge of Peter and the paddling of the disciples. And there was the moment they reached the shore and found Jesus next to a fire of coals. The fish were sizzling, and the bread was waiting, and the defeater of hell and the ruler of heaven invited his friends to sit down and have a bite to eat.

No one could have been more grateful than Peter. The one Satan had sifted like wheat was eating bread at the hand of God. Peter was welcomed to the meal of Christ. Right there for the devil and his tempters to see, Jesus "prepared a table in the presence of his enemies."

OK, so maybe Peter didn't say it that way. But David did. "You prepare a table before me in the presence of my enemies" (Ps. 23:5 NKJV). What the shepherd did for the sheep sounds a lot like what Jesus did for Peter.

At this point in the psalm, David's mind seems to be lingering in the high country with the sheep. Having guided the flock through the valley to the alp lands for greener grass, he remembers the shepherd's added responsibility. He must prepare the pasture.

This is new land, so the shepherd must be careful. Ideally, the grazing area will be flat, a mesa or tableland. The shepherd searches for poisonous plants and ample water. He looks for signs of wolves, coyotes, and bears.

Of special concern to the shepherd is the adder, a small brown snake that lives underground. Adders are known to pop out of their holes and nip the sheep on the nose. The bite often infects and can even kill. As defense against the snake, the shepherd pours a circle of oil at the top of each adder's hole. He also applies the oil to the noses of the animals. The oil on the snake's hole lubricates the exit, preventing the snake from climbing out. The smell of the oil on the sheep's nose drives the serpent away. The shepherd, in a very real sense, has prepared the table.[1]

What if your Shepherd did for you what the shepherd did for his flock? Suppose he dealt with your enemy, the devil, and prepared for you a safe place of nourishment? What if Jesus did for you what he did for Peter? Suppose he, in the hour of your failure, invited you to a meal?

What would you say if I told you he has done exactly that?

On the night before his death, Jesus prepared a table for his followers.

> On the first day of the Festival of Unleavened Bread, the day the lambs for the Passover meal were killed, Jesus' disciples asked him, "Where do you want us to go and get the Passover meal ready for you?"
>
> Then Jesus sent two of them with these instructions: "Go into the city, and a man carrying a jar of water will meet you. Follow him to the house he enters, and say to the owner of the house: 'The Teacher says, Where is the room where my disciples and I will eat the Passover meal?' Then he will show you a large, upstairs room, fixed up and furnished, where you will get everything ready for us." (Mark 14:12–15 TEV)

Look who did the "preparing" here. Jesus reserved a large room and arranged for the guide to lead the disciples. Jesus made certain the room was furnished and the food set out. What did the disciples do? They faithfully complied and were fed.

The Shepherd prepared the table.

Not only that, he dealt with the snakes. You'll remember that only one of the disciples didn't complete the meal that night. "The devil had already persuaded Judas Iscariot, the son of Simon, to turn against Jesus" (John 13:2). Judas started to eat, but Jesus didn't let him finish. On the command of Jesus, Judas left the room. "'The thing that you will do—do it quickly.' . . . Judas took the bread Jesus gave him and immediately went out. It was night" (John 13:27, 30).

There is something dynamic in this dismissal. Jesus prepared a table in the presence of the enemy. Judas was allowed to see the supper, but he wasn't allowed to stay there.

You are not welcome here. This table is for my children. You may tempt them. You may trip them. But you will never sit with them. This is how much he loves us.

And if any doubt remains, lest there be any "Peters" who wonder if there is a place at the table for them, Jesus issues a tender reminder as he passes the cup. "Every one of you drink this. This is my blood which is the new agreement that God makes with his people. This blood is poured out for many to forgive their sins" (Matt. 26:27–28).

"*Every one* of you drink this." Those who feel unworthy, drink this. Those who feel ashamed, drink this. Those who feel embarrassed, drink this.

May I share a time when I felt all three?

By the age of eighteen I was well on my way to a drinking problem. My system had become so resistant to alcohol that a six-pack of beer had little or no impact on me. At the age of twenty, God not only saved me from hell after this life, he saved me from hell during it. Only he knows where I was headed, but I have a pretty good idea.

For that reason, part of my decision to follow Christ included no more beer. So I quit. But, curiously, the thirst for beer never left. It hasn't hounded me or consumed me, but two or three times a week the thought of a good beer sure entices me. Proof to me that I have to be careful is this—nonalcoholic beers have no appeal. It's not the flavor of the drink; it's the buzz. But for more than twenty years, drinking has never been a major issue.

A couple of years ago, however, it nearly became one. I lowered my guard a bit. *One beer with barbecue won't hurt.* Then another time with Mexican food. Then a time or two with no food at all. Over a period of two months I went from no beers to maybe one or two a week. Again, for most people, no problem, but for me it could become one.

You know when I began to smell trouble? One hot Friday afternoon I was on my way to speak at our annual men's retreat. Did I say the day was hot? Brutally hot. I was thirsty. Soda wouldn't do. So I began to plot. Where could I buy a beer and not be seen by anyone I knew?

With that thought, I crossed a line. What's done in secret is best not done at all. But I did it anyway. I drove to an out-of-the-way convenience store, parked, and waited until all patrons had left. I entered, bought my beer, held it close to my side, and hurried to the car.

That's when the rooster crowed.

It crowed because I was sneaking around. It crowed because I knew better. It crowed because, and this really hurt, the night before I'd scolded one of my daughters for keeping secrets from me. And now, what was I doing?

I threw the beer in the trash and asked God to forgive me. A few days later I shared my struggle with the elders and some members of the congregation and was happy to chalk up the matter to experience and move on.

But I couldn't. The shame plagued me. Of all the people to do such a thing. So many could be hurt by my stupidity. And of all the times to do such a thing. En route to minister at a retreat. What hypocrisy!

I felt like a bum. Forgiveness found its way into my head, but the elevator designed to lower it eighteen inches to my heart was out of order.

And, to make matters worse, Sunday rolled around. I found myself on the front row of the church, awaiting my turn to speak. Again, I had been honest with God, honest with the elders, honest with myself. But still, I struggled. Would God want a guy like me to preach?

The answer came in the Supper. The Lord's Supper. The same Jesus who'd prepared a meal for Peter had prepared one for me. The same Shepherd who had trumped the devil trumped him again. The same Savior who had built a fire on the shore stirred a few embers in my heart.

"*Every one* of you drink this." And so I did. It felt good to be back at the table.

15

Slippery Sheep and Healed Hurts

The Burden of Disappointment

You anoint my head with oil.

PSALM 23:5 NKJV

D*is* changes everything. With *dis,* "obey" becomes "*dis*obey." "Respect" is changed to "*dis*respect." "Regard" is suddenly "*dis*regard." What was an "ability" becomes a "*dis*ability." "Engage" is now "*dis*engage," and "grace" is transformed into "*dis*grace." All because of *dis.*

We'd be hard pressed to find a more potent trio of letters. And we'd be hard pressed to find a better example of their power than the word *appointment*.

Most of us like appointments. Even the organizationally inept like appointments. Appointments create a sense of predictability in an unpredictable world. Down deep we know we control the future as much as a caboose controls the train, yet our Day-Timers give us the illusion that we do.

A disappointment reminds us that we don't. A disappointment is a missed appointment. What we hoped would happen, didn't. We wanted health; we got disease. We wanted retirement; we got reassignment. Divorce instead of family. Dismissal instead of promotion. Now what? What do we do with our disappointments?

We could do what Miss Haversham did. Remember her in Charles Dickens's *Great Expectations*? Jilted by her fiancé just prior to the wedding, her appointment became a missed appointment and a disappointment. How did she respond? Not too well. She closed all the blinds in the house, stopped every clock, left the wedding cake on the table to gather cobwebs, and continued to wear her wedding dress until it hung in yellow decay around her shrunken form. Her wounded heart consumed her life.

We can follow the same course.

Or we can follow the example of the apostle Paul. His goal was to be a missionary in Spain. Rather than send Paul to Spain, however, God sent him to prison. Sitting in a Roman jail, Paul could have made the same choice as Miss Haversham, but he didn't. Instead he said, "As long as I'm here, I might as well write a few letters." Hence your Bible has the Epistles to Philemon, the Philippians, the Colossians, and the Ephesians.[1] No doubt Paul would have done a great work in Spain. But would it have compared with the work of those four letters?

You've sat where Paul sat. I know you have. You were hotter than a two-dollar pistol on the trail to Spain or college or marriage or independence . . . but then came the layoff or the pregnancy or the sick parent. And you ended up in prison. So long, Spain. Hello, Rome. So long, appointment. Hello, disappointment. Hello, pain.

How did you handle it? Better asked, how are you handling it? Could you use some help? I've got just what you need. Six words in the fifth verse of the Twenty-third Psalm: "You anoint my head with oil."

Don't see the connection? What does a verse on oil have to do with the hurts that come from the disappointments of life?

A little livestock lesson might help. In ancient Israel shepherds used oil for three purposes: to repel insects, to prevent conflicts, and to heal wounds.

Bugs bug people, but they can kill sheep. Flies, mosquitoes, and gnats can turn the summer into a time of torture for the livestock. Consider nose flies, for example. If they succeed in depositing their eggs into the soft membrane of the sheep's nose, the eggs become wormlike larvae, which drive the sheep insane. One shepherd explains: "For relief from this agonizing annoyance sheep will deliberately beat their heads against trees, rocks, posts, or brush. . . . In extreme cases of intense infestation a sheep may even kill itself in a frenzied endeavor to gain respite from the aggravation."[2]

When a swarm of nose flies appears, sheep panic. They run. They hide. They toss their heads up and down for hours. They forget to eat. They aren't able to sleep. Ewes stop milking, and lambs stop growing. The entire flock can be disrupted, even destroyed by the presence of a few flies.

For this reason, the shepherd anoints the sheep. He covers their heads with an oil-like repellent. The fragrance keeps the insects at bay and the flock at peace.

At peace, that is, until mating season. Most of the year, sheep are calm, passive animals. But during mating season, everything changes. The rams put the "ram" in *rambunctious*. They strut around the pasture and flex their necks, trying to win the attention of the new gal on the block. When a ram catches her eye, he tosses his head back and says, "I want ewe, baby." About that time her boyfriend shows up and tells her to go someplace safe. "Ewe better move, sweetie. This could get ugly." The two rams lower their heads and POW! An old-fashioned head butt breaks out.

To prevent injury, the shepherd anoints the rams. He smears a slippery, greasy substance over the nose and head. This lubricant causes them to glance off rather than crash into each other.

They still tend to get hurt, however. And these wounds are the third reason the shepherd anoints the sheep.

Most of the wounds the shepherd treats are simply the result of living in a pasture. Thorns prick or rocks cut or a sheep rubs its head too hard against a tree. Sheep get hurt. As a result, the shepherd regularly, often daily, inspects the sheep, searching for cuts and abrasions. He doesn't want the cut to worsen. He doesn't want today's wound to become tomorrow's infection.

Neither does God. Just like sheep, we have wounds, but ours are wounds of the heart that come from disappointment after disappointment. If we're not careful, these wounds lead to bitterness. And so just like sheep, we need to be treated. "He made us, and we belong to him; we are his people, the sheep he tends" (Ps. 100:3).

Sheep aren't the only ones who need preventive care, and sheep aren't the only ones who need a healing touch. We also get irritated with each other, butt heads, and then get wounded. Many of our disappointments in life begin as irritations. The large portion of our problems are not lion-sized attacks, but rather the day-to-day swarm of frustrations and mishaps and heartaches. You don't get invited to the dinner party. You don't make the team. You don't get the scholarship. Your boss doesn't notice your hard work. Your husband doesn't notice your new dress. Your neighbor doesn't notice the mess in his yard. You find yourself more irritable, more gloomy, more . . . well, more hurt.

Like the sheep, you don't sleep well, you don't eat well. You may even hit your head against a tree a few times.

Or you may hit your head against a person. It's amazing how hard-headed we can be with each other. Some of our deepest hurts come from butting heads with people.

Like the sheep, the rest of our wounds come just from living in the pasture. The pasture of the sheep, however, is much more appealing. The sheep have to face wounds from thorns and thistles. We have to face aging, loss, and illness. Some of us face betrayal and injustice. Live long enough in this world, and most of us will face deep, deep hurts of some kind or another.

So we, like the sheep, get wounded. And we, like the sheep, have a shepherd. Remember the words we read? "We belong to him; we are his people, the sheep he tends" (Ps. 100:3). He will do for you what the shepherd does for the sheep. He will tend to you.

If the Gospels teach us anything, they teach us that Jesus is a Good Shepherd. "I am the good shepherd," Jesus announces. "The good shepherd gives his life for the sheep" (John 10:11).

Didn't Jesus spread the oil of prevention on his disciples? He prayed for them. He equipped them before he sent them out. He revealed to them the secrets of the parables. He interrupted their arguments and calmed their fears. Because he was a good shepherd, he protected them against disappointments.

Not only did Jesus prevent wounds, he healed them. He touched the eyes of the blind man. He touched the disease of the leper. He touched the body of the dead girl. Jesus tends to his sheep. He touched the searching heart of Nicodemus. He touched the open heart of Zacchaeus. He touched the broken heart of Mary Magdalene. He touched the confused heart of Cleopas. And he touched the stubborn heart of Paul and the repentant heart of Peter. Jesus tends to his sheep. And he will tend to you.

If you will let him. How? How do you let him? The steps are so simple.

First, go to him. David would trust his wounds to no other person but God. He said, "*You* anoint my head with oil." Not, "your prophets," "your teachers," or "your counselors." Others may guide us to God. Others may help us understand God. But no one does the work of God, for only God can heal. God "heals the brokenhearted" (Ps. 147:3).

Have you taken your disappointments to God? You've shared them with your neighbor, your relatives, your friends. But have you taken them to God? James says, "Anyone who is having troubles should pray" (James 5:13).

Before you go anywhere else with your disappointments, go to God.

Maybe you don't want to trouble God with your hurts. *After all, he's got famines and pestilence and wars; he won't care about my little struggles,* you think. Why don't you let him decide that? He cared enough about a wedding to provide the wine. He cared enough about Peter's tax payment to give him a coin. He cared enough about the woman at the well to give her answers. "He cares about you" (1 Pet. 5:7).

Your first step is to go to the right person. Go to God. Your second step is to assume the right posture. Bow before God.

In order to be anointed, the sheep must stand still, lower their heads, and let the shepherd do his work. Peter urges us to "be humble under God's powerful hand so he will lift you up when the right time comes" (1 Pet. 5:6).

When we come to God, we make requests; we don't make demands. We come with high hopes and a humble heart. We state what we want, but we pray for what is right. And if God gives us the prison of Rome instead of the mission of Spain, we accept it because we know "God will always give what is right to his people who cry to him night and day, and he will not be slow to answer them" (Luke 18:7).

We go to him. We bow before him, and we *trust in him.*

The sheep doesn't understand why the oil repels the flies. The sheep doesn't understand how the oil heals the wounds. In fact, all the sheep knows is that something happens in the presence of the shepherd. And that's all we need to know as well. "LORD, I give myself to you; my God, I trust you" (Ps. 25:1–2).

Go.

Bow.

Trust.

Worth a try, don't you think?

16

Jam Session

The Burden of Envy

My cup overflows with blessings.

Psalm 23:5 NLT

A member of our church gave me a jar of homemade peach preserves a couple of weeks ago. Few delicacies in life compare with her peach preserves. Should I someday face a firing squad, I'll pass on the cigarette but be the first to perk up if Sarah's peach preserves are offered. Each spoonful is a celestial experience. The only problem with her gift was that it didn't last. I'm sad to report that the bottom of my jar is in sight. I'll soon be shaking out the last drop like a lost cowboy shakes his canteen.

To be quite honest, I'm dreading the moment. Its proximity has affected my behavior. Anyone who requests a taste of my peach preserves is met with a Clint Eastwood snarl, "Don't even think about it."

If I were Sarah's husband, Keith, I wouldn't have such a problem. He gets all the peach preserves he wants. Does the clinking of the spoon at the bottom of the jar trigger tears for Keith? Hardly, he has an unlimited supply. One might even say that he has more than he deserves. And one might wonder why he has so much and I have so little. Why should he have a pantryful and I just a jarful? Who gave him the key to the jam-and-jelly castle? Who made him the master of marmalades? Who crowned Keith the king of confitures? It's not fair. It's not right. In fact, the more I think about it . . .

Which is exactly what I shouldn't do. I shouldn't think about it. For resting at the end of this trail of thought is the deadly briefcase of envy.

If you haven't seen one in real life, you've seen one in the spy movies. The assassin carries it up the back stairs into the vacated room at the top of the building. When he is sure no one can see him, he opens the case. The disassembled rifle sits in cushioned slots. The scope, the barrel, the stock—all await the hand of the marksman. The marksman awaits the arrival of his victim.

Who is his victim? Anyone who has more than he has. More karats, more horsepower, more office space, more church members. Jealousy sets her cross hairs on the one who has more. "You want something you don't have, and you will do anything to get it. You will even kill!" (James 4:2 CEV).

Honestly, Max, I would never do that. I would never kill.

With a rifle, maybe not. But with your tongue? With your glare? Your gossip? "Jealousy," informs Proverbs 6:34, "enrages a man" (NASB). Are your sights set on someone? If so, be careful; "jealousy will rot your bones" (Prov. 14:30).

Need a deterrent for envy? An antidote for jealousy? The psalm we are studying offers one. Rather than bemoan the peach preserves you don't have, rejoice in the abundant cup you do. "My cup overflows with blessings" (Ps. 23:5 NLT).

Is an overflowing cup full? Absolutely. The wine reaches the rim and then tumbles over the edge. The goblet is not large enough to contain the quantity. According to David, our hearts are not large enough to contain the blessings that God wants to give. He pours and pours until they literally flow over the edge and down on the table. You'll like the paragraph penned a century ago by F. B. Meyer:

> Whatever the blessing is in our cup, it is sure to run over. With him the calf is always the fatted calf; the robe is always the best robe; the joy is unspeakable; the peace passeth understanding. . . . There is no

> grudging in God's benevolence; He does not measure out his goodness as an apothecary counts his drops and measures his drams, slowly and exactly, drop by drop. God's way is always characterized by multitudinous and overflowing bounty.[1]

The last thing we need to worry about is not having enough. Our cup overflows with blessings.

Let me ask a question—a crucial question. If focusing on our diminishing items leads to envy, what would happen if we focused on the unending items? If awareness of what we don't have creates jealousy, is it possible that an awareness of our abundance will lead to contentment? Let's give it a try and see what happens. Let's dedicate a few paragraphs to a couple of blessings that, according to the Bible, are overflowing in our lives.

Abounding grace. "The more we see our sinfulness, the more we see God's *abounding grace* forgiving us" (Rom. 5:20 TLB, emphasis mine). To abound is to have a surplus, an abundance, an extravagant portion. Should the fish in the Pacific worry that it will run out of ocean? No. Why? The ocean abounds with water. Need the lark be anxious about finding room in the sky to fly? No. The sky abounds with space.

Should the Christian worry that the cup of mercy will run empty? He may. For he may not be aware of God's abounding grace. Are you? Are you aware that the cup God gives you *overflows* with mercy? Or are you afraid your cup will run dry? Your warranty will expire? Are you afraid your mistakes are too great for God's grace?

We can't help but wonder if the apostle Paul had the same fear. Before he was Paul the apostle, he was Saul the murderer. Before he encouraged Christians, he murdered Christians. What would it be like to live with such a past? Did he ever meet children whom he had made orphans? Did their faces haunt his sleep? Did Paul ever ask, "Can God forgive a man like me?"

The answer to his and our questions is found in a letter he wrote to Timothy: "The grace of our Lord was poured out on me abundantly, along with the faith and love that are in Christ Jesus" (1 Tim. 1:14 NIV).

God is not a miser with his grace. Your cup may be low on cash or clout, but it is overflowing with mercy. You may not have the prime parking place, but you have sufficient pardon. "He will abundantly pardon" (Isa. 55:7 NKJV). Your cup overflows with grace.

Hope. And because it does, your cup overflows with hope. "God will help you overflow with hope in him through the Holy Spirit's power within you" (Rom. 15:13 TLB).

Heaven's hope does for your world what the sunlight did for my grandmother's cellar. I owe my love of peach preserves to her. She canned her own and stored them in an underground cellar near her West Texas house. It was a deep hole with wooden steps, plywood walls, and a musty smell. As a youngster I used to climb in, close the door, and see how long I could last in the darkness. Not even a slit of light entered that underground hole. I would sit silently, listening to my breath and heartbeats, until I couldn't take it anymore and then would race up the stairs and throw open the door. Light would avalanche into the cellar. What a change! Moments before I couldn't see anything—all of a sudden I could see everything.

Just as light poured into the cellar, God's hope pours into your world. Upon the sick, he shines the ray of healing. To the bereaved, he gives the promise of reunion. For the dying, he lit the flame of resurrection. To the confused, he offers the light of Scripture.

God gives hope. So what if someone was born thinner or stronger, lighter or darker than you? Why count diplomas or compare résumés?

What does it matter if they have a place at the head table? You have a place at God's table. And he is filling your cup to overflowing.

The overflowing cup was a powerful symbol in the days of David. Hosts in the ancient East used it to send a message to the guest. As long as the cup was kept full, the guest knew he was welcome. But when the cup sat empty, the host was hinting that the hour was late. On those occasions, however, when the host really enjoyed the company of the person, he filled the cup to overflowing. He didn't stop when the wine reached the rim; he kept pouring until the liquid ran over the edge of the cup and down on the table.[2]

Have you noticed how wet your table is? God wants you to stay. Your cup overflows with joy. Overflows with grace. Shouldn't your heart overflow with gratitude?

The heart of the boy did. Not at first, mind you. Initially he was full of envy. But, in time, he was full of gratitude.

According to the fable, he lived with his father in a valley at the base of a large dam. Every day the father would go to work on the mountain behind their house and return home with a wheelbarrow full of dirt. "Pour the dirt in the sacks, Son," the father would say. "And stack them in front of the house."

And though the boy would obey, he also complained. He was tired of dirt. He was weary of bags. Why didn't his father give him what other fathers gave their sons? They had toys and games; he had dirt. When he saw what the others had, he grew mad at them. "It's not fair," he said to himself.

And when he saw his father, he objected. "They have fun. I have dirt."

The father would smile and place his arm on the boy's shoulders and say, "Trust me, Son. I'm doing what is best."

But it was so hard for the boy to trust. Every day the father would bring the load. Every day the boy would fill bags. "Stack them as high as you can," the father would say as he went for more. And so the boy filled the bags and piled them high. So high he couldn't see over them.

"Work hard, Son," the father said one day. "We're running out of time." As the father spoke, he looked at the darkening sky. The boy stared at the clouds and turned to ask about them, but when he did, the thunder cracked and the sky opened. The rain poured so hard he could scarcely see his father through the water. "Keep stacking, Son!" And as he did, the boy heard a mighty crash.

The water of the river poured through the dam and toward the little village. In a moment the tide swept everything in its path, but the dike of dirt gave the boy and the father the time they needed. "Hurry, Son. Follow me."

They ran to the side of the mountain behind their house and into a tunnel. In a matter of moments they exited the other side and scampered up the hill and came upon a new cottage.

"We'll be safe here," the father said to the boy.

Only then did the son realize what the father had done. He had burrowed an exit. Rather than give him what he wanted, the father gave his boy what he needed. He gave him a safe passage and a safe place.

Hasn't our Father given us the same? A strong wall of grace to protect us? A sure exit to deliver us? Of whom can we be envious? Who has more than we do? Rather than want what others have, shouldn't we wonder if they have what we do? Instead of being jealous of them, how about zealous for them? For heaven's sake, drop the rifles and hold out the cup. There is enough to go around.

One thing is certain. When the final storm comes and you are safe in your Father's house, you won't regret what he didn't give. You'll be stunned at what he did.

17

God's Loving Pursuit

The Burden of Doubt

Surely goodness and mercy shall follow me
all the days of my life.

PSALM 23:6 NKJV

Eric Hill had everything you'd need for a bright future. He was twenty-eight years old and a recent college grad with an athletic frame and a soft smile. His family loved him, girls took notice of him, and companies had contacted him about working for them. Although Eric appeared composed without, he was tormented within. Tormented by voices he could not still. Bothered by images he could not avoid. So, hoping to get away from them all, he got away from it all. On a gray rainy day in February 1982, Eric Hill walked out the back door of his Florida home and never came back.

His sister Debbie remembers seeing him leave, his tall frame ambling down the interstate. She assumed he would return. He didn't. She hoped he would call. He didn't. She thought she could find him. She couldn't. Where Eric journeyed, only God and Eric know, and neither of them has chosen to tell. What we do know is Eric heard a voice. And in that voice was an "assignment." And that assignment was to pick up garbage along a roadside in San Antonio, Texas.

To the commuters on Interstate 10, his lanky form and bearded face became a familiar sight. He made a home out of a hole in a vacant lot. He made a wardrobe out of split trousers and a torn sweatshirt. An old hat deferred the summer sun. A plastic bag on his shoulders softened the winter chill. His weathered skin and stooped shoulders made him look twice his forty-four years. But then, sixteen years on the side of the road would do that to you.

That's how long it had been since Debbie had seen her brother. She might never have seen him again had it not been for two events. The first was the construction of a car dealership on Eric's vacant lot. The second was a severe pain in his abdomen. The dealership took his home. The pain nearly took his life.

EMS found him curled in a ball on the side of the road, clutching his stomach. The hospital ran some tests and found that Eric had cancer. Terminal cancer. Another few months and he would be dead. And with no known family or relatives, he would die alone.

His court-appointed attorney couldn't handle this thought. "Surely someone is looking for Eric," he reasoned. So the lawyer scoured the Internet for anyone in search of a brown-haired, adult male with the last name Hill. That's how he met Debbie.

His description seemed to match her memory, but she had to know for sure.

So Debbie came to Texas. She and her husband and two children rented a hotel room and set out to find Eric. By now he'd been released from the hospital, but the chaplain knew where he was. They found him sitting against a building not far from the interstate. As they approached, he stood. They offered fruit; he refused. They offered juice; he declined. He was polite but unimpressed with this family who claimed to be his own.

His interest perked, however, when Debbie offered him a pin to wear, an angel pin. He said yes. Her first time to touch her brother in sixteen years was the moment he allowed her to pin the angel on his shirt.

Debbie intended to spend a week. But a week passed, and she stayed. Her husband returned home, and she stayed. Spring became summer, and Eric improved, and still she stayed. Debbie rented an apartment and began homeschooling her kids and reaching out to her brother.

It wasn't easy. He didn't recognize her. He didn't know her. One day he cursed her. He didn't want to sleep in her apartment. He didn't want her food. He didn't want to talk. He wanted his vacant lot. He wanted his "job." Who was this woman anyway?

But Debbie didn't give up on Eric. She understood that he didn't understand. So she stayed.

I met her one Sunday when she visited our congregation. When she shared her story, I asked what you might want to ask. "How do you keep from giving up?"

"Simple," she said. "He's my brother."

I told her that her pursuit reminded me of another pursuit—that her heart reminded me of another heart. Another kind heart who left home in search of the confused. Another compassionate soul who couldn't bear the thought of a brother or sister in pain. So, like Debbie, he left home. Like Debbie, he found his sibling.

And when Jesus found us, we acted like Eric. Our limitations kept us from recognizing the One who came to save us. We even doubted his presence—and sometimes we still do.

How does he deal with our doubts? He follows us. As Debbie followed Eric, God follows us. He pursues us until we finally see him as our Father, even if it takes *all the days of our lives.*

"Surely goodness and mercy shall follow me all the days of my life; and I will dwell in the house of the LORD forever" (Ps. 23:6 NKJV).

This must be one of the sweetest phrases ever penned. Can we read it from a few other translations?

"Goodness and love unfailing, these will follow me all the days of my life, and I shall dwell in the house of the LORD my whole life long" (NEB).

"I know that your goodness and love will be with me all my life; and your house will be my home as long as I live" (TEV).

"Your beauty and love chase after me every day of my life. I'm back home in the house of YAHWEH for the rest of my life" (MSG).

To read the verse is to open a box of jewels. Each word sparkles and begs to be examined in the face of our doubts: *goodness, mercy, all the days, dwell in the house of the LORD, forever.* They sweep in on insecurities like a SWAT team on a terrorist.

Look at the first word: *surely*. David didn't say, "*Maybe* goodness and mercy shall follow me." Or "*Possibly* goodness and mercy shall follow me." Or "*I have a hunch* that goodness and mercy shall follow me." David could have used one of those phrases. But he didn't. He believed in a sure God, who makes sure promises and provides a sure foundation. David would have loved the words of one of his great-great-grandsons, the apostle James. He described God as the one "with whom there is never the slightest variation or shadow of inconsistency" (James 1:17 PHILLIPS).

Our moods may shift, but God's doesn't. Our minds may change, but God's doesn't. Our devotion may falter, but God's never does. Even if we are faithless, he is faithful, for he cannot betray himself (2 Tim. 2:13). He is a sure God. And because he is a sure God, we can state confidently, "Surely goodness and mercy shall follow me all the days of my life."

And what follows the word *surely*? "Goodness and mercy." If the Lord is the shepherd who leads the flock, goodness and mercy are the two sheepdogs that guard the rear of the flock. Goodness *and* mercy. Not goodness alone, for we are sinners in need of mercy. Not mercy alone, for we are fragile, in need of goodness. We need them both. As one man wrote, "Goodness to supply every want. Mercy to forgive every sin. Goodness to provide. Mercy to pardon."[1]

Goodness and mercy—the celestial escort of God's flock. If that duo doesn't reinforce your faith, try this phrase: "all the days of my life."

What a huge statement. Look at the size of it! Goodness and mercy follow the child of God each and every day! Think of the days that lie ahead. What do you see? Days at home with only toddlers? God will be at your side. Days in a dead-end job? He will walk you through. Days of loneliness? He will take your hand. Surely goodness and mercy shall follow me—not some, not most, not nearly all—but all the days of my life.

And what will he do during those days? (Here is my favorite word.) He will "follow" you.

What a surprising way to describe God! We're accustomed to a God who remains in one place. A God who sits enthroned in the heavens and rules and ordains. David, however, envisions a mobile and active God. Dare we do the same? Dare we envision a God who follows us? Who pursues us? Who chases us? Who tracks us down and wins us over? Who follows us with "goodness and mercy" all the days of our lives?

Isn't this the kind of God described in the Bible? A God who follows us? There are many in the Scriptures who would say so. You have to go no farther than the third chapter of the first book before you find God in the role of a seeker. Adam and Eve are hiding in the bushes, partly to cover their bodies, partly to cover their sin. But does God wait for them to come to him? No, the words ring in the garden: "Where are you?" (Gen. 3:9). With that question God began a quest for the heart of humanity that continues up to and through the moment you read these words.

Moses can tell you about it. He was forty years in the desert when he looked over his shoulder and saw a bush blazing. God had followed him into the wilderness.

Jonah can tell you about it. He was a fugitive on a boat when he looked over his shoulder and saw clouds brewing. God had followed him onto the ocean.

The disciples of Jesus knew the feeling of being followed by God. They were rain soaked and shivering when they looked over their shoulders and saw Jesus walking toward them. God had followed them into the storm.

An unnamed Samaritan woman knew the same. She was alone in life and alone at the well when she looked over her shoulder and heard a Messiah speaking. God had followed her through her pain.

John the Apostle was banished on Patmos when he looked over his shoulder and saw the skies begin to open. God had followed him into his exile.

Lazarus was three days dead in a sealed tomb when he heard a voice, lifted his head, and looked over his shoulder and saw Jesus standing. God had followed him into death.

Peter had denied his Lord and gone back to fishing when he heard his name and looked over his shoulder and saw Jesus cooking breakfast. God had followed him in spite of his failure.

God is the God who follows. I wonder . . . have you sensed him following you? We often miss him. Like Eric, we don't know our Helper when he is near. But he comes.

Through the kindness of a stranger. The majesty of a sunset. The mystery of romance. Through the question of a child or the commitment of a spouse. Through a word well spoken or a touch well timed, have you sensed his presence?

If so, then release your doubts. Set them down. Be encumbered by them no longer. You are no candidate for insecurity. You are no longer a client of timidity. You can trust God. He has given his love to you; why don't you give your doubts to him?

Not easy to trust, you say? Maybe not, but neither is it as difficult as you think. Try these ideas:

Trust your faith and not your feelings. You don't feel spiritual each day? Of course you don't. But your feelings have no impact on God's presence. On the days you don't feel close to God, trust your faith and not your feelings. Goodness and mercy shall follow you all the days of your life.

Measure your value through God's eyes, not your own. To everyone else, Eric Hill was a homeless drifter. But to Debbie, he was a brother. There are times in our lives when we are gangrels—homeless, disoriented, hard to help, and hard to love. In those seasons remember this simple fact: God loves you. He follows you. Why? Because you are family, and he will follow you all the days of your life.

See the big picture, not the small. Eric's home was taken. His health was taken. But through the tragedy, his family was returned to him. Perhaps your home and health have been threatened as well. The immediate result might be pain. But the long-term result might be finding a Father you never knew. A Father who will follow you all the days of your life.

By the way, the last chapter in Eric Hill's life is the best one. Days before he died he recognized Debbie as his sister. And, in doing so, he discovered his home.

We will as well. Like Eric, we have doubted our Helper. But like Debbie, God has followed us. Like Eric, we are quick to turn away. But like Debbie, God is slow to anger and determined to stay. Like Eric, we don't accept God's gifts. But like Debbie, God still gives them. He gives us his angels, not just pinned on a lapel, but placed on our path.

And most of all, God gives us himself. Even when we choose our hovel over his house and our trash over his grace, still he follows. Never forcing us. Never leaving us. Patiently persistent. Faithfully present. Using all of his power to convince us that he is who he is and that he can be trusted to lead us home.

His goodness and mercy will follow us all the days of our lives.

18

Almost Heaven

The Burden of Homesickness

I will dwell in the house of the Lord *forever.*

Psalm 23:6 NKJV

For the last twenty years, I've wanted a dog. A big dog. But there were always problems. The apartment was too small. The budget was too tight. The girls were too young. But most of all, Denalyn was unenthusiastic. Her logic? She'd already married one slobbering, shedding beast, why put up with a second? So we compromised and got a small dog.

I like Salty, but small dogs aren't really dogs. They don't bark; they yelp. They don't eat; they nibble. They don't lick you; they sniff you. I like Salty, but I wanted a real dog. A man's-best-friend type of dog. A fat-pawed, big-eating, slurp-you-on-the-face type of dog you could saddle or wrestle or both.

I was alone in my passion until Sara was born. She loves dogs. And the two of us were able to sway the household vote. Denalyn gave in, and Sara and I began the search. We discovered a woman in South Carolina who breeds golden retrievers in a Christian environment. From birth the dogs are surrounded by inspirational music and prayers. (No, I don't know if they tithe with dog biscuits.) When the trainer told me that she had read my books, I got on board. A woman with such good taste is bound to be a good breeder, right?

So we ordered a pup. We mailed the check, selected the name Molly, and cleared a corner for her dog pillow. The dog hadn't even been born, and she was named, claimed, and given a place in the house.

Can't the same be said about you? Long before your first whimper, your Master claimed you, named you, and hung a reserved sign on your room. You and Molly have more in common than odor and eating habits. (Just teasing.)

You're both being groomed for a trip. We prefer the terms *maturation* and *sanctification* to *weaning* and *training,* but it's all the same. You're being prepared for your Master's house. You don't know the departure date or flight number, but you can bet your puppy chow that you'll be seeing your Owner someday. Isn't this the concluding promise of David?

"And I will dwell in the house of the LORD forever" (Ps. 23:6 NKJV).

Where will you live forever? In the house of the Lord. If his house is your "forever house," what does that make this earthly house? You got it! Short-term housing. This is not our home. "Our homeland is in heaven" (Phil. 3:20).

This explains the homesickness we feel.

Have you ever longed to be home? May I share a time when I did? I was spending the summer of my nineteenth year working in northern Georgia. The folks in that region are very nice, but no one is too nice to a door-to-door salesman. There were times that summer when I was so lonely for home I felt my bones would melt.

One of those occasions came on the side of a country road. The hour was late, and I was lost. I'd stopped to pull out a flashlight and a map. To my right was a farmhouse. In the farmhouse was a family. I knew it was a family because I could see them. Right through the big plate-glass window, I could see the mother and father and boy and girl. Norman Rockwell would have placed them on a canvas. The mom was spooning out food, and the dad was telling a story, and the kids were laughing, and it was all I could do to keep from ringing the doorbell and asking for a place at the table. I felt so far from home.

What I felt that night, some of you have felt ever since . . .

your husband died.

your child was buried.

you learned about the lump in your breast or the spot in your lung.

Some of you have felt far from home ever since your home fell apart.

The twists and turns of life have a way of reminding us—we aren't home here. This is not our homeland. We aren't fluent in the languages of disease and death. The culture confuses the heart, the noise disrupts our sleep, and we feel far from home.

And, you know what? That's OK.

Homesickness is one of the burdens God doesn't mind if we carry. We, like Molly, are being prepared for another house. And we, like the parakeet from Green Bay, know we aren't there yet.

Pootsie was her name. She escaped from her owner and came into the keeping of the humane society. When no one else claimed her, Sue Gleason did. They hit it off. They talked and bathed together, becoming fast friends. But one day the little bird did something incredible. It flew over to Mrs. Gleason, put her beak in her ear, and whispered, "Fifteen hundred South Oneida Street, Green Bay."

Gleason was dumbfounded. She researched and found that the address existed. She went to the house and found a seventy-nine-year-old man named John Stroobants.

"Do you have a parakeet?" she asked.

"I used to; I miss him terribly."

When he saw his Pootsie, he was thrilled. "You know, he even knows his phone number."[1]

The story isn't as crazy as you might think. You have an eternal address fixed in your mind as well. God has "set eternity in the hearts of men" (Eccles. 3:11 NIV). Down deep you know you are not home yet.

So be careful not to act like you are. Don't lower the duffel bag too soon. Would you hang pictures on the wall of a Greyhound bus? Do you set up a bedroom at the roadside rest stop? Do you load your king-size bed on a commercial flight?

Would you treat this world like home? It isn't. The greatest calamity is not to feel far from home when you are, but to feel right at home when you are not. Don't quench, but rather, stir this longing for heaven.

God's home is a *forever* home. "And I will dwell in the house of the LORD forever" (Ps. 23:6 NKJV).

My friends Jeff and Carol just adopted two small children. Christopher, the older, is only three, but he knows the difference between Jeff's house and the foster home from which he came. He tells all visitors, "This is my forever home."

Won't it be great when we say the same? Couldn't we use a forever home? This home we're in won't last forever. Birthdays remind us of that.

During the writing of this book I turned forty-six. I'm closer to ninety than I am to infancy. All those things they say about aging are coming true. I'm patting myself less on the back and more under the chin. I have everything I had twenty years ago, except now it's all lower. The other day I tried to straighten out the wrinkles in my socks and found out I wasn't wearing any. I can relate to Dave Barry's description of aging:

> . . . dental problems, intestinal malfunctions, muscle deterioration, emotional instability, memory lapses, hearing and vision loss, impotence, seizures, growths, prostate problems, greatly reduced limb function, massive coronary failure, death, and, of course, painful hemorrhoidal swelling.[2]

Aging. It's no fun. The way we try to avoid it, you'd think we could. We paint the body, preserve the body, protect the body. And well we should. These bodies are God's gifts. We should be responsible. But we should also be realistic. This body must die so the new body can live. "Flesh and blood cannot have a part in the kingdom of God. Something that will ruin cannot have a part in something that never ruins" (1 Cor. 15:50).

Aging is God's idea. It's one of the ways he keeps us headed homeward. We can't change the process, but we can change our attitude. Here is a thought. What if we looked at the aging body as we look at the growth of a tulip?

Do you ever see anyone mourning over the passing of the tulip bulb? Do gardeners weep as the bulb begins to weaken? Of course not. We don't purchase tulip girdles or petal wrinkle cream or consult plastic-leaf surgeons. We don't mourn the passing of the bulb; we celebrate it. Tulip lovers rejoice the minute the bulb weakens. "Watch that one," they say. "It's about to blossom."

Could it be heaven does the same? The angels point to our bodies. The more frail we become, the more excited they become. "Watch that lady in the hospital," they say. "She's about to blossom." "Keep an eye on the fellow with the bad heart. He'll be coming home soon."

"We are waiting for God to finish making us his own children, which means our bodies will be made free" (Rom. 8:23).

Are our bodies now free? No. Paul describes them as our "earthy bodies" (Phil. 3:21 MSG). Or as other translations state:

"our lowly body" (NKJV)

"the body of our humble state" (NASB)

"these weak mortal bodies" (NLT)

"our vile body" (KJV)

"our simple bodies" (NCV)

You could add your own adjective, couldn't you? Which word describes your body? My *cancerous* body? My *arthritic* body? My *deformed* body? My *crippled* body? My *addicted* body? My *ever-expanding* body? The word may be different, but the message is the same: These bodies are weak. They began decaying the minute we began breathing.

And, according to God, that's a part of the plan. Every wrinkle and every needle take us one step closer to the last step when Jesus will change our simple bodies into forever bodies. No pain. No depression. No sickness. No end.

This is not our forever house. It will serve for the time being. But there is nothing like the moment we enter his door.

Molly can tell you. After a month in our house she ran away. I came home one night to find the place unusually quiet. Molly was gone.

She'd slipped out unnoticed. The search began immediately. Within an hour we knew that she was far, far from home. Now, if you don't like pets, what I'm about to say is going to sound strange. If you do like pets, you will understand.

You'll understand why we walked up and down the street, calling her name. You'll understand why I drove around the neighborhood at 10:30 P.M. You'll understand why I put up a poster in the convenience store and convened the family for a prayer. (Honestly, I did.) You'll understand why I sent e-mails to the staff, asking for prayers, and to her breeder, asking for advice. And you'll understand why we were ready to toss the confetti and party when she showed up.

Here is what happened. The next morning Denalyn was on her way home from taking the girls to school when she saw the trash truck. She asked the workers to keep an eye out for Molly and then hurried home to host a moms' prayer group. Soon after the ladies arrived, the trash truck pulled into our driveway, a worker opened the door, and out bounded our dog. She had been found.

When Denalyn called to tell me the news, I could barely hear her voice. It was Mardi Gras in the kitchen. The ladies were celebrating the return of Molly.

This story pops with symbolism. The master leaving his house, searching for the lost. Victories in the midst of prayer. Great things coming out of trash. But most of all: the celebration at the coming home. That's something else you have in common with Molly—a party at your homecoming.

By that moment only one bag will remain. Not guilt. It was dropped at Calvary. Not the fear of death. It was left at the grave. The only lingering luggage will be this God-given longing for home. And when you see him, you'll set it down. Just as a returning soldier drops his duffel when he sees his wife, you'll drop your longing when you see your Father. Those you love will shout. Those you know will applaud. But all the noise will cease when he cups your chin and says, "Welcome home." And with scarred hand he'll wipe every tear from your eye. And you will dwell in the house of your Lord—forever.

Conclusion

I fell asleep in the Louvre.

The most famous museum in the world. The best-known building in Paris. Tourists are oohing and aahing, and that's me, nodding and snoring. Seated on a bench. Back to the wall. Chin to my chest. Conked out.

The crown jewels are down the hall. Rembrandt is on the wall. Van Gogh is one floor up. The *Venus de Milo* is one floor down. I should have been star struck and wide eyed.

Denalyn was. You'd have thought she was at Foley's Red Apple sale. If there was a tour, she took it. If there was a button to push, she pushed it. If there was a brochure to read, she read it. She didn't even want to stop to eat.

But me? I gave the *Mona Lisa* five minutes.

Shameful, I know.

I should have been more like the fellow next to me. When I dozed off, he was transfixed on a seventeenth-century Dutch artist's rendering of a flower. When I awoke, the guy was still staring. I closed my eyes again. When I opened them, he hadn't moved.

I leaned toward him and tried to sound reflective. "Awesome, eh?" No response. "The shades are masterful." Still no reply. "Do you think it's a number painting?" He sighed and said nothing, but I knew what he was thinking, *Uncultured klutz.*

He's right. I was. But it wasn't my fault. I like seventeenth-century art as much as the next guy . . . well, maybe not that much. But at least I can usually stay awake.

But not that day. Why did I fall asleep at the Louvre?

Blame it on the bags, baby; blame it on the bags. I was worn out from lugging the family luggage. We checked more suitcases than the road show of the *Phantom of the Opera.*

I can't fault my wife and daughters. They learned it from me. Remember, I'm the one who travels prepared for an underwater wedding and a bowling tournament. It's bad enough for one person to travel like that, but five? It'll wear you out.

You think I'll ever learn to travel light?

I tell you what. Let's make a pact. I'll reduce the leather bags, and we'll both reduce the emotional ones. After all, it's one thing to sleep through the Louvre but quite another to sleep through life.

We can, you know. Do we not dwell in the gallery of our God? Isn't the sky his canvas and humanity his magnum opus? Are we not encircled by artistry? Sunsets burning. Waves billowing.

And isn't the soul his studio? The birthing of love, the bequeathing of grace. All around us miracles pop like fireflies—souls are touched, hearts are changed, and . . .

Yawn. We miss it. We sleep through it. We can't help it. It's hard work carrying yesterday's guilt around. This burlap bag of worry has my neck in a knot. The dread of death is enough to break a back.

It's also enough to make you miss the magic of life. Many miss it every Sunday. Good, well-meaning folks sitting in church, fighting to keep the eyes—if not of their heads at least of their hearts—awake.

And what do we miss? We miss God parting the heavens to hear us sing. Shouldn't we be stretching heavenward, tiptoed on our pews?

What do we miss? God is meeting us in communion! Shouldn't we be distributing, along with the wafers and wine, ammonia sticks so we could awaken each other from our faints of awe?

What do we miss? God's Word. Should we not hold it like nitroglycerin? Shouldn't we be wide-awake? We should, but we dragged that trunk of dissatisfaction all over town last week. And, besides that, we couldn't sleep last night; we kept rolling over on our duffel bag of disappointments.

Then let's get rid of the bags! Once and for all, let's give our luggage to him. Let's take him at his word! "Come to me, all of you who are weary and carry heavy burdens, and I will give you rest" (Matt. 11:28 NLT).

Rest from the burden of a small god. Why? Because I have found **the Lord.**

Rest from doing things my way. Why? Because **the Lord is my Shepherd.**

Rest from endless wants. Why? Because **I shall not want.**

Rest from weariness. Why? Because **he makes me to lie down.**

Rest from worry. Why? Because **he leads me.**

Rest from hopelessness. Why? Because **he restores my soul.**

Rest from guilt. Why? Because **he leads me in the paths of righteousness.**

Rest from arrogance. Why? Because of **his name's sake.**

Rest from the valley of death. Why? Because **he walks me through it.**

Rest from the shadow of grief. Why? Because **he guides me.**

Rest from fear. Why? Because **his presence comforts me.**

Rest from loneliness. Why? Because **he is with me.**

Rest from shame. Why? Because **he has prepared a place for me in the presence of my enemies.**

Rest from my disappointments. Why? Because **he anoints me.**

Rest from envy. Why? Because **my cup overflows.**

Rest from doubt. Why? Because **he follows me.**

Rest from homesickness. Why? Because **I will dwell in the house of my Lord forever.**

And tomorrow, when out of habit you pick your luggage back up, set it down again. Set it down again and again until that sweet day when you find you aren't picking it back up.

And on that day, when you feel the load lifted, when you've taken a step toward traveling light, when you have the energy to ponder the mysteries of life, do me a favor. Walk down the hall and turn to the left. Wait your turn behind the scarlet ropes. Take a good, long look at the *Mona Lisa,* and tell me, what's the big deal about her anyway?

Notes

Chapter 2: The Middle C of Life

1. Or, in Hebrew, fifty-four words describe the first one.
2. Around A.D. 200 Christian scholars began writing the vowels for *Adonai* beneath the Tetragrammaton (YHWH), reminding the reader to say "Adonai." The word was still unpronounceable until German scholars in the middle of the nineteenth century inserted the vowels of *Adonai* between the *Yahweh* consonants creating the name *Jehovah*—a name that had never existed in any language.
3. Nathan Stone, *Names of God* (Chicago: Moody Press, 1944), 20.
4. Donald W. McCullough, *The Trivialization of God: The Dangerous Illusion of a Manageable Deity* (Colorado Springs: NavPress, 1995), 66.
5. Ibid., 54.

Chapter 3: I'll Do It My Way

1. With appreciation to Rick Reilly and his chapter on Jean Van de Velde, "*Mon Dieu!* Better Safe Than Sorry!" in *The Life of Reilly* (New York: Total Sports Illustrated, 2000), 175–77.

Chapter 4: The Prison of Want

1. Randy C. Alcorn, *Money, Possessions, and Eternity* (Wheaton, Ill.: Tyndale Publishers, 1989), 55.

2. Chris Seidman, *Little Buddy* (Orange, Calif.: New Leaf Books, 2001), 138. Used with permission.

3. Rick Atchley, "I Have Learned the Secret," audiotape 7 of the 1997 Pepperdine Lectures (Malibu, Calif., 1997). Used with permission.

4. Used with permission.

Chapter 5: I Will Give You Rest

1. Robert Sullivan, "Sleepless in America," *Life,* February 1998, 56–66 and *Prime Time Live,* 2 March 1998.

2. Sullivan, "Sleepless," 63.

3. Ibid.

4. Phillip Keller, *A Shepherd Looks at Psalm 23* (Grand Rapids, Mich.: Zondervan Publishing, 1970; reprint, in *Phillip Keller: The Inspirational Writings,* New York: Inspirational Press, 1993), 28–29 (page citations are to the reprint edition).

5. Helmut Thielicke, *Encounter with Spurgeon,* trans. John W. Doberstein (Philadelphia: Fortress Press, 1963; reprint, Grand Rapids, Mich.: Baker Book House, 1975), 220 (page citation is to the reprint edition).

Chapter 6: Whaddifs and Howells

1. Og Mandino, *The Spellbinder's Gift* (New York: Fawcett Columbine, 1995), 70–71.

2. From "Worrier and Warrior," a sermon by Ted Schroder, Christ Episcopal Church, San Antonio, Texas, on 10 April 1994.

3. See Psalm 119:105.

Chapter 9: Get Over Yourself

1. Rick Reilly, *The Life of Reilly* (New York: Total Sports Illustrated, 2000), 73.

2. Paul Lee Tan, *Encyclopedia of 7700 Illustrations* (Rockville, Md.: Assurance Publishers, 1979), 211.

3. Ibid., 1100.

4. William J. Bennett, ed., *The Spirit of America: Words of Advice from the Founders in Stories, Letters, Poem and Speeches* (New York: Touchstone, 1997), 161.

Chapter 10: I Will Lead You Home

1. Phillip Keller, *A Shepherd Looks at Psalm 23* (Grand Rapids, Mich.: Zondervan Publishing, 1970; reprint, in *Phillip Keller: The Inspirational Writings,* New York: Inspirational Press, 1993), 70 (page citation is to the reprint edition).

2. F. W. Boreham, *Life Verses: The Bible's Impact on Famous Lives,* vol. 2 (Grand Rapids, Mich.: Kregel Publications, 1994), 211.

Chapter 11: When Mourning Comes

1. Michael P. Green, ed., *Illustrations for Biblical Preaching* (Grand Rapids, Mich.: Baker Book House, 1989), 91.

Chapter 14: The Crowing Rooster and Me

1. Charles W. Slemming, *He Leadeth Me: The Shepherd's Life in Palestine* (Fort Washington, Pa.: Christian Literature Crusade, 1964), quoted in Charles R. Swindoll, *Living Beyond the Daily Grind, Book 1: Reflections on the Songs and Sayings in Scripture* (Nashville: W Publishing Group, 1988), 77–78.

Chapter 15: Slippery Sheep and Healed Hurts

1. "Paul was in prison several times: Philippi (Acts 16:23); Jerusalem (Acts 23:18); Caesarea (Acts 23:33; 24:27; 25:14); and Rome (Acts 28:16, 20, 30)." Robert B. Hughes and J. Carl Laney, *New Bible Companion* (Wheaton, Ill.: Tyndale House Publishers, 1990), 681.

2. Phillip Keller, *A Shepherd Looks at Psalm 23* (Grand Rapids, Mich.: Zondervan Publishing, 1970; reprint, in *Phillip Keller: The Inspirational Writings,* New York: Inspirational Press, 1993), 99 (page citation is to the reprint edition).

Chapter 16: Jam Session

1. F. B. Meyer, *The Shepherd Psalm* (Grand Rapids, Mich.: Kregel Publications, 1991), 115.
2. From a sermon entitled "God's Antidote to Your Hurt" by Rick Warren.

Chapter 17: God's Loving Pursuit

1. F. B. Meyer, *The Shepherd Psalm* (Grand Rapids, Mich.: Kregel Publications, 1991), 125.
2. Though originally written for this book, this story initially appeared in *The Gift for All People.* Thanks to Multnomah Publishing for allowing us to use it in *Traveling Light*.

Chapter 18: Almost Heaven

1. Calvin Miller, *Into the Depths of God: Where Eyes See the Invisible, Ears Hear the Inaudible, and Minds Conceive the Inconceivable* (Minneapolis: Bethany House, 2000), 217.
2. Dave Barry, *Dave Barry Turns 40* (New York: Crown, 1990), quoted in Helen Exley, *A Spread of Over 40s Jokes* (New York: Exley Giftbooks, 1992).

Study Guide

Traveling Light

Prepared by Steve Halliday

1

The Luggage of Life

Traveling Back

1. *The bags we grab are not made of leather; they're made of burdens. The suitcase of guilt. A sack of discontent. You drape a duffel bag of weariness on one shoulder and a hanging bag of grief on the other. Add on a backpack of doubt, an overnight bag of loneliness, and a trunk of fear. Pretty soon you're pulling more stuff than a skycap. No wonder you're so tired at the end of the day. Lugging luggage is exhausting.*

   A. Which of the "bags" listed here trouble you the most? Why?

   B. Have you left any luggage behind? How did it feel to do so?

2. *God is saying to you, "Set that stuff down! You're carrying burdens you don't need to bear."*

   A. Why do you think we carry burdens we don't need to bear?

   B. What keeps you from setting down burdens you needn't bear?

3. *Traveling light means trusting God with the burdens you were never intended to bear.*

   A. What does it mean to trust God with a burden? How does one do this?

   B. What have you learned from observing others with their "luggage"?

Traveling Up

1. Read Psalm 23.

   A. What pictures leap to mind when you read this psalm?

   B. What memories does this psalm conjure up for you?

C. What part of this psalm means the most to you? Why?

D. How does this psalm teach us to give up personal burdens?

2. Read Matthew 11:28–30.

A. To whom are these words addressed? Does this include you?

B. What promise does Jesus give to those who respond to his invitation?

C. Are you taking advantage of Jesus' invitation? Why or why not?

3. Read 1 Peter 5:7.

A. What does this verse instruct us to do? (How are we to obey?)

B. What reason does Peter give for obeying this command?

C. What benefit can we expect to receive when we obey?

Traveling On

1. Set aside at least a half-hour for prayer, and ask the Lord to reveal any burdens you need to lay down. Pray with a piece of paper and a pen in hand, and write down any burdens the Lord brings to mind. Show your completed list to your closest friend, and ask him or her to pray with you that God will show you how to release these burdens.

2. What burdens are your loved ones needlessly bearing? What can you do to help them lay down those unnecessary burdens?

2

The Middle C of Life

The Burden of a Lesser God

Traveling Back

1. *With his very first words in [Psalm 23], David sets out to deliver us from the burden of a lesser deity.*

   A. What lesser deities hold an attraction for your acquaintances?

   B. Why would anyone settle for a lesser deity?

2. Max says that many people settle for one of three lesser deities: God as a genie in a bottle, as a sweet grandpa, or as a busy dad.

   A. Describe in your own words each of these lesser deities. What seems attractive about them?

   B. Have any of these three lesser deities appealed to you? Why or why not?

3. *God is the "One who is" and the "One who causes." Why is that important? Because we need a big God. And if God is the "One who is," then he is an unchanging God.*

   A. Why do we need a big God? Why do we need an unchanging God?

   B. What would be different about your life if God were smaller than he is? How would you feel if he changed capriciously?

4. *Unchanging. Uncaused. Ungoverned. These are only a fraction of God's qualities, but aren't they enough to give you a glimpse of your Father? Don't we need this kind of shepherd? Don't we need an unchanging shepherd?*

   A. How do you answer Max's questions?

   B. Give an example of how God has been an unchanging shepherd in your life.

Traveling Up

1. Read Exodus 3:13–17; 6:2–8.

   A. What do you learn about God from his name?

   B. What do you learn about God from his track record?

   C. What do you learn about God's concern for his people?

2. Read Psalm 102:25–27; 139:7–12.

   A. What do you learn about God from these passages? How do these verses affect your view of God?

3. Read 1 Timothy 6:13–16.

   A. What do you learn about God from this text?

   B. How does Paul suggest we respond to this God?

4. Read Isaiah 40:21–31.

   A. What does this text reveal about God?

   B. What does God think of pretenders to his throne?

   C. How does God intend for this majestic picture of him to encourage our weary hearts?

Traveling On

1. Do a study on the false gods described in Scripture. Start with names such as "Chemosh," "Baal," "Asherah," and the generic "gods." Do other research, perhaps in a good Bible dictionary, to discover something about these "lesser gods." How do they compare to the God of Jesus?

2. Spend some time meditating and concentrating on the attributes of the real God of the Bible. Consider using a daily devotional such as *How Great Thou Art* (Sister, Ore.: Multnomah, 1999), which focuses for a full year on the majesty and greatness of God.

3

I'll Do It My Way

The Burden of Self-Reliance

Traveling Back

1. *We humans want to do things our way. Forget the easy way. Forget the common way. Forget the best way. Forget God's way. We want to do things our way.*

   A. What is it about us that causes us to desire our own way?

   B. When we rely on ourselves rather than God, what is the result?

2. *When David, who was a warrior, minstrel, and ambassador for God, searched for an illustration of God, he remembered his days as a shepherd. . . . And the way he cared for the sheep reminded him of the way God cares for us. David rejoiced to say, "The Lord is my shepherd," and in so doing he proudly implied, "I am his sheep."*

   A. Why do you think David chose to picture God through the image of a shepherd? Why not use another image?

   B. Do you proudly think of yourself as a sheep? Explain.

3. *Will you humor me and take a simple quiz? See if you succeed in self-reliance. Raise your hand if any of the following describe you.*

   You can control your moods.
   You are at peace with everyone.
   You have no fears.
   You need no forgiveness.

   A. Describe someone you know who believes he or she fits one of the previous four statements.

B. Which of these four areas of life cause you the most struggles? Explain.

C. Why is it that the ones who most need a shepherd resist him so?

Traveling Up

1. Read Jeremiah 17:5–8.

   A. What does the Lord think of someone who relies on himself (v. 5)?

   B. What is the result of relying on yourself (v. 6)?

   C. How does the Lord feel about those who trust in him (v. 7)?

   D. What is the result of trusting in God (v. 8)?

2. Read Deuteronomy 8:10–18.

   A. What are we to do in times of prosperity (v. 10)?

   B. In what way can prosperity create a spiritual threat (vv. 11–14)?

   C. Why is it always foolish to believe that we are self-sufficient (vv. 15–18)?

3. Read 1 Corinthians 4:6–7.

   A. What does it mean to "not go beyond what is written" (v. 6 NIV)? Why does the Bible warn us to "not go beyond what is written"?

   B. How would you answer Paul's three questions in verse 7?

Traveling On

1. Consciously get out of your comfort zone, and do something that requires you to rely on another person. Make it as exotic as a parachute jump or as mundane as asking directions to a place you've never visited.

2. Read the classic *A Shepherd Looks at Psalm 23* by Phillip Keller to gain a better picture of what it means to be a sheep in the fold of God.

4

The Prison of Want

The Burden of Discontent

Traveling Back

1. *The prison of want. You've seen her prisoners. They are "in want." They want something. They want something bigger. Nicer. Faster. Thinner. They want.*

   A. Are you in prison?

   B. What things in life are most likely to send you to this prison? Describe them.

2. *David has found the pasture where discontent goes to die. It's as if he is saying, "What I have in God is greater than what I don't have in life."*

   A. What do you have in God? List the first ten things that come to mind.

   B. Can you say that what you have in God is greater than what you don't have in life? Explain.

3. *Are you hoping that a change in circumstances will bring a change in your attitude? If so, you are in prison, and you need to learn a secret of traveling light.*

   A. Answer the question above and explain your answer.

   B. What is this secret of traveling light? How does one master it?

4. *What is the one thing separating you from joy? How do you fill in this blank: "I will be happy when __________________"? When I am healed. When I am promoted. When I am married. When I am single. When I am rich. How would you finish that statement?*

   A. Answer the question above.

B. How does this thing separate you from joy? How long has it been doing so? How can you deprive it of its power over you?

Traveling Up

1. Read Luke 12:13–21.
   A. What warning does Jesus give in verse 15? What declaration does he make?
   B. What error did the rich man make in the parable Jesus told?
   C. What does it mean to be "rich toward God" (v. 21)? Are you rich toward God? Explain.
2. Read Philippians 4:10–13.
   A. Why did Paul "rejoice greatly in the Lord" (v. 10 NIV)?
   B. What secret does Paul describe in verse 12? How did he gain access to this secret? Do you know this secret? Explain.
   C. How does verse 13 relate to the context of the passage? How does it relate specifically to contentment?
3. Read 1 Timothy 6:3–10.
   A. How does Paul characterize those who teach that godliness is a means to financial gain (v. 5)?
   B. What does Paul say *is* "great gain" (v. 6 NIV)?
   C. What reason does Paul give for his statement (vv. 7–8)?
   D. What warning does Paul give in verses 9–10? Why do so many people ignore this warning? What do you think of his warning? Explain.

Traveling On

1. Make a list of at least a dozen things you possess, whether spiritual or material, that came to you as a result of your relationship with God.
2. Do a Bible study on contentment. Use a good concordance to look up words such as *content* and *contented,* then study the verses that you find. Also see what a good Bible dictionary or encyclopedia has to say on the topic. What do you learn?

5

I Will Give You Rest

The Burden of Weariness

Traveling Back

1. *People with too much work and too little sleep step over to the baggage claim of life and grab the duffel bag of weariness. You don't carry this one. You don't hoist it onto your shoulder and stride down the street. You drag it as you would a stubborn St. Bernard.*

   A. What sorts of things tend to make you weary?

   B. How do you normally deal with weariness? What did you do the last time weariness struck hard?

2. *In our book, busyness is next to godliness. We idolize Thomas Edison, who claimed he could live on fifteen-minute naps. Somehow we forget to mention Albert Einstein, who averaged eleven hours of sleep a night.*

   A. How often do you tell others, "I'm really busy right now"? What keeps you so busy?

   B. How much sleep do you normally get? Is it sufficient for you to function well? Explain.

3. *God's message is plain: "If creation didn't crash when I rested, it won't crash when you do." Repeat these words after me: It is not my job to run the world.*

   A. Name some of the reasons you have heard (or used yourself) for not getting adequate rest.

   B. Why do you think God so emphasized the fourth commandment, about resting on the Sabbath day?

4. *In a world rocky with human failure, there is a land lush with divine mercy. Your Shepherd invites you there. He wants you to lie down. Nestle*

deeply until you are hidden, buried, in the tall shoots of his love, and there you will find rest.

A. What is your favorite way of nestling deeply "in the tall shoots of his love"? Describe what most refreshes you.

B. What is keeping you from resting in God's love right now?

Traveling Up

1. Read Exodus 20:8–11.

   A. What does it mean to keep the Sabbath day "holy"?

   B. What does God command Israel in verses 9–10?

   C. What reason does God give in verse 11 for his command?

   D. Why do you think God so highly values our rest?

2. Read Isaiah 30:15–18.

   A. According to verse 15, Israel's salvation consisted in what? How did the nation respond to this direction?

   B. What response is described in verse 16? How do we often respond in a similar way?

   C. What is the result of ignoring God's command to rest (v. 17)?

   D. Despite our foolishness, how does the Lord treat us (v. 18)?

3. Read Hebrews 4:1–11.

   A. What does the writer warn us about in verse 1?

   B. What keeps people from entering God's rest (vv. 2–6)?

   C. When is the best time to obey God's command (v. 7)?

   D. What kind of rest is the writer describing in verse 9?

   E. How do we "labour" to enter God's rest (v. 11 KJV)?

Traveling On

1. What activities or events keep you busy? Try an experiment to judge the accuracy of your assumptions. Keep a "busyness journal"

for one week, recording the things that occupy your time. Write down not only what you did but also how long each took. Then at the end of the week evaluate your journal. Are you busy doing the things that matter most? Or do you need to make some changes?

2. How much sleep do you get? Keep a chart for one month, accurately recording the amount and quality of your sleep. Do the results surprise you? What changes, if any, do you need to make?

6

Whaddifs and Howells

The Burden of Worry

Traveling Back

1. *Worry is the burlap bag of burdens. It's overflowing with "whaddifs" and "howells." "Whaddif it rains at my wedding?" "Howell I know when to discipline my kids?" "Whaddif I marry a guy who snores?" "Howell we pay our baby's tuition?"*

   A. What "whaddifs" trouble you the most?

   B. What "howells" give you the most grief?

   C. How do you typically deal with these "whaddifs" and "howells"?

2. *Worry divides the mind. The biblical word for* worry (merimnao) *is a compound of two Greek words,* merizo *("to divide") and* nous *("the mind"). Anxiety splits our energy between today's priorities and tomorrow's problems. Part of our mind is on the now; the rest is on the not yet. The result is half-minded living.*

   A. What practical things can we do to keep from spending today's energies on tomorrow's problems?

   B. What issues are most likely to nudge you toward half-minded living? Why?

3. *God leads us. God will do the right thing at the right time. And what a difference that makes.*

   A. How has God led you in the past? Describe at least one incident.

   B. Do we believe that God will do the right thing at the right time? How would our lives change if we really believed this?

C. What in your life would change *right now* if you believed this fully?

4. *Meet today's problems with today's strength. Don't start tackling tomorrow's problems until tomorrow. You do not have tomorrow's strength yet. You simply have enough for today.*

   A. How many of the things you have worried about actually have come to pass?

   B. What issues that should be dealt with today are you avoiding by trying to tackle tomorrow's problems?

Traveling Up

1. Read Matthew 6:25–34.

   A. What reason does Jesus give for refusing to worry (vv. 25–27)?

   B. Why should worry not trouble Christians in the same way it troubles nonbelievers (vv. 31–32)?

   C. If we are not to worry, what are we to do (v. 33)? What does this mean in practical terms?

   D. What additional reason for not worrying does Jesus give in verse 34?

2. Read Philippians 4:6–8.

   A. How does Paul recommend that we combat worry?

   B. According to Paul, what will we enjoy when we follow his counsel?

   C. Rather than worry, what kinds of things should fill our minds (v. 8)?

3. Read Hebrews 4:14–16.

   A. Describe the high priest pictured in this passage.

   B. How is verse 16 designed to combat our worry?

Traveling On

1. Make a list of the things in life that worry you the most. Then, one by one, commit these items to the Lord in prayer. As you pray for each concern, tear it off your sheet of paper and throw it in the trash.

2. Use a good concordance to do a word study on worry. Look up terms such as *worry, worried, anxious,* and *anxiety,* and study the verses that you find. What do you learn about how to combat worry?

7

It's a Jungle Out There

The Burden of Hopelessness

Traveling Back

1. *Hopelessness is an odd bag. Unlike the others, it isn't full. It is empty, and its emptiness creates the burden. Unzip the top and examine all the pockets. Turn it upside down and shake it hard. The bag of hopelessness is painfully empty.*

   A. Describe a time when you felt hopeless. What made you feel that way?

   B. What in your life right now threatens your hope? How will you deal with it?

2. *If you have only a person but no renewed vision, all you have is company. If he has a vision but no direction, you have a dreamer for company. But if you have a person with direction—who can take you from this place to the right place—ah, then you have one who can restore your hope.*

   A. Why does it take a competent guide to restore hope?

   B. Do you have such a guide? Explain.

3. *God, your rescuer, has the right vision. He also has the right direction. He made the boldest claim in the history of man when he declared, "I am the way."*

   A. What did Jesus mean when he said, "I am the way"?

   B. Why wasn't it arrogant of Jesus to say that he was *the* way? Then what about Muhammad, the Dalai Lama, or spiritual leaders of other faiths?

4. *We ask God, "Where are you taking me? Where is the path?" And he, like the guide, doesn't tell us. Oh, he may give us a hint or two, but that's*

all. If he did, would we understand? Would we comprehend our location? No, like the traveler, we are unacquainted with this jungle. So rather than give us an answer, Jesus gives us a far greater gift. He gives us himself.

A. How does it make you feel that God almost never tells us what lies ahead for us? Do you wish he did things differently? Explain.

B. In what ways has Jesus guided you in the past? How are you depending upon his guidance right now?

Traveling Up

1. Read Psalm 121.

   A. From where did the psalmist expect his hope to arrive (v. 2)?

   B. How much sleep does God get each night (vv. 3–4)? Why is this important?

   C. What kinds of things is the Lord said to watch over in verses 5–8? How can this give you hope?

2. Read Psalm 33:16–22.

   A. What *cannot* save a king or a warrior (vv. 16–17)? Why are these things vain hopes?

   B. On whom does the Lord fix his eyes (v. 18)? What difference does this make?

   C. What does it mean to "wait in hope" (v. 20 NIV)? How can you put your hope in the Lord?

3. Read Romans 8:18–25.

   A. Why should we avoid attaching too much importance to our present sufferings (v. 18)?

   B. Why do we need hope in the first place (vv. 19–23)?

   C. How does Paul define real hope (v. 24)?

   D. Why is it always too soon to give up hope (v. 25)?

Traveling On

1. Take a guided tour of a place you've never visited. During the tour, consciously remind yourself of how your Savior desires to guide you through life. What unexpected discoveries or parallels do you uncover?

2. Do a Bible study on hope. Use a good concordance to look up the word *hope* and its derivatives, like *hoping, hoped, hopeful,* etc. What do you learn?

8

A Heavenly Exchange

The Burden of Guilt

Traveling Back

1. *God is never wrong. He has never rendered a wrong decision, experienced the wrong attitude, taken the wrong path, said the wrong thing, or acted the wrong way. He is never too late or too early, too loud or too soft, too fast or too slow. He has always been and always will be right. He is righteous.*

   A. Has it ever felt as if God made a mistake with your life? If so, how did you deal with this feeling?

   B. Who is the most "righteous" person you know? What makes you say this about him or her?

2. *The weight of weariness pulls you down. Self-reliance misleads you. Disappointments discourage you. Anxiety plagues you. But guilt? Guilt consumes you. So what do we do? Our Lord is right, and we are wrong. His party is for the guiltless, and we are anything but. What do we do?*

   A. Answer the question above.

   B. How do you deal with disappointments? With anxiety? Guilt?

3. *It was, at once, history's most beautiful and most horrible moment. Jesus stood in the tribunal of heaven. Sweeping a hand over all creation, he pleaded, "Punish me for their mistakes. See the murderer? Give me his penalty. The adulteress? I'll take her shame. The bigot, the liar, the thief? Do to me what you would do to them. Treat me as you would a sinner." And God did.*

   A. Why did innocent Jesus request to take the punishment due to murderers, adulterers, and other sinners?

B. Have you allowed Jesus to take on himself your own sin? Explain.

4. *The path of righteousness is a narrow, winding trail up a steep hill. At the top of the hill is a cross. At the base of the cross are bags. Countless bags full of innumerable sins. Calvary is the compost pile for guilt.*

   A. In what way is Calvary "the compost pile for guilt"?

   B. If you have set your bag of guilt at the foot of Calvary, describe how this came to be. If you have not already done so, why not?

Traveling Up

1. Read Romans 3:9–18.

   A. What does it mean to be "under sin" (NIV)? Who is "under sin" (v. 9)?

   B. List the characteristics of being "under sin" (vv. 10–17).

   C. How does verse 18 summarize all the characteristics you just listed?

2. Read Isaiah 45:21–25.

   A. How does God describe himself in verse 21?

   B. What command does God give in verse 22?

   C. What prediction does God give in verses 23–24?

   D. What promise does God give in verse 25? To whom is he referring?

3. Read Romans 5:6–11 and 1 Peter 3:18.

   A. According to Romans 5:6, for whom did Christ die?

   B. What drove Christ to die for us (v. 8)?

   C. What is the difference between being "justified" and "saved" (v. 9 NIV)?

   D. What is the normal response of one who has been "reconciled" (v. 11 NIV)? Is this your response? Explain.

Traveling On

1. Read a contemporary book by an author who exchanged his or her guilt for the forgiveness of God. How does this remind you of your own need for forgiveness?

2. Is there someone in your life whom you need to forgive but haven't? Remember Jesus' words: "But if you do not forgive men their sins, your Father will not forgive your sins" (Matthew 6:15 NIV). Commit today to forgive this person—and if possible, let him or her know what you've done.

9

Get Over Yourself

The Burden of Arrogance

Traveling Back

1. *God . . . doesn't dislike arrogance. He doesn't disapprove of arrogance. He's not unfavorably disposed toward arrogance. God hates arrogance. What a meal of maggots does for our stomach, human pride does for God's.*

   A. Why do you think God dislikes human pride?

   B. Would you consider yourself a prideful person? Would others agree with you? Explain.

2. *God . . . hates arrogance because we haven't done anything to be arrogant about. Do art critics give awards to the canvas? Is there a Pulitzer for ink? Can you imagine a scalpel growing smug after a successful heart transplant? Of course not. They are only tools, so they get no credit for the accomplishments.*

   A. In what way are we "tools" in God's hands?

   B. Is there any room at all for taking pride in one's accomplishments? Explain.

3. *Why does God have anything to do with us?* For his name's sake. *No other name on the marquee. No other name up in lights. No other name on the front page. This is all done for God's glory.*

   A. Why isn't it vain of God to associate with us for *his* name's sake?

   B. What is meant by "God's glory"? Why is God's glory so important?

4. Consider several ways to cultivate humility and kill ungodly pride:

- Assess yourself honestly.
- Don't take success too seriously.
- Celebrate the significance of others.
- Don't demand your own parking place.
- Never announce your success before it occurs.
- Speak humbly.
- Live at the foot of the cross.

A. Who can help you assess yourself honestly? What does such an assessment reveal?

B. How can you celebrate the significance of others? Who in your immediate circle do you need to celebrate right now?

C. How can you "live at the foot of the cross"? What does this mean?

Traveling Up

1. Read Proverbs 16:5, 18–19.

   A. What does the Lord think of the proud (v. 5)? How will he respond to them?

   B. What is the outcome of pride (v. 18)?

   C. What contrast is made in verse 19? Why is this true?

2. Read Isaiah 57:15–19; 66:2.

   A. How does the Lord describe himself in verse 15? With whom is he pleased to live?

   B. Why will God not "accuse forever" (v. 16)?

   C. How will the Lord respond to those who turn to him in faith (vv. 18–19)?

   D. Whom does God esteem, according to Isaiah 66:2? Why does the Lord delight in men and women like this?

3. Read Philippians 2:3–11.

   A. What does verse 3 instruct us not to do? What should we do instead?

   B. What overall instruction do we receive in verse 5?

   C. How did Jesus follow this instruction during his earthly ministry (vv. 6–8)?

   D. How will God reward Jesus for his faithfulness (vv. 9–11)?

   E. In what way are we to emulate Jesus' example? How are you doing in this regard? Explain.

Traveling On

1. Watch a classic movie such as *Citizen Kane* to see how even Hollywood sometimes recognizes the deadly poison of human pride. How does pride ultimately destroy the person who lets it control him or her?

2. Do a Bible study on how God does everything for the sake of his name. Look up references to "the name," "my name," "his name," etc. What do you discover?

10

I Will Lead You Home

The Burden of the Grave

Traveling Back

1. *Someday our Shepherd . . . will take us to the mountain by way of the valley. He will guide us to his house through the valley of the shadow of death.*

   A. Do you think of your own death, or do you avoid the thought? Explain.

   B. Has a believer you were close to ever died? If so, describe how the Shepherd guided him or her through the valley of the shadow of death.

2. *David grants us two important reminders that can help us surrender our fear of the grave.* We all have to face it. . . . *And though his first reminder sobers us, his second reminder encourages us:* We don't have to face death alone.

   A. If you were to face your own death tomorrow, would you be ready? Explain.

   B. Do you feel as though you would be facing death alone? Explain.

3. *Don't face death without facing God. Don't even speak of death without speaking to God. He and he alone can guide you through the valley. Others may speculate or aspire, but only God knows the way to get you home. And only God is committed to getting you there safely.*

   A. Name a few ways in which God helps his children face death.

   B. How can we be certain God is committed to getting us to heaven safely?

4. *[Jesus] may send missionaries to teach you, angels to protect you, teachers to guide you, singers to inspire you, and physicians to heal you, but he sends no one to take you. He reserves this job for himself.*

   A. When Jesus comes to take you home, what do you think you might say to him first?

   B. Why do you think Jesus insists on coming in person to get you? How does this make you feel?

Traveling Up

1. Read Psalm 116:15; 139:16.

   A. What does Psalm 116:15 say is "precious" to God? Why is this so?

   B. What claim does Psalm 139:16 make? Does this give you comfort? Explain.

2. Read 1 Thessalonians 4:13–18.

   A. What do you learn from this passage about those who die in Christ?

   B. How are these words intended to "encourage" us? Why are we instructed to repeat these words to others?

3. Read 2 Corinthians 5:1–10.

   A. What does Paul mean by "earthly tent" (v. 1 NIV)? Why use this picture?

   B. What is life like in this "tent"? How does Paul contrast life in the "heavenly dwelling" (v.2 NIV)?

   C. What token has God given us to assure us that what he says will one day happen, will actually happen (v. 5)?

   D. How is the information in this passage supposed to make us "confident" (v. 6 NIV)?

   E. What preference does Paul express in verse 8? Why does he prefer this?

   F. How is verse 10 both a promise and a warning?

Traveling On

1. Visit a nearby cemetery, and spend at least an hour reading the gravestones to remind yourself both of death's reality and of the hope believers can have despite its cold embrace.

2. Read Herbert Lockyer's classic book. *Last Words of Saints and Sinners*. How do the deaths of the two groups compare?

11

When Mourning Comes

The Burden of Grief

Traveling Back

1. *The black bag of sorrow is hard to bear. It's hard to bear because not everyone understands your grief. They did at first. They did at the funeral. They did at the graveside. But they don't now; they don't understand. Grief lingers.*

    A. How do you personally deal with sorrow?

    B. How can we help someone whose grief just won't go away?

2. *Only God knows the reasons behind his actions. But here is a key truth on which we can stand.* Our God is a good God.

    A. Why do you think God seldom "explains" his actions in our lives?

    B. How have you personally experienced that God is a good God?

3. *Death is God's way of taking people away from evil. From what kind of evil? An extended disease? An addiction? A dark season of rebellion? We don't know. But we know that no person lives one day more or less than God intends.*

    A. Have you ever thought about death in this way? That it's God's way of taking people away from evil? How do you respond to this idea?

    B. How can the idea of God's sovereignty bring comfort in a time of death? How can the doctrine be used to increase someone's pain?

4. *God will lead you* through, *not around, the valley of the shadow of death. And, by the way, aren't you glad it's just a shadow?*

A. If God really loves us, why doesn't he lead us *around* the valley of the shadow of death? Why lead us *through* it?

B. Is death merely a shadow for you? Explain.

Traveling Up

1. Read Lamentations 3:31–33.

    A. How can verse 31 give you hope when you find yourself engulfed in grief?

    B. What do you learn about God in verse 32?

    C. Why is it important that God does not "willingly" bring us grief (v. 33 NIV)? Why does he bring us grief at all?

2. Read John 16:20–22.

    A. What two promises did Jesus give his disciples in verse 20?

    B. What illustration did Jesus use in verse 21 to picture his promises of verse 20? What can we learn from this illustration?

    C. What promise does Jesus give in verse 22? How certain is this promise? On what is it based? How can it continue to help you today when you face grief?

3. Read 1 Peter 1:3–9.

    A. What great blessing does Peter describe in verses 3–4? Do you share in this blessing? Explain.

    B. What kind of shield are we promised in verse 5?

    C. Does genuine faith exempt one from grief (v. 6)? Why or why not?

    D. How do trials and the grief they bring fit in with the Christian life (v. 7)?

    E. What blessing comes to those who believe in Christ (v. 8)?

    F. What blessing does faith ultimately bring to those who exercise it (v. 9)?

Traveling On

1. Interview someone you know to be gifted in the art of comforting the grieving. Look for someone whom others seek out in a time of loss. Ask the person what he or she does at these times. What do you learn?

2. Do a Bible study on the words *tear* and *tears.* What do you learn?

12

From Panic to Peace

The Burden of Fear

Traveling Back

1. *Jesus flat on the ground? Face in the dirt? Extended hands gripping grass? Body rising and falling with sobs? Face as twisted as the olive trees that surround him? What do we do with this image of Jesus? Simple. We turn to it when we look the same.*

   A. Describe the last time you felt the way Jesus is described above.

   B. How does it help us to know that Jesus felt this way?

2. *When you feel the panic, don't focus on the people; focus on the opening. Good counsel in golf. Good counsel in life. Rather than focus on the fear, focus on the solution.*

   A. What kind of situations make you most fearful?

   B. When you face one of these frightening events, how can you "focus on the opening"? What "solution" can you call upon?

3. *Don't avoid life's Gardens of Gethsemane. Enter them. Just don't enter them alone. And while there, be honest. Pounding the ground is permitted. Tears are allowed. And if you sweat blood, you won't be the first. Do what Jesus did; open your heart.*

   A. How do we try to avoid life's Gardens of Gethsemane? Describe the last time you tried to avoid one.

   B. Is it easy or hard for you to express your emotions like this? Explain.

4. *Don't measure the size of the mountain; talk to the One who can move it. Instead of carrying the world on your shoulders, talk to the One who holds the universe on his. Hope is a look away.*

   A. How do we often try to "measure the size of the mountain"? Why is this a bad idea?

   B. In what way is hope "a look away"? How can prayer help to restore our hope? Does it help restore yours? Explain.

Traveling Up

1. Read Psalm 56:3–4.

   A. How does the psalmist deal with his own fears? Do you follow his example? Explain.

   B. Why is the psalmist unafraid of "mortal man" (v. 4 NIV)? Is this a statement of ignorance or something else? Explain.

2. Read Isaiah 41:10–14.

   A. Why does God tell Israel not to fear (v. 10)?

   B. What promise does God give in verses 11–12?

   C. What reason does God give for his promise in verse 13?

   D. What command and promise does God give in verse 14? How can his words encourage you today?

3. Read 1 John 4:16–19.

   A. On what should we rely when we are afraid (v. 16)?

   B. How does John describe God in verse 16? What difference does this make?

   C. How can we have "confidence on the day of judgment" (v. 17 NIV)?

   D. What antidote to fear does John give in verse 18? How does this antidote work?

   E. How is this antidote to be shared? How does this show that we really have the antidote?

Traveling On

1. In your journal write about a time you had "garden" experiences. Explain what situation took you there, how you felt, what prayers you prayed, and how God ministered to you.

2. Read *Foxe's Book of Martyrs* to see how many of God's choicest saints overcame their fear even as they faced death.

13

Silent Nights and Solitary Days

The Burden of Loneliness

Traveling Back

1. *By now you've learned that you don't have to be alone to feel lonely.*

   A. What's the difference between being alone and feeling lonely?

   B. Do you avoid being alone? Explain.

   C. How often, in a normal week, would you say you feel lonely?

2. *Loneliness is not the absence of faces. It is the absence of intimacy. Loneliness doesn't come from being alone; it comes from feeling alone.*

   A. How would you define nonsexual intimacy? With how many friends can you speak intimately? Are you satisfied with this number? Explain.

   B. How do you deal with loneliness? When you feel lonely, what do you do?

3. *Could it be that loneliness is not a curse but a gift? A gift from God? . . . I wonder if loneliness is God's way of getting our attention.*

   A. Do you agree that loneliness can be a gift from God? Explain.

   B. Why might God want to get your attention through loneliness? To what might he want to call your attention?

4. *God changes your* n *into a* v. *You go from* lonely *to* lovely. *When you know God loves you, you won't be desperate for the love of others.*

   A. How does assurance of God's love for you, personally, change everything?

   B. Does knowledge of God's love eliminate the need for intimate friends? Explain.

C. What's the difference between desiring the love of others and being desperate for it?

Traveling Up

1. Read Psalm 88.

   A. How would you describe the man who wrote this psalm?

   B. Why do you think God included this psalm in the Bible?

   C. Have you ever felt as the psalmist did in verses 13–14? Explain.

   D. Most psalms do not end as this one does (v. 18). Why do you think it ends like this? Is this a comfort to you? Explain.

2. Read Deuteronomy 31:6–8.

   A. What command does God give the Israelites in verse 6? What encouragement does he give them?

   B. Why do you suppose that Moses repeats to Joshua both the command and the encouragement in verses 7–8? What does this suggest to you about dealing with your own fears?

3. Read John 14:16–18; Matthew 28:16–20.

   A. What request did Jesus say he would make of the Father in John 14:16?

   B. What promise did Jesus make in John 14:18? How is he fulfilling this promise today?

   C. How can we take courage from Jesus' words in Matthew 28:18?

   D. What encouragement can we get from Jesus' final words in Matthew 28:20? Are you relying on this promise? Why or why not?

Traveling On

1. Examine your schedule, and find an entire day when you can plan to get alone, just you and God. Go to a retreat center, a solitary spot, a place in the woods, any place where you can spend a whole

day in solitude. Bring your Bible, and make no other plans than to spend the day alone with God.

2. Get a group of your believing friends together, and spend a few hours visiting some of your church's shut-ins, whether at their homes or in care centers. Relieve their loneliness for a while.

14

The Crowing Rooster and Me

The Burden of Shame

Traveling Back

1. *Is Peter the only person to do the very thing he swore he'd never do? "Infidelity is behind me!" "From now on, I'm going to bridle my tongue." "No more shady deals. I've learned my lesson." Oh, the volume of our boasting. And, oh, the heartbreak of our shame.*

   A. Describe a time when you followed Peter's example and did the very thing you swore you'd never do. What happened?

   B. Why do you think we engage in such foolish boasting? What do we think we'll gain?

2. *We weep as Peter wept, and we do what Peter did. We go fishing. We go back to our old lives. We return to our pre-Jesus practices. We do what comes naturally, rather than what comes spiritually. And we question whether Jesus has a place for folks like us.*

   A. Have you ever "gone fishing" or returned to your pre-Jesus practices after a spiritual failure? If so, how did you feel at the time?

   B. Why do we question whether Jesus has a place for folks like us? Have you ever felt this way? Explain.

3. *Jesus prepared a table in the presence of the enemy. Judas was allowed to see the supper, but he wasn't allowed to stay there.* You are not welcome here. This table is for my children. You may tempt them. You may trip them. But you will never sit with them. *This is how much he loves us.*

A. Why do you think Jesus allowed Judas to see the supper? Why not banish him before the disciples gathered?

B. What does the Lord's Supper mean to you personally? What goes through your mind during the service?

4. *The same Jesus who'd prepared a meal for Peter had prepared one for me. The same Shepherd who had trumped the devil trumped him again. The same Savior who had built a fire on the shore stirred a few embers in my heart.* "Every one *of you drink this." And so I did. It felt good to be back at the table.*

A. Why do you think Jesus prepared a meal for Peter, who denied him, but not for Judas, who betrayed him? What was the difference?

B. How do the stories of both Peter and Max show true repentance? How does Jesus always respond to true repentance? Why is this important to understand?

Traveling Up

1. Read Joel 2:25–27.

A. What promise does God make to his people who repent (v. 25)?

B. Why do you think God twice says in verses 26–27 that his people will never again be shamed? Why does God care about getting rid of shame?

2. Read 2 Timothy 2:15–16.

A. What instruction is given in verse 15? How can you comply with this command?

B. How can we avoid being ashamed, according to verse 15?

C. How does verse 16 continue to tell us how to avoid being ashamed?

3. Read Hebrews 12:2–3.

A. What are we instructed to do in verse 2? How can this keep us from being ashamed?

B. How did Jesus react to the shame of the cross? Why was there shame at the cross?

C. How are we to benefit from the example of Jesus on the cross?

Traveling On

1. Think of Max's story and how shame kept him from fellowship with God. Be honest with yourself, and ask if you're dealing with anything similar. If so, follow Max's courageous example, and admit this "shameful thing" to a trusted and godly friend. Break its power over you by confessing and forsaking it—and be glad at the Lord's table once more.

2. If you ever have the opportunity, attend a Seder prepared by someone who can explain the Messianic significance of this ancient Jewish meal. Enrich your appreciation of the Lord's Supper.

15

Slippery Sheep and Healed Hurts

The Burden of Disappointment

Traveling Back

1. *A disappointment is a missed appointment. What we hoped would happen, didn't. We wanted health; we got disease. We wanted retirement; we got reassignment. Divorce instead of family. Dismissal instead of promotion.*

   A. What disappointments have you had to face recently?

   B. What do you do with your disappointments?

2. *Just like sheep, we have wounds, but ours are wounds of the heart that come from disappointment after disappointment. If we're not careful, these wounds lead to bitterness. And so just like sheep, we need to be treated.*

   A. How do repeated disappointments lead to bitterness?

   B. What kinds of things have made you bitter? How do you deal with bitterness?

3. *The large portion of our problems are not lion-sized attacks, but rather the day-to-day swarm of frustrations and mishaps and heartaches.*

   A. What little things in life tend to frustrate you the most?

   B. What help can you offer to someone plagued with a swarm of mishaps or heartaches?

4. *Jesus tends to his sheep. And he will tend to you. If you will let him. How? How do you let him? The steps are so simple. First, go to him. Second, assume the right posture. Bow before God. Third, trust in him.*

   A. How can you "go to" Jesus? What does it mean to "go to" him?

   B. Why is it necessary to "bow" before God? What does this mean?

C. What does it mean to "trust" in God? How do we do this, practically speaking?

Traveling Up

1. Read Psalm 22:2–5.

   A. What disappointment did David suffer in verse 2? Have you ever felt like this? Explain.

   B. How did David combat his disappointment in verses 3–5?

   C. What was the result of the ancestors' trust described in verses 4–5? How is this meant to encourage us?

   D. Consider that this is the psalm Jesus quoted while hanging on the cross. What do you think the psalm taught him about disappointment?

2. Read Romans 5:1–5.

   A. How do we gain peace with God (v. 1)?

   B. What benefit does this peace gain us (v. 2)? How should this make us feel?

   C. What relationship does sufferings have to hope (vv. 3–5)?

   D. Why does hope not disappoint us (v. 5)? How does this matter to us on a day-to-day level?

3. Read Psalm 147:1–3.

   A. How did the Israelites deal with their disappointments (v. 1)?

   B. What encouragement does God give his people in verse 3?

   C. How do you think God heals the brokenhearted? What has he done in your own life?

Traveling On

1. Make a list of your biggest disappointments in life. Write them down. Then take each one, in order, to God in prayer. Give them to him explicitly, one by one.

2. Make a new commitment to get involved in regular prayer. Set a time. Set a place. Set a specific period. Prepare a list of concerns and thanks to bring to God. Then do it.

16

Jam Session

The Burden of Envy

Traveling Back

1. *Jealousy sets her cross hairs on the one who has more.*

   A. Describe a time when you felt jealous of someone. What prompted your jealousy?

   B. Why do most of us want "more"? What keeps us from being content with what we have?

2. *If focusing on our diminishing items leads to envy, what would happen if we focused on the unending items? If awareness of what we don't have creates jealousy, is it possible that an awareness of our abundance will lead to contentment?*

   A. Answer both of the preceding questions.

   B. Try to itemize the "unending items" that you possess. What's on your list?

   C. Try to list your "abundance." What does this tell you about God's provision?

3. *God is not a miser with his grace. Your cup may be low on cash or clout, but it is overflowing with mercy. You may not have the prime parking place, but you have sufficient pardon.*

   A. How often do you ponder God's grace to you? His mercy?

   B. How has God been gracious to you this week? This month? This year?

4. *One thing is certain. When the final storm comes and you are safe in your Father's house, you won't regret what he didn't give. You'll be stunned at what he did.*

A. Try to imagine the day you arrive safe in your Father's house. Look around. What has he given you?

B. How can meditating on your eternal future with God help you to deal with what exists today?

Traveling Up

1. Read Proverbs 14:30; 23:17.

    A. With what does Proverbs 14:30 contrast envy? How is this significant?

    B. In what ways do believers sometimes envy "sinners" (Prov. 23:17)?

    C. What does it mean to be "zealous for the fear of the Lord" (NIV)?

2. Read James 3:13–4:5.

    A. What in verse 13 does James contrast with "bitter envy" in verse 14?

    B. Where does envy come from (v. 15)?

    C. What always accompanies envy (v. 16)?

    D. What causes fights and quarrels among spiritual brothers (4:1)?

    F. God himself is said to "envy" in 4:5 (NIV). How does this differ from human envy?

3. Read Titus 3:3–7.

    A. How does Paul describe his pre-Christian life (v. 3)? What do you think he envied?

    B. How did God deliver us from envy (vv. 4–5)?

    C. To what extent did God pour out his Holy Spirit on us (v. 6)? How is this meant to nip envy in the bud?

    D. What was the purpose of God's saving us (v. 7)? How can meditating on this truth destroy envy?

Traveling On

1. Draw a line down a sheet of paper, creating two columns. On the left side, list some of the things you envy in others. On the right side, list what God has supplied you in abundance and, if possible, include a Scripture reference. For example, in the left column you might say "I wish I had better health," and beside it, in the right column, you might list "God will give me a glorious, eternal body (Phil. 3:20–21)."

2. Make a date to serve dinner at a local rescue mission or homeless shelter. Try not to schedule your visit at Thanksgiving or Christmas (since such service organizations usually have more than enough help during those two holidays). And be thankful for what God has given you.

17

God's Loving Pursuit

The Burden of Doubt

Traveling Back

1. *When Jesus found us, we acted like Eric. Our limitations kept us from recognizing the One who came to save us. We even doubted his presence—and sometimes we still do.*

   A. Do you ever doubt God's presence? If so, why?

   B. How do our limitations keep us from recognizing the One who came to save us? How can we overcome these limitations?

2. *If the Lord is the shepherd who leads the flock, goodness and mercy are the two sheepdogs who guard the rear of the flock.*

   A. How does "goodness" differ from "mercy"? How are they the same?

   B. Where in your life do you most need God's goodness and mercy right now? Why don't you take the time to talk to him about your need?

3. *Trust your faith and not your feelings. . . . Measure your value through God's eyes, not your own. . . . See the big picture, not the small.*

   A. How do we sometimes trust our feelings and not our faith? How can we stop making this mistake?

   B. Take a few minutes to describe your value in God's eyes. What has he said about you in the Bible?

   C. How can we see the big picture, not the small?

4. *Most of all, God gives us himself. Even when we choose our hovel over his house and our trash over his grace, still he follows. Never forcing us.*

Never leaving us. Patiently persistent. Faithfully present. Using all of his power to convince us that he is who he is and that he can be trusted to lead us home.

A. How do you know God has given you himself? How can you be sure of this?

B. How has God used his power to convince you he is who he is? What most convinces you that God can be trusted to lead you home?

Traveling Up

1. Read James 1:5–8.

   A. To whom is verse 5 addressed? Do you qualify? Explain.

   B. What promise does verse 5 make?

   C. What condition is placed in verse 6 on the promise of verse 5?

   D. To what does James compare someone who doubts God's promise? Why is this picture appropriate?

   E. What warning is given in verses 7 and 8? In what way are these individuals "double-minded" (NIV)? How can one correct such a serious problem?

2. Read Jude 20–22.

   A. What instruction is given in verse 20? How is this instruction to be carried out?

   B. What instruction is given in verse 21? What future event empowers us to follow this instruction?

   C. What instruction is given in verse 22? Why do you think the command was given? How can we comply with this command?

3. Read Romans 14:19–23.

   A. Describe the command in verse 19. What is the purpose of this command? How well do you fulfill it? Explain.

B. How is it possible to destroy someone for the sake of food (v. 20)?

C. How does verse 21 relate to doubt?

D. What command is given in verse 22? What blessing is available? What does this blessing mean?

E. How is verse 23 an effective guideline for the entire Christian life? What rule is laid out here?

Traveling On

1. Realize that there is a great difference between doubt and questions. Doubt disbelieves in the promises and good character of God; questions merely wonder how God might pull off some incredible feat. To get a "feel" for the difference between doubt and questions, study the vastly different ways God responded to Zechariah in Luke 1:5–20 and Mary in Luke 1:26–38. They asked similar questions ("How can I be sure of this?" versus "How will this be?" [NIV]) regarding miraculous pregnancies, but one was judged and the other blessed. Why?

2. Read Os Guinness's book *God in the Dark* for a clear and helpful discussion on doubt.

18

Almost Heaven

The Burden of Homesickness

Traveling Back

1. *The twists and turns of life have a way of reminding us—we aren't home here. This is not our homeland. We aren't fluent in the languages of disease and death. The culture confuses the heart, the noise disrupts our sleep, and we feel far from home. And, you know what? That's OK.*

   A. Why do we often forget that this is not our real home?

   B. In what ways do you feel like a foreigner on this earth? Are you OK with that? Explain.

2. *Homesickness is one of the burdens God doesn't mind if we carry. We . . . are being prepared for another house. And we . . . know we aren't there yet.*

   A. Do you feel "homesick" for heaven? Explain.

   B. How is God preparing you for "another house"?

3. *The greatest calamity is not to feel far from home when you are, but to feel right at home when you are not.*

   A. Could it be that much of the disappointment we feel in life comes from trying to feel right at home when we're not? Explain.

   B. How can we consciously guard against feeling at home in this world? Name several practical things we can do.

4. *Every wrinkle and every needle take us one step closer to the last step when Jesus will change our simple bodies into forever bodies. No pain. No depression. No sickness. No end.*

   A. How does your own body remind you that this is not your forever home?

B. How would you respond to someone who says this desire for an eternal, painless body is merely wishful thinking and you'd be better off getting all the gusto while you can?

Traveling Up

1. Read Philippians 1:20–23.

   A. Describe Paul's firm expectation in verse 20. What challenge faced him?

   B. In your own words, explain what Paul meant in verse 21.

   C. Describe Paul's dilemma in verse 22. Why was he so torn?

   D. What did Paul mean by "depart" in verse 23 (NIV)? Depart where? Why would this be "better"?

2. Read Philippians 3:17–4:1.

   A. How does Paul describe the enemies of Christ in verses 18–19? What traits characterize them?

   B. Describe the main contrast of these people with believers in Christ (v. 20).

   C. For whom are Christians waiting (vv. 20–21)? What are they waiting for him to do?

   D. What effect should meditating on this truth have on believers (4:1)? Does it have this effect on you? Explain.

3. Read 1 Corinthians 15:50–57.

   A. What two contrasts does Paul make in verse 50? Why should this matter to us? Why is it important?

   B. What "secret" or "mystery" does Paul describe in verses 51–52?

   C. What kind of "clothes" will believers wear in heaven (v. 53)? Why is this important?

   D. Restate the message of verses 54–57 in your own words. Imagine that you are describing this situation to an eight-year-old.

   E. Are you "homesick"? Why or why not?

Traveling On

1. Do a study in the four Gospels and in the Book of Acts on the Lord Jesus' postresurrection body. Describe it. Then realize that our resurrection bodies will look and act similar to his!

2. Read Joni Eareckson Tada's book titled *Heaven*. Joni has lived in a wheelchair for decades since a diving accident at age seventeen, so she expresses a uniquely powerful vision of heaven.

A LOVE WORTH GIVING

LIVING *in the* OVERFLOW
of GOD'S LOVE

Published in Nashville, Tennessee by Thomas Nelson. Thomas Nelson is a trademark of Thomas Nelson, Inc.

Thomas Nelson, Inc. titles may be purchased in bulk for educational, business, fund-raising, or sales promotional use. For information, please e-mail SpecialMarkets@ThomasNelson.com.

Library of Congress Cataloging-in-Publication data

Lucado, Max.
A love worth giving : living in the overflow of God's love / by Max Lucado.
p. cm.
Includes bibliographical references.
ISBN-10: 0-8499-1759-X (hc)
ISBN-13: 978-0-8499-1759-2
ISBN-10: 0-8499-1346-2 (sc)
ISBN-13: 978-0-8499-1346-4
1. God—Love. 2. Love—Religious aspects—Christianity. 3. Christian life. I. Title.
BT140 .L83 2002
231'.6—dc21 2002008238

Printed in the United States of America

To my daughter Jenna on her eighteenth birthday.
A higher joy and deeper pride no father could know.
I love you.

Acknowledgments

The fingerprints of many dear ones are on these pages.

Liz Heaney and Karen Hill—Your patience is exceeded only by your skill. Thanks for the brilliant editing.

Steve and Cheryl Green—Can you believe it? Three decades of friendship! Thanks for keeping this ship on course.

Susan Perry—Thanks for the sweet spirit you add to our office.

The Oak Hills Church of Christ—We're living in an era of answered prayer. And you are the answer to one of mine.

The Thomas Nelson team—You're not just my publishers; you're my family.

Carol Bartley and Laura Kendall—For the constellation of corrections you gave this manuscript, I'm in your debt.

Charles Shinn—Prayer partner, golf buddy, shepherd, and just all-around good guy. Thanks for showing up.

Charles Prince—Gentleman scholar and dear adviser.

Steve Halliday—Your discussion guide is terrific! Thanks for another great job.

Jenna, Andrea, and Sara—You make other dads jealous and this dad beam. I love you.

Denalyn—A guy could get lost in your brown eyes.

To you, the reader—May you find a love worth giving.

And to you, our heavenly Father—Can an ocean be captured in a thimble? Can the tone deaf play Mozart? Can a mouse understand the majesty of the Rocky Mountains? Of course not. And can any words capture your love? By no means. But what joy is found in the attempt.

CHAPTER ONE

THE 7:47 PRINCIPLE

We love, because He first loved us.

1 JOHN 4:19 NASB

God loves you. Personally. Powerfully. Passionately.

Others have promised and failed.

But God has promised and succeeded.

He loves you with an unfailing love.

And his love—if you will let it—can fill you

and leave you with a love worth giving.

Could two people be more different?

He is looked up to. She is looked down on.

He is a church leader. She is a streetwalker.

He makes a living promoting standards. She's made a living breaking them.

He's hosting the party. She's crashing it.

Ask the other residents of Capernaum to point out the more pious of the two, and they'll pick Simon. Why, after all, he's a student of theology, a man of the cloth. Anyone would pick him. Anyone, that is, except Jesus. Jesus knew them both. And Jesus would pick the woman. Jesus does pick the woman. And, what's more, he tells Simon why.

Not that Simon wants to know. His mind is elsewhere. *How did this whore get in my house?* He doesn't know whom to yell at first, the woman or the servant who let her in. After all, this dinner is a formal affair. Invitation only. Upper crust. Crème de la crème. Who let the riffraff in?

Simon is angry. *Just look at her—groveling at Jesus' feet. Kissing them, no less! Why, if Jesus were who he says he is, he would have nothing to do with this woman.*

One of the lessons Simon learned that day was this: Don't think thoughts you don't want Jesus to hear. For Jesus heard them, and when he did, he chose to share a few of his own.

> "Simon," he said to the Pharisee, "I have something to say to you."
>
> "All right, Teacher," Simon replied, "go ahead."
>
> Then Jesus told him this story: "A man loaned money to two people—five hundred pieces of silver to one and fifty pieces to the other. But neither of them could repay him, so he kindly forgave them both, canceling their debts. Who do you suppose loved him more after that?"
>
> Simon answered, "I suppose the one for whom he canceled the larger debt."
>
> "That's right," Jesus said. Then he turned to the woman and said to Simon, "Look at this woman kneeling here. When I entered your home, you didn't offer me water to wash the dust from my feet, but she has washed them with her tears and wiped them with her hair. You didn't give me a kiss of greeting, but she has kissed my feet again and again from the time I first came in. You neglected the courtesy of olive oil to anoint my head, but she has anointed my feet with rare perfume. I tell you, her sins—and they are many—have been forgiven, so she has shown me much love. But a person who is forgiven little shows only little love." (Luke 7:40–47 NLT)

Simon invites Jesus to his house but treats him like an unwanted step-uncle. No customary courtesies. No kiss of greeting. No washing his feet. No oil for his head.

Or, in modern terms, no one opened the door for him, took his coat, or shook his hand. Count Dracula has better manners.

Simon does nothing to make Jesus feel welcome. The woman, however, does everything that Simon didn't. We aren't told her name. Just her reputation—a sinner. A prostitute most likely. She has no invitation to the party and no standing in the community. (Imagine a hooker in a tight dress showing up at the parsonage during the pastor's Christmas party. Heads turn. Faces blush. Gasp!)

But people's opinions didn't stop her from coming. It's not for them she has come. It's for him. Her every move is measured and meaningful. Each gesture extravagant. She puts her cheek to his feet, still dusty from the path. She has no water, but she has tears. She has no towel, but she has her hair. She uses both to bathe the feet of Christ. As one translation reads, "she rained tears" on his feet (v. 44 MSG). She opens a vial of perfume, perhaps her only possession of worth, and massages it into his skin. The aroma is as inescapable as the irony.

You'd think Simon of all people would show such love. Is he not the reverend of the church, the student of Scripture? But he is harsh, distant. You'd think the woman would avoid Jesus. Is she not the woman of the night, the town hussy? But she can't resist him. Simon's "love" is calibrated and stingy. Her love, on the other hand, is extravagant and risky.

How do we explain the difference between the two? Training? Education? Money? No, for Simon has outdistanced her in all three.

But there is one area in which the woman leaves him eating dust. Think about it. What one discovery has she made that Simon hasn't? What one treasure does she cherish that Simon doesn't? Simple. God's love. We don't know when she received it. We aren't told how she heard about it. Did she overhear Jesus' words "Your Father is merciful" (Luke 6:36 ESV)? Was she nearby when Jesus had compassion on the widow of Nain? Did someone tell her how Jesus touched lepers and turned tax collectors into disciples? We don't know. But we know this. She came thirsty. Thirsty from guilt. Thirsty from regret. Thirsty from countless nights of making love and finding none. She came thirsty.

And when Jesus hands her the goblet of grace, she drinks. She doesn't just taste or nip. She doesn't dip her finger and lick it or take the cup and sip it. She lifts the liquid to her lips and drinks, gulping and swallowing like the parched pilgrim she is. She drinks until the mercy flows down her chin and onto her neck and chest. She drinks until every inch of her soul is moist and soft. She comes thirsty and she drinks. She drinks deeply.

Simon, on the other hand, doesn't even know he is thirsty. People like Simon don't need grace; they analyze it. They don't request mercy; they debate and prorate it. It wasn't that Simon couldn't be forgiven; he just never asks to be.

So while she drinks up, he puffs up. While she has ample love to give, he has no love to offer. Why? The 7:47 Principle. Read again verse 47 of chapter 7: "A person who is forgiven little shows only little love." Just like the jumbo jet, the 7:47 Principle has wide wings. Just like the aircraft, this truth can lift you to another level. Read it one more time. "A person who is forgiven little shows only little love." In other words, we can't give what we've never received. If we've never received love, how can we love others?

But, oh, how we try! As if we can conjure up love by the sheer force of will. As if there is within us a distillery of affection that lacks only a piece of wood or a hotter fire. We poke it and stoke it with resolve. What's our typical strategy for treating a troubled relationship? Try harder.

"My spouse needs my forgiveness? I don't know how, but I'm going to give it."

"I don't care how much it hurts, I'm going to be nice to that bum."

"I'm supposed to love my neighbor? Okay. By golly, I will."

So we try. Teeth clinched. Jaw firm. We're going to love if it kills us! And it may do just that.

Could it be we are missing a step? Could it be that the first step of love is not toward them but toward him? Could it be that the secret to loving is receiving? You give love by first receiving it. "We love, because he first loved us" (1 John 4:19 NASB).

Long to be more loving? Begin by accepting your place as a dearly loved child. "Be imitators of God, therefore, as dearly loved children and live a life of love, just as Christ loved us" (Eph. 5:1–2 NIV).

Want to learn to forgive? Then consider how you've been forgiven. "Be kind and compassionate to one another, forgiving each other, just as in Christ God forgave you" (Eph. 4:32 NIV).

Finding it hard to put others first? Think of the way Christ put you first. "Though he was God, he did not demand and cling to his rights as God" (Phil. 2:6 NLT).

Need more patience? Drink from the patience of God (2 Pet. 3:9). Is generosity an elusive virtue? Then consider how generous God has been with you (Rom. 5:8). Having trouble putting up with ungrateful relatives or cranky neighbors? God puts up with you when you act the same. "He is kind to the ungrateful and wicked" (Luke 6:35 NIV).

Can't we love like this?

Not without God's help we can't. Oh, we may succeed for a time. We, like Simon, may open a door. But our relationships need more than a social gesture. Some of our spouses need a foot washing. A few of our friends need a flood of tears. Our children need to be covered in the oil of our love.

But if we haven't received these things ourselves, how can we give them to others? Apart from God, "the heart is deceitful above all things" (Jer. 17:9 NIV). A marriage-saving love is not within us. A friendship-preserving devotion cannot be found in our hearts. We need help from an outside source. A transfusion. Would we love as God loves? Then we start by receiving God's love.

We preachers have been guilty of skipping the first step. "Love each other!" we tell our churches. "Be patient, kind, forgiving," we urge. But instructing people to love without telling them they are loved is like telling them to write a check without our making a deposit in their accounts. No wonder so many relationships are overdrawn. Hearts have insufficient love. The apostle John models the right sequence. He makes a deposit before he tells us to write the check. First, the deposit:

> God showed how much he loved us by sending his only Son into the world so that we might have eternal life through him. This is real love. It is not that we loved God, but that he loved us and sent his Son as a sacrifice to take away our sins. (1 John 4:9–10 NLT)

And then, having made such an outrageous, eye-opening deposit, John calls on you and me to pull out the checkbook: "Dear friends, since God loved us that much, we surely ought to love each other" (v. 11 NLT).

The secret to loving is living loved. This is the forgotten first step in relationships. Remember Paul's prayer? "May your roots go down deep into the soil of God's marvelous love" (Eph. 3:17 NLT). As a tree draws nutrients from the soil, we draw nourishment from the Father. But what if the tree has no contact with the soil?

I was thinking of this yesterday as I disassembled our Christmas tree. That's my traditional New Year's Day chore. Remove the ornaments, carry out the tree, and sweep up all the needles. There are thousands of them! The tree is falling apart. Blame it on bad rooting. For two weeks this tree has been planted in a metal bowl. What comes from a tree holder?

Old Simon had the same problem. Impressive to look at, nicely decorated, but he falls apart when you give him a shove or two.

Sound familiar? Does bumping into certain people leave you brittle, breakable, and fruitless? Do you easily fall apart? If so, your love may be grounded in the wrong soil. It may be rooted in their love (which is fickle) or in your resolve to love (which is frail). John urges us to "rely on the love *God* has for us" (1 John 4:16 NIV, emphasis mine). He alone is the power source.

Many people tell us to love. Only God gives us the power to do so.

We know what God wants us to do. "This is what God commands: . . . that we love each other" (1 John 3:23). But how can we? How can we be kind to the vow breakers? To those who are unkind to us? How can we be patient with people who have the warmth of a vulture and the tenderness of a porcupine? How can we forgive the moneygrubbers and backstabbers we meet, love, and marry? How can we love as God loves? We want to. We long to. But how can we?

By living loved. By following the 7:47 Principle: Receive first, love second.

Want to give it a try? Let's carry this principle up the Mount Everest of love writings. More than one person has hailed 1 Corinthians 13 as the finest chapter in the Bible. No words get to the heart of loving people like these verses. And no verses get to the heart of the chapter like verses 4 through 8.

> Love is patient, love is kind. It does not envy, it does not boast, it is not proud. It is not rude, it is not self-seeking, it is not easily angered, it keeps no record of wrongs. Love does not delight in evil but rejoices with the truth. It always protects, always trusts, always hopes, always perseveres. Love never fails. (NIV)

Several years ago someone challenged me to replace the word *love* in this passage with my name. I did and became a liar. "Max is patient, Max is kind. Max does not envy, he does not boast, he is not proud. . . ." That's enough! Stop right there! Those words are false. Max is not patient. Max is not kind. Ask my wife and kids. Max can be an out-and-out clod! That's my problem.

And for years that was my problem with this paragraph. It set a standard I could not meet. No one can meet it. No one, that is, except Christ. Does this passage not describe the measureless love of God? Let's insert Christ's name in place of the word *love,* and see if it rings true.

> Jesus is patient, Jesus is kind. Jesus does not envy, he does not boast, he is not proud. Jesus is not rude, he is not self-seeking, he is not easily angered, he keeps no record of wrongs. Jesus does not delight in evil but rejoices with the truth. Jesus always protects, always trusts, always hopes, always perseveres. Jesus never fails.

Rather than let this scripture remind us of a love we cannot produce, let it remind us of a love we cannot resist—God's love.

Some of you are so thirsty for this type of love. Those who should have loved you didn't. Those who could have loved you didn't. You were left at the hospital. Left at the altar. Left with an empty bed. Left with a broken heart. Left with your question "Does anybody love me?"

Please listen to heaven's answer. God loves you. Personally. Powerfully. Passionately. Others have promised and failed. But God has promised and succeeded. He loves you with an unfailing love. And his love—if you will let it—can fill you and leave you with a love worth giving.

So come. Come thirsty and drink deeply.

CHAPTER
TWO

Love's Flagship

Love is patient.

1 Corinthians 13:4

Patience is the red carpet upon which God's grace approaches us.

See the people hiding in the house? That's us. The folks ducking behind the stairwell? That's you and me. We're avoiding the bill collectors. This is the eve of eviction. The bank has given us one day to pay the mortgage. Credit-card agents are camped on the front lawn. Loan sharks have our number on speed dial. But we are broke. We've peddled our last food stamp. The water is disconnected, the car repossessed, the furniture picked up, and now the IRS agent is knocking on the door. He wants back taxes. "I know you are in there. Open up!"

So we do. He tells us how much we owe; we remind him that turnips give no blood. He mentions jail, and at this point a warm bed out of the reach of creditors doesn't sound half bad.

Just as he motions for the sheriff, his cell phone rings. It's Washington. The president wants a word with us, an explanation from us. We have none. No defense. Only a plea for patience. He listens in silence and asks to speak with the agent again. As the president speaks, the suit nods and says, "Yessir . . . Yessir . . . Yessir." He closes his phone and looks first at you and then at me. "I don't know who you know, but your debt is paid," he says, tearing up the papers and letting the pieces fall.

Maybe you didn't know God did that for us. Maybe no one has told you about "God's . . . patience and willingness to put up with you" (Rom. 2:4 CEV). Could be you dozed off the day the minister read Psalm 103:8: "The LORD is compassionate and gracious, slow to anger, abounding in love" (NIV). If so, no wonder you've been edgy. No wonder you've been impatient. Bankruptcy can put the best of us in a foul mood. You know what you need to do?

Step out on the porch. Stand where the IRS guy stood, and look at those papers—the torn pieces scattered and strewn across the lawn. Stare at the proof of God's patience.

You were in debt!

Those times you used his name only when you cussed? God could have blown up at you. But he didn't. He was patient.

Those thousand sunsets you never thanked him for? He could have put you on beauty rations. But he didn't. He was patient with you.

Those Sundays you strutted into church to show off the new dress? It's a wonder he didn't strike you naked. But he didn't. He was patient.

And, oh my, those promises: "Get me out of this, and I'll never tell another lie." "Count on me to stand up for you from now on." "I'm done with temper tantrums, Lord." Goodness gracious. If broken promises were lumber, we could build a subdivision. Doesn't God have ample reason to walk out on us?

But he doesn't. Why? Because "God is being patient with you" (2 Pet. 3:9).

Paul presents patience as the premiere expression of love. Positioned at the head of the apostle's Love Armada—a boat-length or two in front of kindness, courtesy, and forgiveness—is the flagship known as patience. "Love is patient" (1 Cor. 13:4).

The Greek word used here for *patience* is a descriptive one. It figuratively means "taking a long time to boil." Think about a pot of boiling water. What factors determine the speed at which it boils? The size of the stove? No. The pot? The utensil may have an influence, but the primary factor is the intensity of the flame. Water boils quickly when the flame is high. It boils slowly when the flame is low. Patience "keeps the burner down."

Helpful clarification, don't you think? Patience isn't naive. It doesn't ignore misbehavior. It just keeps the flame low. It waits. It listens. It's slow to boil. This is how God treats us. And, according to Jesus, this is how we should treat others.

He once told a parable about a king who decides to settle his accounts with his debtors. His bookkeeper surfaces a fellow who owes not thousands or hundreds of thousands but millions of dollars. The king summarily declares that the man and his wife and kids are to be sold to pay the debt. Because of his inability to pay, the man is about to lose everything and everyone dear to him. No wonder

> the man fell down before the king and begged him, "Oh, sir, be *patient* with me, and I will pay it all." Then the king was filled with pity for him, and he released him and forgave his debt. (Matt. 18:26–27 NLT, emphasis mine)

The word *patience* makes a surprise appearance here. The debtor does not plead for mercy or forgiveness; he pleads for patience. Equally curious is this singular appearance of the word. Jesus uses it twice in this story and never again. It appears nowhere else in the Gospels. Perhaps the scarce usage is the first-century equivalent of a highlighter. Jesus reserves the word for one occasion to make one point. Patience is more than a virtue for long lines and slow waiters. Patience is the red carpet upon which God's grace approaches us.

Had there been no patience, there would have been no mercy. But the king was patient, and the man with the multimillion-dollar debt was forgiven.

But then the story takes a left turn. The freshly forgiven fellow makes a beeline from the courthouse to the suburbs. There he searches out a guy who owes him some money.

> But when the man left the king, he went to a fellow servant who owed him a few thousand dollars. He grabbed him by the throat and demanded instant payment. His fellow servant fell down before him and begged for a little more time. "Be *patient* and I will pay it," he pleaded. But his creditor wouldn't wait. He had the man arrested and jailed until the debt could be paid in full. (vv. 28–30 NLT, emphasis mine)

The king is stunned. How could the man be so impatient? How *dare* the man be so impatient! The ink of the CANCELED stamp is still moist on the man's bills. Wouldn't you expect a little Mother Teresa–ness out of him? You'd think that a person who'd been forgiven so much would love much. But he didn't. And his lack of love led to a costly mistake.

The unforgiving servant is called back to the castle.

> "You evil servant!" [the king, a.k.a. God, declares.] "I forgave you that tremendous debt because you pleaded with me. Shouldn't you have mercy on your fellow servant, just as I had mercy on you?" Then the angry king sent the man to prison until he had paid every penny. (Matt. 18:32–34 NLT)

The king's patience made no difference in the man's life. To the servant, throne-room mercy was nothing more than a canceled test, a dodged bullet, a get-out-of-jail-free card. He wasn't stunned by the royal grace; he was relieved he hadn't been punished. He was given much patience but gave none, which makes us wonder if he actually understood the gift he had received.

If you find patience hard to give, you might ask the same question. How infiltrated are you with God's patience? You've heard about it. Read about it. Perhaps underlined Bible passages regarding it. But have you received it? The proof is in your patience. Patience deeply received results in patience freely offered.

But patience never received leads to an abundance of problems, not the least of which is prison. Remember where the king sent the unforgiving servant? "Then the angry king sent the man to prison until he had paid every penny" (Matt. 18:34 NLT).

Whew! we sigh. *Glad that story is a parable. It's a good thing God doesn't imprison the impatient in real life.* Don't be so sure he doesn't. Self-absorption and ingratitude make for thick walls and lonely jails.

Impatience still imprisons the soul. For that reason, our God is quick to help us avoid it. He does more than demand patience from us; he offers it to us. Patience is a fruit of his Spirit. It hangs from the tree of Galatians 5:22: "The Spirit produces the fruit of love, joy, peace, patience." Have you asked God to give you some fruit? *Well I did once, but . . .* But what? Did you, h'm, grow impatient? Ask him again and again and again. He won't grow impatient with your pleading, and you will receive patience in your praying.

And while you're praying, ask for understanding. "Patient people have great understanding" (Prov. 14:29). Could it be your impatience stems from a lack of understanding? Mine has.

Sometime ago our church staff attended a leadership conference. Especially interested in one class, I arrived early and snagged a front-row seat. As the speaker began, however, I was distracted by a couple of voices in the back of the room. Two guys were mumbling to each other. I was giving serious thought to shooting a glare over my shoulder when the speaker offered an explanation. "Forgive me," he said. "I forgot to explain why the two fellows at the back of the class are talking. One of them is an elder at a new church in Romania. He has traveled here to learn about church leadership. But he doesn't speak English, so the message is being translated."

All of a sudden everything changed. Patience replaced impatience. Why? Because patience always hitches a ride with understanding. The wise man says, "A man of understanding holds his tongue" (Prov. 11:12 NIV). He also says, "A man of understanding is even-tempered" (Prov. 17:27 NIV). Don't miss the connection between understanding and patience. Before you blow up, listen up. Before you strike out, tune in. "It takes wisdom to have a good family, and it takes understanding to make it strong" (Prov. 24:3).

Before anything else, love is patient.

For an example, come with me to Paris, France, 1954. Elie Wiesel is a correspondent for a Jewish newspaper. A decade earlier he was a prisoner in a Jewish concentration camp. A decade later he would be known as the author of *Night,* the Pulitzer Prize–winning account of the Holocaust. Eventually he'll be awarded the Congressional Medal of Achievement and the Nobel Peace Prize.

But tonight Elie Wiesel is a twenty-six-year-old unknown newspaper correspondent. He is about to interview the French author François Mauriac, who is a devout Christian. Mauriac is France's most recent Nobel laureate for literature and an expert on French political life.

Wiesel shows up at Mauriac's apartment, nervous and chain-smoking—his emotions still frayed from the German horror, his comfort as a writer still raw. The older Mauriac tries to put him at ease. He invites Wiesel in, and the two sit in the small room. Before Wiesel can ask a question, however, Mauriac, a staunch Roman Catholic, begins to speak about his favorite subject: Jesus. Wiesel grows uneasy. The name of Jesus is a pressed thumb on his infected wounds.

Wiesel tries to reroute the conversation but can't. It is as though everything in creation leads back to Jesus. Jerusalem? Jerusalem is where Jesus ministered. The Old Testament? Because of Jesus, the Old is now enriched by the New. Mauriac turns every topic toward the Messiah. The anger in Wiesel begins to heat. The Christian anti-Semitism he'd grown up with, the layers of grief from Sighet, Auschwitz, and Buchenwald—it all boils over. He puts away his pen, shuts his notebook, and stands up angrily.

> "Sir," he said to the still-seated Mauriac, "you speak of Christ. Christians love to speak of him. The passion of Christ, the agony of Christ, the death of Christ. In your religion, that is all you speak of. Well, I want you to know that ten years ago, not very far from here, I knew Jewish children every one of whom suffered a thousand times more, six million times more, than Christ on the cross. And we don't speak about them. Can you understand that, sir? We don't speak about them."[1]

Mauriac is stunned. Wiesel turns and marches out the door. Mauriac sits in shock, his woolen blanket still around him. The young reporter is pressing the elevator button when Mauriac appears in the hall. He gently reaches for Wiesel's arm. "Come back," he implores. Wiesel agrees, and the two sit on the sofa. At this point Mauriac begins to weep. He looks at Wiesel but says nothing. Just tears.

Wiesel starts to apologize. Mauriac will have nothing of it. Instead he urges his young friend to talk. He wants to hear about it—the camps, the trains, the deaths. He asks Wiesel why he hasn't put this to paper. Wiesel tells him the pain is too severe. He's made a vow of silence. The older man tells him to break it and speak out.

The evening changed them both. The drama became the soil of a lifelong friendship. They corresponded until Mauriac's death in 1970. "I owe François Mauriac my career," Wiesel has said . . . and it was to Mauriac that Wiesel sent the first manuscript of *Night.*[2]

What if Mauriac had kept the door shut? Would anyone have blamed him? Cut by the sharp words of Wiesel, he could have become impatient with the angry young man and have been glad to be rid of him. But he didn't and he wasn't. He reacted decisively, quickly, and lovingly. He was "slow to boil." And, because he was, a heart began to heal.

May I urge you to do the same?

"God is being patient with you" (2 Pet. 3:9). And if God is being patient with you, can't you pass on some patience to others? Of course you can. Because before love is anything else:

Love is patient.

CHAPTER THREE

Your Kindness Quotient

Love is kind.

1 Corinthians 13:4 NIV

The kindness of Jesus.

We are quick to think of his power,

his passion, and his devotion.

But those near him knew and know

God comes cloaked in kindness.

Three messages were on my answering machine this morning. All three making the same request. They'd heard the topic of this chapter and wanted to contribute. God had been kind to them. They had a story to share. I invited them over.

The first to arrive was a young couple freshly married. Both showed evidence of a recent wedding—she was thin from the weight she'd lost; he was wide eyed at the bride he'd gained. Sitting cuddly close on the couch, they told me their story. She did most of the talking. He nodded and smiled and would finish a sentence when she stopped for breath.

"My mother and Mary had been friends since they were teens. So we invited Mary and Jesus to the wedding."

"My wife knew Jesus when he ran the family business," he added.

"We were thrilled when Jesus came. But a bit surprised at the vanload of buddies. There was a bunch."

"Fifteen or twenty," he offered.

"But that was fine. After all, Jesus is like family. Besides, we had a great time. Long after the ceremony ended, people lingered. Eating and drinking."

"Drinking a bit too much," the groom explained.

"Yeah, soon the wine was gone, and the waiters were nervous because the people still wanted to party."

The young girl slid to the front of the couch. "I didn't even know about the problem until it was solved. No one told me. Someone told Jesus, though, and he took care of it. Not only did he produce more wine, he improved it!" She went on to say that the wedding coordinator reported that the vintage tasted like the hundred-dollar-a-bottle Bordeaux she tasted once at a wine festival.

The young man moved up to the front of the couch with his wife. "Here is what impresses us." As he spoke, she looked at him and nodded as if she knew what he was going to say. "This is his first miracle, right? His debut, and he uses it on us! To save us from looking like poor hosts."

"He didn't have to do that," she jumped in. "Our town had sick people, poor people. Why, raising the dead would have made the headlines. But he used his premiere miracle on a social miscue. Wasn't that kind of him?" She smiled. He smiled.

So did I.

As they left a businessman came in. Told me his name was Zacchaeus. A short fellow in an Italian suit. All tan and teeth. Cole Haans. Ray·Bans. You could tell he had done well for himself. "Don't let the appearance fool you," he said. "I had the bucks but not the friends. Built this big house on the edge of town. But no one ever came to see me, not even the Jehovah's Witnesses. Can't say I blamed them. I paid for the place with money I'd skimmed off their taxes. No, no one ever visited me till the day Jesus came. 'I'm coming to your house today,' he announced. Right there in the middle of town where all could hear. He didn't have to do that, you know. The diner was down the block, or I would have bought him lunch at the club. But, no, he wanted to come to my house. And he wanted everyone to know where he was going. His is the first signature in my guest book. That was kind of him, don't you think? Unbelievably kind."

Later in the day a woman came by. Middle aged. Hair streaked with gray and pulled back. Dress was simple. Reminded me of a middle-school librarian. Face was wrinkled and earnest. Said she'd been sick for a dozen years. HIV positive.

"That's a long time," I said.

Long enough, she agreed, to run out of doctors, money, even hope. But worst of all, she had run out of friends. "They were afraid of me," she said. "Worried about catching the disease. My church hadn't turned me out, but they hadn't helped me out either. I hadn't been home in years. Been living in a shelter. But then Jesus came to town. He was on his way to treat the mayor's daughter, who was dying. The crowd was thick, and people were pushing, but I was desperate."

She spoke of following Jesus at a distance. Then she drew near and stepped back for fear of being recognized. She told of inching behind a broad-shouldered man and staying in his wake until, as she said, "There were only two people between him and me. I pressed my arm through the mob and reached for the hem of his jacket. Not to grab, just to touch it. And when I did, my body changed. Instantly. My face rushed with warmth. I could breathe deeply. My back seemed to straighten. I stopped, letting the people push past. He stopped too. 'Who touched me?' he asked. I slid behind the big man again and said nothing. As he and the crowd waited, my heart pounded. From the healing? From fear? From both? I didn't know. Then he asked again, 'Who touched me?' He didn't sound angry—just curious. So I spoke up. My voice shook; so did my hands. The big man stepped away. Jesus stepped forward, and I told the whole story."

"The whole story?" I asked.

"The whole story," she replied.

I tried to imagine the moment. Everyone waiting as Jesus listened. The crowd waiting. The city leaders waiting. A girl was dying, people were pressing, disciples were questioning, but Jesus . . . Jesus was listening. Listening to the whole story. He didn't have to. The healing would have been enough. Enough for her. Enough for the crowd. But not enough for him. Jesus wanted to do more than heal her body. He wanted to hear her story—all of it. The whole story. What a kind thing to do. The miracle restored her health. The kindness restored her dignity.

And what he did next, the woman never forgot. "As if he hadn't done enough already"—her eyes began to water—"he called me 'daughter.' 'Daughter, be of good cheer; your faith has made you well. Go in peace.' I've been told he never used that word with anyone else. Just me."[1]

After she left, I checked. She was right.

The kindness of Jesus. We are quick to think of his power, his passion, and his devotion. But those near him knew and know God comes cloaked in kindness. Kind enough to care about a faux pas. Kind enough to have lunch with a crook. Kind enough to bless a suffering sister.

"Love is kind," writes Paul.

Nehemiah agrees: "You are God, ready to pardon, gracious and merciful, slow to anger, abundant in kindness" (Neh. 9:17 NKJV).

David agrees, "Your lovingkindness is better than life" (Ps. 63:3 NASB).

Paul speaks of "the kindness and love of God our Savior" (Titus 3:4 NIV). He is exuberant as he announces: "Now God has us where he wants us, with all the time in this world and the next to shower grace and kindness upon us in Christ Jesus. Saving is all his idea, and all his work. All we do is trust him enough to let him do it" (Eph. 2:7–8 MSG).

But Jesus' invitation offers the sweetest proof of the kindness of heaven:

> Come to Me, all you who labor and are heavy laden, and I will give you rest. Take My yoke upon you and learn from Me, for I am gentle and lowly in heart, and you will find rest for your souls. For My yoke is easy and My burden is light. (Matt. 11:28–30 NKJV)

Farmers in ancient Israel used to train an inexperienced ox by yoking it to an experienced one with a wooden harness. The straps around the older animal were tightly drawn. He carried the load. But the yoke around the younger animal was loose. He walked alongside the more mature ox, but his burden was light. In this verse Jesus is saying, "I walk alongside you. We are yoked together. But I pull the weight and carry the burden."

I wonder, how many burdens is Jesus carrying for us that we know nothing about? We're aware of some. He carries our sin. He carries our shame. He carries our eternal debt. But are there others? Has he lifted fears before we felt them? Has he carried our confusion so we wouldn't have to? Those times when we have been surprised by our own sense of peace? Could it be that Jesus has lifted our anxiety onto his shoulders and placed a yoke of kindness on ours?

And how often do we thank him for his kindness? Not often enough. But does our ingratitude restrict his kindness? No. "Because he is kind even to people who are ungrateful and full of sin" (Luke 6:35).

In the original language, the word for *kindness* carries an added idea the English word does not. Chiefly it refers to an act of grace. But it also refers to a deed or person who is "useful, serviceable, adapted to its purpose."[2] *Kindness* was even employed to describe food that was tasty as well as healthy. Sounds odd to our ears. "Hey, honey, what a great meal. The salad is especially *kind* tonight."

But the usage makes sense. Isn't kindness good *and* good for you? Pleasant *and* practical? Kindness not only says good morning, kindness makes the coffee. Again, doesn't Jesus fit this description? He not only attended the wedding, he rescued it. He not only healed the woman, he honored her. He did more than call Zacchaeus by name; he entered his house.

Hasn't he acted similarly with you? Hasn't he helped you out of a few jams? Hasn't he come into your house? And has there ever been a time when he was too busy to listen to your story? The Bible says, "Whoever is wise will observe these things, and they will understand the lovingkindness of the LORD" (Ps. 107:43 NKJV). Hasn't God been kind—pleasantly useful—to you? And since God has been so kind to you (you know what I am about to say), can't you be kind to others?

Paul's question is for all of us: "Do you think lightly of the riches of His kindness and tolerance and patience, not knowing that the kindness of God leads you to repentance?" (Rom. 2:4 NASB). Repentance from what? Certainly from ungodliness, rebellion, and sin. But can't we equally state that God's kindness leads to repentance from unkindness?

Some may think that all this talk of kindness sounds, well . . . it sounds a bit wimpy. Men in particular tend to value more dramatic virtues—courage, devotion, and visionary leadership. We attend seminars on strategizing and team building. But I can't say I've ever attended or even heard of one lecture on kindness. Jesus, however, would take issue with our priorities. "Go and learn what this means," he commands. "'I want kindness more than I want animal sacrifices'" (Matt. 9:13). Paul places kindness toward the top of the pyramid when he writes, "Love is kind" (1 Cor. 13:4 NIV).

How kind are you? What is your kindness quotient? When was the last time you did something kind for someone in your family—e.g., got a blanket, cleaned off the table, prepared the coffee—without being asked?

Think about your school or workplace. Which person is the most overlooked or avoided? A shy student? A grumpy employee? Maybe he doesn't speak the language. Maybe she doesn't fit in. Are you kind to this person?

Kind hearts are quietly kind. They let the car cut into traffic and the young mom with three kids move up in the checkout line. They pick up the neighbor's trash can that rolled into the street. And they are especially kind at church. They understand that perhaps the neediest person they'll meet all week is the one standing in the foyer or sitting on the row behind them in worship. Paul writes: "When we have the opportunity to help anyone, we should do it. But we should give special attention to those who are in the family of believers" (Gal. 6:10).

And, here is a challenge—what about your enemies? How kind are you to those who want what you want or take what you have?

A friend of mine witnessed a humorous act of kindness at an auction. The purpose of the gathering was to raise money for a school. Someone had donated a purebred puppy that melted the heart and opened the checkbooks of many guests. Two in particular.

They sat on opposite sides of the banquet room, a man and a woman. As the bidding continued, these two surfaced as the most determined. Others dropped off, but not this duo. Back and forth they went until they'd one-upped the bid to several thousand dollars. This was no longer about a puppy. This was about victory. This was the Wimbledon finals, and neither player was backing off the net. (Don't you know the school president was drooling?)

Finally the fellow gave in and didn't return the bid. "Going once, going twice, going three times. Sold!" The place erupted, and the lady was presented with her tail-wagging trophy. Her face softened, then reddened. Maybe she'd forgotten where she was. Never intended to go twelve rounds at a formal dinner. Certainly never intended for the world to see her pit-bull side.

So you know what she did? As the applause subsided, she walked across the room and presented the puppy to the competition.

Suppose you did that with your competition. With your enemy. With the boss who fired you or the wife who left you. Suppose you surprised them with kindness? Not easy? No, it's not. But mercy is the deepest gesture of kindness. Paul equates the two. "Be kind to one another, tenderhearted, forgiving one another, even as God in Christ forgave you" (Eph. 4:32 NKJV). Jesus said:

> Love your enemies. Do good to those who hate you, bless those who curse you. . . . If you love only the people who love you, what praise should you get? . . . [L]ove your enemies, do good to them, and lend to them without hoping to get anything back. Then you will have a great reward, and you will be children of the Most High God, because he is kind even to people who are ungrateful and full of sin. Show mercy, just as your Father shows mercy. (Luke 6:27–28, 32, 35–36)

Kindness at home. Kindness in public. Kindness at church and kindness with your enemies. Pretty well covers the gamut, don't you think? Almost. Someone else needs your kindness. Who could that be? You.

Don't we tend to be tough on ourselves? And rightly so. Like the young couple at the wedding, we don't always plan ahead. Like Zacchaeus, we've cheated our share of friends. We've been self-serving. And like the woman with the illness, our world sometimes seems out of control.

But did Jesus scold the couple? No. Did he punish Zacchaeus? No. Was he hard on the woman? No. He is kind to the forgetful. He is kind to the greedy. He is kind to the sick.

And he is kind to us. And since he is so kind to us, can't we be a little kinder to ourselves? *Oh, but you don't know me, Max. You don't know my faults and my thoughts. You don't know the gripes I grumble and the complaints I mumble.* No, I don't, but he does. He knows everything about you, yet he doesn't hold back his kindness toward you. Has he, knowing all your secrets, retracted one promise or reclaimed one gift?

No, he is kind to you. Why don't you be kind to yourself? He forgives your faults. Why don't you do the same? He thinks tomorrow is worth living. Why don't you agree? He believes in you enough to call you his ambassador, his follower, even his child. Why not take his cue and believe in yourself?

In the book entitled *Sweet Thursday,* John Steinbeck introduces us to Madam Fauna. She runs a brothel and takes a liking to a prostitute by the name of Suzy. Madam Fauna sets Suzy up on a real date with a man, not a client. She buys Suzy a nice dress and helps her get ready for the evening. As Suzy is leaving, she, moved by Madam Fauna's kindness, asks her, "You have done so much for me. Can I do anything for you?"

"Yes," the older woman replies, "you can say, 'I'm Suzy and no one else.'"

Suzy does. Then Madam Fauna requests, "Now say, 'I'm Suzy, and I'm a good thing.'"

And so Suzy tries. "I'm Suzy, and I'm a good . . ." And Suzy begins to cry.

Wouldn't God want you to say the same words? In his book you are a *good thing.* Be kind to yourself. God thinks you're worth his kindness. And he's a good judge of character.

CHAPTER FOUR

INFLAMED

Love does not envy.

1 CORINTHIANS 13:4 NKJV

God offers authentic love.

His devotion is the real deal.

But he won't give you the genuine

until you surrender the imitations.

Nancy is single. Forty-something and single. Her friends chat about diapers and schools, the oddities of husbands, and the curiosities of family life. She just listens and smiles.

She is single. Forty-something and single. Her friends drive minivans. A high-school classmate has kids bound for college. Nancy drives a compact car and eats most meals alone and feels awkward at baby showers.

She is single. People wonder why. They never say it, but their eyes betray it. "You aren't married?" is the question. *Why not?* is the thought. Is something wrong? Something awry? Abnormal?

Serving on a church staff exacerbates the contrast. She dutifully nods as members tell family holiday stories and husband-wife vacation adventures. She spent last Christmas with her parents, then drove home alone. And she'd enjoy a trip, but travel partners are hard to come by. How can she love the church family when they have what she wants?

She occasionally feels vulnerable at night. What was that noise? She feels self-conscious at parties. *Do I go alone?* And she's having to cope with envy. Not anger. Not red-hot jealousy. Certainly not hatred. Just envy. A flicker of resentment toward women who have what she doesn't. And she's concerned.

Well she should be. For what is a flicker today can turn into a fire tomorrow.

Suppose you spotted a flame in your house. Not a blaze and certainly not a fire, but tiny tongues of heat dancing on the hem of a curtain, on the fringe of the carpet, to the side of the stove. What would you do? How would you react? Would you shrug your shoulders and walk away, saying, "A little fire never hurt any house."

Of course not. You'd put it out. Douse it, stamp it, cover it—anything but allow it. You would not tolerate a maverick flame in your house. Why? Because you know the growth pattern of fire. What is born in innocence is deadly in adolescence. Left untended, fire consumes all that is consumable. You know, for the sake of your house, you don't play with fire.

For the sake of your heart, the same is true. A warning should be offered about the fire in the heart, which, left unchecked, can burst into a hungry flame and consume all that is consumable. The name of the fire? Solomon tagged it. "Jealousy is cruel as the grave. Its flashes are flashes of fire" (Song of Sol. 8:6 RSV).

Paul was equally aggressive in his declaration. "Love does not envy" (1 Cor. 13:4 NKJV). No doubt he'd read about and seen the results of unmanaged jealousy.

Look at Joseph's brothers. They started out taunting and teasing Joseph. Harmless sibling rivalry. But then the flicker became a flame. "His brothers were jealous of him" (Gen. 37:11 NIV). Soon it was easier to dump Joseph into a pit than see him at the dinner table. Before long, Joseph was in Egypt, the brothers were in cahoots, and Jacob, the father, was in the dark. He thought his boy was dead. All because of envy.

And what about the Pharisees? Were they evil men? Criminals? Thugs?

No, they were the pastors and teachers of their day. Little League coaches and carpool partners. But what did they do with Jesus? "They had handed Him over because of envy" (Matt. 27:18 NKJV).

And Max, don't forget Max. As long as we are listing the names of people prone to jealousy, put my name on the list. I began smelling smoke when I learned of a church across town. A friend came back with this report: "The church is great! It's bursting at the seams! It's the largest one in town."

A more spiritual Max would have rejoiced. A more mature Max would have thanked God. But the Max who heard the report didn't act mature or spiritual. He acted jealous. Can you believe it? Rather than celebrate God's work, I was obsessed with my own. I wanted our church to be the biggest.

Sickening. The Lord didn't leave me to indulge in such territorialism for long. In a profound moment of conviction, he let me know that the church is his church, not mine. The work is his work, not mine. And my life is his life, not mine.

My job was not to question him but to trust him. "Don't be jealous. . . . Trust the LORD and do good" (Ps. 37:1, 3). The cure for jealousy? Trust. The cause of jealousy? Distrust. The sons of Jacob didn't trust God to meet their needs. The Pharisees didn't trust God to solve their problems. The writer of this book didn't trust God to expand his kingdom. I didn't do so at great risk. What are the consequences of envy?

Loneliness tops the list. Solomon says, "Anger is cruel and destroys like a flood, but no one can put up with jealousy!" (Prov. 27:4). Who wants to hang out with a jealous fool? In a cemetery in England stands a grave marker with the inscription: SHE DIED FOR WANT OF THINGS. Alongside that marker is another, which reads: HE DIED TRYING TO GIVE THEM TO HER.[1]

Sickness is another consequence. The wise man also wrote, "Peace of mind means a healthy body, but jealousy will rot your bones" (Prov. 14:30).

Violence is the ugliest fruit. "You want something you don't have, and you will do anything to get it. You will even kill!" (James 4:2 CEV). "Jealousy," informs Proverbs 6:34, "enrages a man" (NASB). The Jews used one word for jealousy, *qua-nah.* It meant "to be intensely red." Let me ask you, have you seen such envy? Have you seen red-faced jealousy? Are you acquainted with the crimson forehead and the bulging veins? And—be honest now—have they appeared on your face?

If so, you need to do what Nancy did. Stop listing what you want, and start trusting God to provide what you need. Listen to her story:

> It was a few days before my . . . annual staff Christmas party. It came to my attention that I might be one of the few singles in attendance. It was such a dreadful thought, and of course, I truly didn't want to go! But as I prayed, I realized that God wanted me to go and HE wanted to be my partner. I didn't know how this could happen, but I began to pray that I would recognize His presence beside me every moment and that I would radiate that presence. So, "we" went to the party!
>
> As "we" entered, I immediately saw a potential male interest with a beautiful woman. It didn't faze me. As "we" walked from room to room, I socialized, encouraged those I saw, and truly practiced putting others first. As "we" left that evening and got into my car for the long drive home, I burst into tears . . . tears of joy and pain. I rejoiced to feel the peace and presence of Jesus in a tangible way, despite the pain of singleness.
>
> The following Monday a friend stopped by my office and said, "I noticed you at the party and wondered if it might be hard for you to be there alone. But I just wanted to tell you that you radiated God's joy that night."

> Since then, I've attended countless weddings, receptions, class reunions, and parties with Jesus as my partner. I can't say it's been easy, but I know that with each event my faith has grown. Jesus is a real, tangible presence—as real to me as any other person. I continue to grow in my understanding of what it means to partner with Him daily in the small things and the big things and what it means for Him to be the ever-present, always available lover of my soul.[2]

God withholds what we desire in order to give us what we need. You desire a spouse; he gives you himself. You seek a larger church; he prefers a stronger church. You want to be healed so you can serve. He wants you confined so you can pray. Such is the testimony of Joni Eareckson Tada. Three decades after a diving accident rendered her a quadriplegic, she and her husband, Ken, visited Jerusalem. Sitting in her wheelchair, she remembered the story of the paralytic Jesus healed at the pool of Bethesda. Thirty years earlier she'd read the account and asked Jesus to do the same for her.

That day in Jerusalem she thanked God that he had answered a higher prayer. Joni now sees her chair as her prayer bench and her affliction as her blessing. Had he healed her legs, thousands of prayers would have been sacrificed to her busy life. She sees that now. She accepts that now. Jealousy was eclipsed by gratitude as she surrendered her will to his.[3]

Nancy trusted her Father with her singleness.

Joni trusted her Father with her disability.

And Susie trusted her father with her pearls. At the age of six her most treasured possession was a string of pearls. The fact that they were fake didn't bother her. She wore them everywhere and played with them every day. She loved the pearls.

She also loved her daddy. His business often took him away for days at a time. The first day home would always be one of celebration. As an adult

Susie can still remember the time he spent a week in the Orient. When he finally returned, the daddy and daughter played all afternoon. As he put her to bed, he asked this question: "Do you love me?"

"Yes, Daddy. I love you more than anything."

"More than anything?"

"More than anything."

He paused for a moment. "More than the pearls? Would you give me your pearls?"

"Oh, Daddy," she replied. "I couldn't do that. I love my pearls."

"I understand," he told her and kissed her good-night.

As she fell asleep, she thought about his request. When she awoke, she thought about it some more. It was on her mind that morning and later in the day. Finally, that night, she went to him with her pearls. "Daddy, I love you more than these. Here, you take them."

"I'm so glad to hear that," he said, standing and opening his attaché case. "I brought you a gift."

She opened the small flat box and gasped. Pearls. Genuine pearls.[4]

You suppose your Father wants to give you some as well? He offers authentic love. His devotion is the real deal. But he won't give you the genuine until you surrender the imitations.

What pearls is he hoping you'll release? What costume jewelry would he love for you to drop? Would you exchange the lesser gifts for the highest gift of knowing God? If you would, then your envy will pass. Jealousy has no fire when true love is received.

CHAPTER FIVE

God's "No Pecking" Zone

Love . . . does not boast,
it is not proud.

1 Corinthians 13:4 NIV

THAT'S WHAT LOVE DOES. IT PUTS THE BELOVED BEFORE ITSELF.

YOUR SOUL WAS MORE IMPORTANT THAN HIS BLOOD.

YOUR ETERNAL LIFE WAS MORE IMPORTANT THAN HIS EARTHLY LIFE.

YOUR PLACE IN HEAVEN WAS MORE IMPORTANT TO HIM

THAN HIS PLACE IN HEAVEN,

SO HE GAVE UP HIS SO YOU COULD HAVE YOURS.

The temperature is in the twenties. The chill factor is single digit. The West Texas wind stings the ears, and frozen grass cracks beneath the step. It is a cold December day. Even the cattle are smart enough to stay in the barn on a morning like this.

Then what am I doing outside? What am I doing standing in a ditch, ankle deep in water, hunkered over a leaking pipe? And, most of all, why aren't the three guys in the truck helping me? Why are they in there while I'm out here? Why are they warm while I'm cold? Why are they dry while I'm wet?

The answer is found in two words: *pecking order.*

We can thank Norwegian naturalists for the term. They are the ones who studied the barnyard caste system. By counting the number of times chickens give and receive pecks, we can discern a chain of command. The alpha bird does most of the pecking, and the omega bird gets pecked. The rest of the chickens are somewhere in between.

That day in the oil field, our alpha bird was the crew chief. Beneath him was a former foreman and beneath the foreman, an illegal immigrant. I was the omega bird. College students on Christmas break come in last.

Our truck-seating assignments revealed our rank. The crew chief drove; second in command got the window seat. Third in line sat in the middle, and the bottom dweller straddled the stick shift. No one announced the system or wrote it down. We just knew it. And when the time came for someone to climb out of the truck and into the ditch, no one had to tell me. I understood the pecking order.

You do too. You know the system. Pecking orders are a part of life. And, to an extent, they should be. We need to know who is in charge. Ranking systems can clarify our roles. The problem with pecking orders is not the order. The problem is with the pecking.

Just ask the shortest kid in class or the janitor whose name no one knows or cares to know. The minority family can tell you. So can the new fellow on the factory line and the family scapegoat. It's not pleasant to be the plankton in the food chain.

A friend who grew up on a farm told me about a time she saw their chickens attacking a sick newborn. She ran and told her mother what was happening. Her mother explained, "That's what chickens do. When one is really sick, the rest peck it to death."

For that reason God says that love has no place for pecking orders. Jesus won't tolerate such thinking. Such barnyard mentality may fly on the farm but not in his kingdom. Just listen to what he says about the alpha birds of his day:

> They do good things so that other people will see them. They make the boxes of Scriptures that they wear bigger, and they make their special prayer clothes very long. Those Pharisees and teachers of the law love to have the most important seats at feasts and in the synagogues. They love people to greet them with respect in the marketplaces, and they love to have people call them "Teacher." (Matt. 23:5–7)

Jesus blasts the top birds of the church, those who roost at the top of the spiritual ladder and spread their plumes of robes, titles, jewelry, and choice seats. Jesus won't stand for it. It's easy to see why. How can I love others if my eyes are only on me? How can I point to God if I'm pointing at me? And, worse still, how can someone see God if I keep fanning my own tail feathers?

Jesus has no room for pecking orders. Love "does not boast, it is not proud" (1 Cor. 13:4 NIV).

His solution to man-made caste systems? A change of direction. In a world of upward mobility, choose downward servility. Go down, not up. "Regard one another as more important than yourselves" (Phil. 2:3 NASB). That's what Jesus did.

He flip-flopped the pecking order. While others were going up, he was going down.

> Your attitude should be the same as that of Christ Jesus: Who, being in very nature God, did not consider equality with God something to be grasped, but made himself nothing, taking the very nature of a servant, being made in human likeness. And being found in appearance as a man, he humbled himself and became obedient to death—even death on a cross! (Phil. 2:5–8 NIV)

Would you do what Jesus did? He swapped a spotless castle for a grimy stable. He exchanged the worship of angels for the company of killers. He could hold the universe in his palm but gave it up to float in the womb of a maiden.

If you were God, would you sleep on straw, nurse from a breast, and be clothed in a diaper? I wouldn't, but Christ did.

If you knew that only a few would care that you came, would you still come? If you knew that those you loved would laugh in your face, would you still care? If you knew that the tongues you made would mock you, the mouths you made would spit at you, the hands you made would crucify you, would you still make them? Christ did. Would you regard the immobile and invalid more important than yourself? Jesus did.

He humbled himself. He went from commanding angels to sleeping in the straw. From holding stars to clutching Mary's finger. The palm that held the universe took the nail of a soldier.

Why? Because that's what love does. It puts the beloved before itself. Your soul was more important than his blood. Your eternal life was more important than his earthly life. Your place in heaven was more important to him than his place in heaven, so he gave up his so you could have yours.

He loves you that much, and because he loves you, you are of prime importance to him.

Christ stands in contrast to the barnyard. He points to the sparrow, the most inexpensive bird of his day, and says, "Five sparrows are sold for only two pennies, and God does not forget any of them. . . . You are worth much more than many sparrows" (Luke 12:6–7).

God remembers the small birds of the world. We remember the eagles. We make bronze statues of the hawk. We name our athletic teams after the falcons. But God notices the sparrows. He makes time for the children and takes note of the lepers. He offers the woman in adultery a second chance and the thief on the cross a personal invitation. Christ is partial to the beat up and done in and urges us to follow suit. "When you give a feast, invite the poor, the crippled, the lame, and the blind" (Luke 14:13).

Want to love others as God has loved you? Come thirsty. Drink deeply of God's love for you, and ask him to fill your heart with a love worth giving. A love that will enable you to:

Put others before yourself. Esther Kim knows what this means. For thirteen years she had one dream. The Summer Olympics. She wanted to represent the United States on the Olympic tae kwon do squad.

From the age of eight, she spent every available hour in training. In fact, it was in training that she met and made her best friend, Kay Poe. The two worked so hard for so long that no one was surprised when they both qualified for the 2000 Olympic trials in Colorado Springs.

Everyone, however, was surprised when they were placed in the same division. They'd never competed against each other, but when the number of divisions was reduced, they found their names on the same bracket. It would be just a matter of events before they found themselves on the same mat. One would win and one would lose. Only one could go to Australia.

As if the moment needed more drama, two facts put Esther Kim in a heartrending position. First, her friend Kay injured her leg in the match prior to theirs. Kay could scarcely walk, much less compete. Because of the injury Esther could defeat her friend with hardly any effort.

But then there was a second truth. Esther knew that Kay was the better fighter. If she took advantage of her crippled friend, the better athlete would stay home.

So what did she do? Esther stepped onto the floor and bowed to her friend and opponent. Both knew the meaning of the gesture. Esther forfeited her place. She considered the cause more important than the credit.[1]

This is a good time for a few poignant questions. What's more important to you—that the work be done or that you be seen? When a brother or sister is honored, are you joyful or jealous? Do you have the attitude of Jesus? Do you consider others more important than yourself?

May I share the first time I felt the force of that challenge?

Harold suffered from cerebral palsy. The condition left him unable to walk, dress, feed himself, or go to the rest room. My job was to help him with each. And I didn't like it. I had moved to St. Louis for spiritual training.

Fresh out of college and ready to change the world. Ready to preach, ready to travel, ready to make history. But I wasn't ready to help Harold.

The director of our internship program had other plans. One day he told me he had a special assignment. I assumed he meant a promotion. I never thought he meant Harold.

Harold loved Bible classes and worship services. My job was to help him attend both. To pick him up, to clean him up. To wheel him in, sit next to him, and take him home. To hold his fork when he ate, to wipe his mouth when he drooled. I don't remember feeling very loving. I do remember the day we studied Philippians 2:3: "In humility consider others better than yourselves" (NIV).

After the teacher read the passage, he asked this question: "Think about the person to your left. Do you consider him more important than yourself?" I looked to my left. Guess who I saw? Harold. His head had fallen forward, mouth open.

Harold more important than me? I had the health, the glib tongue, the (ahem) hours of graduate work. How could I regard him as more important?

But God convicted me of my arrogance and began to work on my attitude. Slowly, but markedly, I became content to be Harold's caretaker. By the end of the year Harold and I had become fast friends. God worked a quiet, yet indelible, miracle in my heart. When word of Harold's death reached me a year ago, I thanked God for letting me know such a teacher as Harold. God uses people like him to remind us: *Put others before yourself.*

And then:

Accept your part in his plan. God uses people like Bob Russell to illustrate this kind of love. Bob ministers at the Southeast Christian Church in Louisville, Kentucky. When Bob began his service there in 1966, the church had 125 members, and Bob was twenty-two years old. During the last three and a half decades, God has built this church into one of his finest and largest families. Over 16,000 people gather each weekend to worship in one of several services.

In 1989 Bob made a choice that surprised many observers. He announced that he was going to share the preaching duties with a twenty-seven-year-old preacher. He and Dave Stone would begin coministering to the church. In the announced plan, each year Bob would preach less and Dave would preach more, thus providing Bob more time to lead the church and the church an experienced successor.

Not everyone could do that. Larger egos in smaller churches have struggled to surrender the pulpit. But Bob understands the danger of the pecking order and is humble enough to invert it.

True humility is not thinking lowly of yourself but thinking accurately of yourself. The humble heart does not say, "I can't do anything." But rather, "I can't do everything. I know my part and am happy to do it."

When Paul writes "*consider* others better than yourselves" (Phil. 2:3 NIV, emphasis mine), he uses a verb that means "to calculate," "to reckon." The word implies a conscious judgment resting on carefully weighed facts.[2] To consider others better than yourself, then, is not to say you have no place; it is to say that you know your place. "Don't cherish exaggerated ideas of yourself or your importance, but try to have a sane estimate of your capabilities by the light of the faith that God has given to you" (Rom. 12:3 PHILLIPS).

And finally:

Be quick to applaud the success of others. To the Romans, Paul gives this counsel: "Give each other more honor than you want for yourselves" (Rom. 12:10).

William Barclay tells of a respected educator of a century past. He was known not just for his success but the way he handled it. On one occasion as he stepped to a seat on a platform, the public noticed who he was and began to applaud. Shocked, he turned and asked the man behind him to go ahead. He then began to applaud the man, assuming the applause was for him, and he was quite willing to share in it.[3]

The humble heart honors others.

Again, is Jesus not our example? Content to be known as a carpenter. Happy to be mistaken for the gardener. He served his followers by washing their feet. He serves us by doing the same. Each morning he gifts us with beauty. Each Sunday he calls us to his table. Each moment he dwells in our hearts. And does he not speak of the day when he as "the master will dress himself to serve and tell the servants to sit at the table, and he will serve them" (Luke 12:37)?

If Jesus is so willing to honor us, can we not do the same for others? Make people a priority. Accept your part in his plan. Be quick to share the applause. And, most of all, regard others as more important than yourself. Love does. For love "does not boast, it is not proud" (1 Cor. 13:4 NIV).

Someone is piecing this all together. His thoughts are something like this: *If I think you are more important than I am . . . and you think I am more important than you are . . . and he thinks she is more important than he is . . . and she thinks he is more important than she is . . . then in the end everyone feels important but no one acts important.*

H'm. You think that's what God had in mind?

CHAPTER SIX

A Call to Common Courtesy

Love is not rude.

1 Corinthians 13:5

Jesus always knocks before entering.

He doesn't have to. He owns your heart.

If anyone has the right to barge in, Christ does.

But he doesn't.

That gentle tap you hear? It's Christ.

"Behold, I stand at the door and knock" (Rev. 3:20 NASB).

And when you answer,

he awaits your invitation to cross the threshold.

See the passenger at gate 26? The fellow looking at the ticket agent with the basset-hound eyes? That's me. Yeah, I know, you can't see very well. DFW Airport is packed. Pass out antennae and extra sets of legs, and you'd have a human anthill. We're all over each other.

It's Canada's fault. A front from the north blasted the Midwest, freezing O'Hare and blowing a thousand itineraries to the wind, including mine. When the plane finally disgorged us, we raced through the concourse like Wal-Mart shoppers on the day after Thanksgiving. Pity anything or anyone in our paths. How else were we supposed to make our connections? Even with perfect weather I'd barely catch the final flight of the day to San Antonio.

That explains my hangdog look. I'm pouring what little charm I have on the kind but hassled ticket agent. The plane is overbooked, and she holds my future in her hands. What will she give me—a boarding pass or a hotel voucher?

"Are there any seats left?" I'm winking, but she doesn't notice. I'm sliding a twenty in her direction, but she doesn't see it. She just looks at the screen and sighs, "I'm afraid . . ."

Afraid? Afraid of what?!

"Afraid you'll have to spend the night in the men's room."

"Afraid the only seat left is in the last row, between two sumo wrestlers."

"Afraid you're milking this illustration like a dairy cow, and if you don't get to the point of the chapter, I'll route you through Afghanistan."

But she said none of these. Want to know how she completed the sentence? (Here, take a tissue. You'll be moved.)

"I'm afraid there are no more seats in coach. We are going to have to bump you up to first class. Do you mind if we do that?"

"Do you mind if I kiss you?" So I boarded the plane and nestled down in the wide seat with the extra leg room and smiled like a prisoner on early parole. Not only was I going home, I was going home in style. I leaned back my head, closed my eyes, and . . .

"Hey! Hey! Lady!" My eyes opened. Two rows in front of me a fellow was standing. A short fellow. Didn't need to watch his head to stand up straight. Did need to watch his tone, however. He was rude.

"How does a guy get an extra pillow around here? And what about my drink? My wife and I paid extra to fly first-class. I am accustomed to better attention. I want some service!"

It's not like the flight attendants had nothing to do, mind you. There was the simple matter of making sure the doors were closed and the bins were shut so this already-hour-late flight could lift off. You'd think a fellow could wait on his pillow and Scotch. Not this guy. After all, as we all knew, he had paid extra to fly first-class.

Which may explain the difference between his behavior and mine. I'm not always a good example, but that night I was a poster child for courtesy. You weren't hearing me grumble. I wasn't complaining. No demands from the window seat in row four. I was just happy to be on board. Mr. Got-to-Have-It-Now may have paid for his place. Not me. Mine was a free gift.

And it wasn't the first. God gave me one long before the airlines did. Talk about an upgrade! Not just coach to first class. How about sinner to saint, hellbent to heavenbound, confused to clarified, guilty to justified? If anyone has been bumped up, I have. I'm not only heading home, I'm heading home in style. And I didn't pay a cent. Nor have any of God's children.

But do we sometimes act as if we did? Do we sometimes behave like the pillowless *prima donna* in the first row? Think about his request for a moment. Was it unreasonable? No. A pillow is part of the flight package. *What* he requested was understandable. *The way* he requested it, however, was not.

His timing was poor; he could have waited a few moments. His tone was harsh; the flight attendants didn't deserve condescension. His agenda was selfish. He didn't just want a pillow; he wanted to be the center of attention.

The Bible has a four-letter word for such behavior: *rude.* When defining what love is not, Paul put *rudeness* on the list. "It is not rude" (1 Cor. 13:5 NIV).

The Greek word for *rude* means shameful or disgraceful behavior.

An example of rudeness was recently taken before the courts in Minnesota. A man fell out of his canoe and lost his temper. Though the river was lined with vacationing families, he polluted the air with obscenities. Some of those families sued him. He said, "I have my rights."

God calls us to a higher, more noble concern. Not "What are my rights?" but "What is loving?"

Do you have the right to dominate a conversation? Yes, but is it loving to do so?

Do you have the right to pretend you don't hear your wife speaking? I suppose so. But is it loving?

Is it within your rights to bark at the clerk or snap at the kids? Yes. But is it loving to act this way?

Denalyn has a right to park in the center of the garage. Which she used to do quite often. I'd open the garage door and see her car overlapping half her space and half mine. My response was always a good-natured hint. "Denalyn," I'd say as I entered the house, "some car is taking up its half of the garage in the middle."

Maybe I said it more firmly one day. Perhaps my tone wasn't as chipper. I honestly don't know what happened, but she began parking on her side. I overheard my daughter ask her why she had quit parking in the middle. "Is it that big of a deal, Mom?"

"It's not that big to me. But it seems to be big to your dad. And if it matters to him, it matters to me."

Wasn't that courteous? Wasn't that Christlike? Perhaps you've never placed the word *courteous* next to Christ. I hadn't until I wrote this chapter.

But you know how you never notice double-cab red trucks until your friend says he wants one—then you see a dozen of them? I had never thought much about the courtesy of Christ before, but as I began looking, I realized that Jesus makes Emily Post look like Archie Bunker.

He always knocks before entering. He doesn't have to. He owns your heart. If anyone has the right to barge in, Christ does. But he doesn't. That gentle tap you hear? It's Christ. "Behold, I stand at the door and knock" (Rev. 3:20 NASB). And when you answer, he awaits your invitation to cross the threshold.

That's how he treated the two disciples on the Emmaus road. The resurrected Jesus didn't presume on their hospitality. When they entered the house, he didn't follow. Only when they "urged" him to enter, did he do so (Luke 24:29 NIV). Astounding! Only days before, he had died for their sin. Only hours before, he had defeated their death. Every angel in the universe would gladly be his doormat, but Jesus, ever the gentleman, walks with no swagger.

And when he enters, he always brings a gift. Some bring Chianti and daisies. Christ brings "the gift of the Holy Spirit" (Acts 2:38). And, as he stays, he serves. "For even the Son of Man did not come to be served, but to serve" (Mark 10:45 NIV). If you're missing your apron, you'll find it on him. He's serving the guests as they sit (John 13:4–5). He won't eat until he's offered thanks, and he won't leave until the leftovers are put away (Matt. 14:19–20).

He is courteous enough to tell you his name (Exod. 3:15) and to call you by yours (John 10:3). And when you talk, he never interrupts. Ever been to a doctor who is so busy that he prescribes the medicine before he hears your problem? Jesus isn't like that. He could be. He "knows what you need before you ask him" (Matt. 6:8 NIV). He also knows what you've done before you ask him for forgiveness. "Nothing in all creation can hide from him. Everything is naked and exposed before his eyes" (Heb. 4:13 NLT). A God of lesser courtesy would stop you midsentence with reminders of your past foibles. Not Christ. He is not rude. He listens.

He is even on time. Never late. Never early. If you're checking your watch, it's because you're on a different itinerary. "There is a time for everything" (Eccles. 3:1). And Christ stays on schedule.

He even opens doors for you. Paul could preach at Troas because "the Lord had opened a door" (2 Cor. 2:12 NIV). When I asked my dad why men should open doors for women, his answer was one word: "respect." Christ must have abundant respect for you.

He knocks before he enters. He always brings a gift. Food is served. The table is cleared. Thanks are offered. He knows your name and tells you his, and here is one more.

He pulls out the chair for you. "He raised us up with Christ and gave us a seat with him in the heavens" (Eph. 2:6).

My wife has a heart for single moms. She loves to include a widow or divorcée at the table when we go to a restaurant. Through the years I've noticed a common appreciation from them. They love it when I pull out their chair. More than once they have specifically thanked me. One mom in particular comes to mind. "My," she blushed, brushing the sudden moisture from her eye, "it's been a while since anyone did that."

Has it been a while for you as well? People can be so rude. We snatch parking places. We forget names. We interrupt. We fail to show up. Could you use some courtesy? Has it been a while since someone pulled out your chair?

Then let Jesus. Don't hurry through this thought. Receive the courtesy of Christ. He's your groom. Does not the groom cherish the bride? Respect the bride? Honor the bride? Let Christ do what he longs to do.

For as you receive his love, you'll find it easier to give yours. As you reflect on his courtesy to you, you'll be likely to offer the same.

Did you notice the first five letters of the word *courteous* spell *court*? In old England, to be courteous was to act in the way of the court. The family and servants of the king were expected to follow a higher standard.

So are we. Are we not called to represent the King? Then "let your light shine before men, that they may see your good deeds and praise your Father in heaven" (Matt. 5:16 NIV).

Occasionally our staff members wear shirts that bear the name of our church. On one such day a staffer needed a special pan, and she phoned around until she located it in a store across town. She endured a long drive through heavy traffic only to encounter a gruff store clerk, who told her they no longer carried the product. The staff member started to return tacky with tacky but then remembered she was wearing the shirt—and she changed her behavior.

The truth is, we are all wearing a shirt. "All of you who were baptized into Christ have clothed yourselves with Christ" (Gal. 3:27 NIV). We wear Jesus. And those who don't believe in Jesus note what we do. They make decisions about Christ by watching us. When we are kind, they assume Christ is kind. When we are gracious, they assume Christ is gracious. But if we are brash, what will people think about our King? When we are dishonest, what assumption will an observer make about our Master? No wonder Paul says, "Be wise in the way you act with people who are not believers, making the most of every opportunity. When you talk, you should always be kind and pleasant so you will be able to answer everyone in the way you should" (Col. 4:5–6). Courteous conduct honors Christ.

It also honors his children. When you surrender a parking place to someone, you honor him. When you return a borrowed book, you honor the lender. When you make an effort to greet everyone in the room, especially the ones others may have overlooked, you honor God's children.

In his book *Handyman of the Lord,* William Borders tells the story of a black man whose poverty had left him begging for food. Ringing the front doorbell at a Southern mansion, the man was told to go around to the back, where he would be given something to eat. The owner of the mansion met him on the back porch and said, "First we will bless the food. Repeat after me, 'Our Father, who art in heaven . . .'"

The hungry man replied, "Your Father, who art in heaven . . ."

"No," the owner of the house corrected. "*Our* Father who art in heaven . . ."

Still the beggar said, "Your Father who art in heaven . . ."

Frustrated, the giver of the food asked, "Why do you insist on saying 'your Father' when I keep telling you to say 'our Father'?"

The man answered, "If I say 'our Father,' that would make you and me brothers, and I'm afraid the Lord wouldn't like it, you askin' your brother to come to the back porch to get a piece of bread."[1]

Common courtesy honors God and his children. "Do your best to live in peace with everyone" (Rom. 12:18). Just do your best. You can't control their attitude, but you can manage yours.

Besides, just look where you are sitting. You could've been bumped off. Instead, you've been bumped up. So loosen up and enjoy the journey. You are going home in style.

CHAPTER SEVEN

Getting the "I" Out of Your Eye

Love . . . is not self-seeking.

1 Corinthians 13:4–5 NIV

Get your self out of your eye

by getting your eye off your self.

Quit staring at that little self,

and focus on your great Savior.

There is a malady that makes the Black Plague appear as mild as the common cold.

Tally the death tolls of all infections, fevers, and epidemics since the beginning of time, and you'll still fall short of the number claimed by this single infirmity.

And, forgive me for being the one to tell you, but you are infected. You suffer from it. You are a victim—a diseased carrier. You have shown the symptoms and manifested the signs. You have a case of—brace yourself—selfishness.

Don't believe me?

Suppose you are in a group photo. The first time you see the picture, where do you look? And if you look good, do you like the picture? If you are the *only* one who looks good, do you still like the picture? If some are cross-eyed and others have spinach in their teeth, do you still like the picture? If that makes you like it even more, you've got a bad case.

What about the physical manifestations?

Clutching hands. Do your fingers ever wrap and close around possessions?

Protruding teeth. Do fangs ever flare when you are interrupted or irritated?

Heavy feet. When a neighboring car wants to cut in front of you, do you sense a sudden heaviness of foot on the accelerator?

Extended shoulder. Any inflammation from patting yourself on the back?

And your neck. Is it sore from keeping your nose in the air?

But most of all, look into your eyes. Look long into your pupils. Do you see a tiny figure? An image of a person? An image of you?

The self-centered see everything through self. Their motto? "It's all about me!" The flight schedule. The traffic. The dress styles. The worship styles. The weather, the work, whether or not one works—everything is filtered through the mini-me in the eye.

Selfishness.

Such a condition can be fatal.

Listen to the words of James. "Whenever people are jealous or selfish, they cause trouble and do all sorts of cruel things" (James 3:16 CEV).

Need proof?

Let's examine one newspaper. Today's edition. How many examples of selfishness will we find in the first few pages?

1. A teenage girl died in a car wreck. Her boyfriend was challenged to a race on a city street. He took the dare and wrapped the car around a telephone pole.
2. The largest petroleum company in the world has filed for bankruptcy. Executives allegedly knew the ship had leaks but told no one until they had time to make huge profits.
3. A prominent citizen is put in jail for child pornography.

Selfishness is to society what the Exxon *Valdez* was to scallops and sea otters—deadly. Is it any wonder that Paul writes: "Do nothing from selfishness or empty conceit, but with humility of mind regard one another as more important than yourselves; do not *merely* look out for your own personal interests, but also for the interests of others" (Phil. 2:3–4 NASB)?

At first glance the standard in the passage seems impossible to meet. Nothing? We shouldn't do *anything* for ourselves? No new dress or suit. What about going to school or saving money—couldn't all of these things be considered selfish?

They could, unless we are careful to understand what Paul is saying. The word the apostle uses for *selfishness* shares a root form with the words *strife* and *contentious.* It suggests a self-preoccupation that hurts others. A divisive arrogance. In fact, first-century writers used the word to describe a politician who procured office by illegal manipulation or a harlot who seduced the client, demeaning both herself and him.[1] *Selfishness is an obsession with self that excludes others, hurting everyone.*

Looking after your personal interests is proper life management. Doing so to the exclusion of the rest of the world is selfishness. The adverb highlighted in verse 4 is helpful. "Do not *merely* look out for your own personal interests, but also for the interests of others."

Desire success? Fine. Just don't hurt others in achieving it. Wish to look nice? That's okay. Just don't do so by making others look bad. Love isn't selfish.

I was. And I made a mess of things in the process.

A couple of Mondays ago I intended to dedicate the day to sermon preparation. But an urgent call changed everything. *No problem,* I told myself, *I'll start on Tuesday.* Kind people had other ideas. A project had been moved up, and some correspondence needed to be read. Then some bills needed to be paid, and—oh, yes, I forgot about the luncheon. It wasn't the agenda I had in mind. But there was always Wednesday.

On Wednesday the staff meeting went long. I drummed my fingers, but no one took the hint. I cleared my throat and wound my battery-run watch, but no one noticed. Finally the meeting ended, and I could study. "Don't forget to call so-and-so," I was reminded as I left the room. "He's leaving in an hour." *So-and-so* was in a good mood. A chatty mood. I was in a fast mood. A focused mood. Sunday was coming, and the clock was moving. I had the Lord's work to do, and people were in my way.

Finally at midafternoon I sat down. The phone rang. It was my wife. She was in a *disgustingly* good mood. "See you at the ceremony?" she reminded.

"Ceremony?"

"Andrea is graduating from middle school today."

What a dumb day to schedule a graduation ceremony. Everyone knows that diplomas wilt on Wednesdays. "And," she continued, still nauseatingly happy, "could you pick up Jenna from school and bring her home?"

Does this woman not know my calling? Is she unaware of my place in history? Hungry souls need my study. Emaciated minds await my insights. The angels themselves are lining up to grab the front-row Sunday seats—and she wants me to be a chauffeur. "Okay," I growled, not disguising my displeasure.

I was upset. And because I was upset, I chided Jenna for not hurrying to the car.

I was upset. And because I was upset, I forgot to be thankful at the graduation service.

I was upset. And because I was upset, I said, "Let's go, Andrea," instead of saying, "Way to go, Andrea."

I was upset. My day hadn't gone my way. The little Max in my eyes had grown so large I couldn't see anything else.

Apparently God was determined to change all that. At 5:00 P.M. on Wednesday, some fifty-six hours later than I intended to start my preparation, I opened my Bible to read the text of the week and found the very words we've been studying.

> Do nothing from selfishness or empty conceit, but with humility of mind regard one another as more important than yourselves; do not *merely* look out for your own personal interests, but also for the interests of others. (Phil. 2:3–4 NASB)

Remember the passage that describes the Word of God as a sword? I was impaled. As a doctor pronounces a disease, so the passage declared mine. Selfishness. Because of the little me in my eyes, I couldn't see my blessings.

Love builds up relationships; selfishness erodes relationships. No wonder Paul is so urgent in his appeal: "Do nothing from selfishness or empty conceit" (Phil. 2:3 NASB).

But aren't we born selfish? And if so, can we do anything about it? Can we get our eyes off of self? Or, better asked, can we get the little self out of our eyes? According to Scripture, we can.

> Therefore if there is any encouragement in Christ, if there is any consolation of love, if there is any fellowship of the Spirit, if any affection and compassion, make my joy complete by being of the same mind. (Phil. 2:1–2 NASB)

Paul's sarcasm is thinly veiled. Is there any encouragement? Any consolation? Any fellowship? Then smile!

What's the cure for selfishness?

Get your self out of your eye by getting your eye off your self. Quit staring at that little self, and focus on your great Savior.

A friend who is an Episcopalian minister explains the reason he closes his prayers with the sign of the cross. "The touching of my forehead and chest makes a capital 'I.' The gesture of touching first one shoulder, then the other, cuts the 'I' in half."

Isn't that a work of the Cross? A smaller "I" and a greater Christ? Don't focus on yourself; focus on all that you have in Christ. Focus on the encouragement in Christ, the consolation of Christ, the love of Christ, the fellowship of the Spirit, the affection and compassion of heaven.

If Christ becomes our focus, we won't be like the physician in Arkansas. He misdiagnosed the patient. He declared the woman to be dead. The family was informed, and the husband was grief-stricken. Imagine the surprise of the nurse when she discovered that the woman was alive! "You better tell the family," she urged the doctor.

The embarrassed physician phoned the husband and said, "I need to talk to you about the condition of your wife."

"The condition of my wife?" he asked. "She's dead."

The doctor's pride only allowed him to concede, "Well, she has seen a slight improvement."

Slight improvement? Talk about an understatement! Lazarus is walking out of the tomb, and he calls that a "slight improvement"?

He was so concerned about his image that he missed an opportunity to celebrate. We laugh, but don't we do the same? We've gone from cremation to celebration. We deserve a lava bath, but we've been given a pool of grace.

Yet to look at our faces you'd think our circumstances had made only a "slight improvement." "How's life?" someone asks. And we who've been resurrected from the dead say, "Well, things could be better." Or "Couldn't get a parking place." Or "My parents won't let me move to Hawaii." Or "People won't leave me alone so I can finish my sermon on selfishness."

Honestly. We worry about acid rain in silver linings. Do you think Paul might like to have a word with us? Are you so focused on what you don't have that you are blind to what you do? Have you received any encouragement? Any fellowship? Any consolation? Then don't you have reason for joy?

Come. Come thirsty. Drink deeply from God's goodness.

You have a ticket to heaven no thief can take,
an eternal home no divorce can break.

Every sin of your life has been cast to the sea.
Every mistake you've made is nailed to the tree.

You're blood-bought and heaven-made.
A child of God—forever saved.

So be grateful, joyful—for isn't it true?
What you don't have is much less than what you do.

CHAPTER EIGHT

The Headwaters of Anger

Love . . . is not easily angered.

1 Corinthians 13:4–5 NIV

God will load your world with flowers.

He hand-delivers a bouquet to your door every day.

Open it! Take them!

Then, when rejections come, you won't be left short-petaled.

A glance at the two brothers would raise no suspicion. To see them exit the worship service would give you no cause for concern. Like any other set of siblings, they had their differences. One more like Mom, the other more like Dad. One with a bent toward livestock, the other interested in farming. Beyond that, they seemed alike. Compatible. Raised in the same culture. Romped in the same hills. Played with the same animals. Spoke with the same accent. Worshiped the same God.

Then why did one kill the other? Why the violent assault? What made one brother turn on the other and spill his blood? Why did Cain kill Abel?

To answer that question is to shed light on a larger one. Looming behind the question of murder is the question of anger. For "Cain was very angry" (Gen. 4:5 NKJV). Angry indeed. Angry enough to kill. What made him so mad?

Anger in and of itself is not a sin. The emotion was God's idea. "Be angry," he urges, "and do not sin" (Eph. 4:26 NKJV). It's possible to feel what Cain felt without doing what Cain did. Anger is not a sin, but it can lead to sin. Perhaps your anger doesn't lead you to shed blood, but does it make you touchy, irritable, quick-tempered, quick to take offense? Do you fly off the handle? Those aren't my terms. They are Paul's. According to the apostle, love is not:

"touchy" (TLB),

"irritable" (NLT),

"quick tempered" (CEV),

"quick to take offence" (NEB),

"easily angered" (NIV),

and love "doesn't fly off the handle" (MSG).

Cain was all of these and more. But why? Why the short fuse? Again the text gives an answer. "The LORD accepted Abel and his gift, but he did not accept Cain and his gift. So Cain became very *angry* and felt *rejected*" (Gen. 4:4–5, emphasis mine).

Interesting. This is the first appearance of Anger in the Bible. He'll pop up some four hundred more times between here and the maps in the back, but this is the first occasion. He pulls up to the curb and gets out of the car, and look who is in the front seat with him—Rejection. Anger and Rejection in the same sentence.

This isn't the only time the couple are spotted in Scripture. Anger singes many pages. And more than once Rejection is charged with arson.

The sons of Jacob were rejected by their father. He pampered Joseph and neglected them. The result? The brothers were angry. Joseph's "brothers saw that their father loved him more than all his brothers; and so they hated him and could not speak to him on friendly terms" (Gen. 37:4 NASB).

Saul was rejected by his people. In choosing heroes, they chose the fair-haired David over the appointed king. The result? Saul was ticked off. "The women sang as they played, and said, 'Saul has slain his thousands, and David his ten thousands.' Then Saul became very angry" (1 Sam. 18:7–8 NASB).

David's work was rejected by God. His plan to move the ark of the covenant by cart didn't please the Father. And when Uzzah touched what he shouldn't have touched, "God smote him . . . and he died" (2 Sam. 6:7 RSV). Before David was afraid, he fumed. "David became angry because of the LORD's outburst against Uzzah" (2 Sam. 6:8 NASB).

And Jonah. The fellow had a whale of a problem with anger. (Sorry, couldn't resist.) He didn't feel the Ninevites were worthy of mercy, but God did. By forgiving them, God rejected Jonah's opinion. And how did the rejection make Jonah feel? "It greatly displeased Jonah and he became angry" (Jon. 4:1 NASB).

I don't want to oversimplify a complex emotion. Anger has many causes: impatience, unmet expectations, stress, referees who couldn't see a pass-interference call if you painted it on their garage door—oops, sorry, a flashback to a high-school football game. The fire of anger has many logs, but according to biblical accounts, the thickest and the hottest block of wood is rejection.

An odd encounter allowed me to experience this formula firsthand. I was tagging along with my wife and daughters as they went shopping. Such is the life of a father of three girls. Not being an avid shopper myself, I tend to pass the time with a book. We enter a store, they look for sales, I look for chairs. (Hint to retailers: A few recliners would lead to greater sales volume.) This particular store didn't have a chair, however. It was a high-priced, uppity purse store that assumed you'd never want to sit in the presence of their creations. So I found a corner, sat on the floor, and entered the world of fiction.

"Ahem."

Lifting my eyes, I saw pointy-toed high-heeled shoes.

"Ahem, ahem."

Looking up, I saw a female employee with bunned-up hair and black thick-framed glasses.

"Don't sit on the floor," she said.

I thought she was feeling sorry for me. "I don't mind. Besides, I couldn't find a chair."

Her response had the tone of a miffed third-grade teacher. "You aren't *allowed* to sit on the floor."

Not allowed to sit on the floor? Isn't that like saying, "You're not allowed to have your wisdom teeth pulled"? If I'd had another choice, I'd have taken it. "I couldn't find a chair," I told her.

"We don't have chairs," she told me, lowering the room temperature with her frost.

"But I just want to sit down," I replied, my throat starting to tighten.

"We don't want people to sit down," she commanded.

My math was off. This didn't add up. I enter the store with four women who have a weakness for puny purses with foreign names. Shouldn't I be offered a soda and a massage? "I'll stand, all right. I'll stand outside." O-o-o-h, Max, the tough guy.

I leaned against the building and fumed.

Now, why was I angry? What stirred my frustration? In the great scheme of things, the event wouldn't bump a seismic needle. So what bothered me? I narrowed it down to one word. *Rejection.* The salesperson had rejected me. She didn't accept me.

Multiply that emotion by a zillion to understand the anger of an abandoned teen or a divorced spouse. I didn't even know the lady, and I was angry. What happens when you feel the same from your boss, friend, or teacher?

You hurt. And because you get hurt, you get hot. Tacky-toned, cold-shouldered, name-calling, door-slamming, get-my-pound-of-flesh sort of hot. Anger is your defense mechanism.

Envision a teenager receiving a lecture. His dad is going down the list:

poor grades, missed curfews, messy room. Each accusation is like a shove in the boy's chest. Back and back and back until he perceives a Grand Canyon between his father and him. His initial response is silence and shame. Lower and lower he bows. But somewhere a line is crossed, and an innate survival technique kicks in, and he lashes back, "I've had it!" And he stands and storms out.

What about the Hispanic immigrant in the small Anglo town? How many times can a man be teased about his accent, mocked because of his name, and overlooked because of his skin color before he takes a swing at someone?

Consider the wife of the insensitive husband. Every other woman in her office received a card or flowers for Valentine's Day. She kept thinking a delivery boy would stop at her desk, but none ever did. She drives home thinking, *Surely there will be something on the table.* The table is empty. The phone rings. It's him. He'll be late for dinner. No word about Valentine's Day. He forgot. How could he forget? When this happened last year, she was sad. When he did something similar at Christmas, she was hurt. But when he forgot their anniversary, she started to harden. And now this? Her tears are hot. Rejection leads to anger.

And if rejection from people makes us angry, what about when we feel rejected by God? Case study #1? Cain.

The account is sketchy and not without gaps, but we are told enough to re-create the crime scene. Cain and Abel went to worship, perhaps at the same time. They each brought an offering. How did they know to do so? God had told them. Hebrews 11:4 says, "It was by faith that Abel offered God a better sacrifice than Cain did." From where does one get faith? "Faith comes by hearing" (Rom. 10:17 NKJV). Cain and Abel had heard God's instructions. And when Abel brought the best parts of a firstborn from his flock, he did so out of obedience to what he had heard.

And when Cain brought "some food" from the ground, he was acting out of disobedience. Surely he had heard what Abel had heard. Would God hold him accountable otherwise? He knew what Abel knew. He knew that forgiveness of sin came through the shedding of blood (Heb. 9:22). But still he was angry that God returned his sacrifice unopened. God cautioned him to be careful.

God asked Cain, "Why are you angry? Why do you look so unhappy? If you do things well, I will accept you, but if you do not do them well, sin is ready to attack you. Sin wants you, but you must rule over it." At this point in the story, Cain had not sinned. A dose of humility and he would have been fine. But Cain had other plans.

"Cain said to his brother Abel, 'Let's go out into the field.' While they were out in the field, Cain attacked his brother Abel and killed him" (Gen. 4:3–8).

Cain gave up. He gave up on God. He gave up on his ability to please him. And he took it out on Abel. Cain would have related to the frustration of the struggling missionary who wrote:

> God's demands of me were so high, and His opinion of me was so low, there was no way for me to live except under His frown. . . . All day long He nagged me: "Why don't you pray more? Why don't you witness more? When will you ever learn self-discipline? How can you allow yourself to indulge in such wicked thoughts? Do this. Don't do that." . . . When I came down to it, there was scarcely a word or a feeling or a thought or a decision of mine that God really liked.[1]

Many have written letters like that. If not with pen and paper, at least with thoughts. Cain would have penned: "I can't satisfy him. I work in the field and bring my crops. I give him my best, and it's not enough."

Others would write:

"Why won't God hear our prayers! We go to church, we pay our bills, but still the crib is empty."

"Why won't God give me a job? I've done nothing wrong. People who curse him have jobs. I've served him all these years and can't even get an interview."

"What do I have to do to be forgiven? Do I have to spend the rest of my life paying for one mistake?"

Such thoughts will heat your collar. Stoke your anger. Make you snap at those shallow minds like Abel who do half the work but get all the blessings—

Stop for a second. Did you just make a discovery? Did a light go on? Have you for the first time found the headwaters of your anger? Can your bitterness be traced upstream to a feeling of divine rejection? If so (I'm glad to tell you this), in finding the cause you have also found the cure.

When I really want a person to listen to me, I scoot my chair a couple of inches in their direction and lower my voice. If you and I were having a chat about your anger, this is where I'd start scooting, and I'd say the next sentence so softly you'd have to lean forward to hear. So incline a tad and listen to this thought.

If rejection causes anger, wouldn't acceptance cure it? If rejection by heaven makes you mad at others, wouldn't acceptance from heaven stir your love for them? This is the 7:47 Principle. Remember the verse? "He who is forgiven little loves little." We can replace the word *forgiven* with *accepted* and maintain the integrity of the passage. "He who is *accepted* little loves little." If we think God is harsh and unfair, guess how we'll treat people. Harshly and unfairly. But if we discover that God has doused us with unconditional love, would that make a difference?

The apostle Paul would say so! Talk about a turnaround. He went from bully to teddy bear. Paul B.C. (Before Christ) sizzled with anger. He "made havoc of the church" (Acts 8:3 NKJV). Paul A.D. (After Discovery) brimmed with love. Could a raving maniac write these words?

To the Corinthians: "I always thank my God for you" (1 Cor. 1:4).

To the Philippians: "I have you in my heart. . . . I long for all of you with the affection of Christ Jesus" (Phil. 1:7–8 NIV).

To the Ephesians: "I have not stopped giving thanks for you, remembering you in my prayers" (Eph. 1:16 NIV).

To the Colossians: "We always thank God, the Father of our Lord Jesus Christ, when we pray for you" (Col. 1:3 NIV).

To the Thessalonians: "We were gentle among you, like a mother caring for her little children" (1 Thess. 2:7 NIV).

His heart was a universe of love. But what about his enemies? It's one thing to love your coworkers, but did Paul love those who challenged him? "I would be willing to be forever cursed—cut off from Christ!—if that would save them" (Rom. 9:1–3 NLT). On every occasion that he had to enter their synagogues and teach, he did so (Acts 13:4–5; 14:1; 17:1–2, 10). His accusers beat him, stoned him, jailed him, mocked him. But can you find one occasion where he responded in kind? One temper tantrum? One angry outburst? *This is a different man.* His anger is gone. His passion is strong. His devotion is unquestioned. But rash outbursts of anger? A thing of the past.

What made the difference? He encountered Christ. Or, to use his phrase, he was hidden in Christ: "Your life is now hidden with Christ in God" (Col. 3:3 NIV).

The Chinese language has a great symbol for this truth. The word for *righteousness* is a combination of two pictures. On the top is a lamb. Beneath the lamb is a person. The lamb covers the person.[2] Isn't that the essence of righteousness? The Lamb of Christ over the child of God? Whenever the Father looks down on you, what does he see? He sees his

Son, the perfect Lamb of God, hiding you. Christians are like their ancestor Abel. We come to God by virtue of the flock. Cain came with the work of his own hands. God turned him away. Abel came, and we come, dependent upon the sacrifice of the Lamb, and we are accepted. Like the Chinese symbol, we are covered by the lamb, hidden in Christ.

When God looks at you, he doesn't see you; he sees Jesus. And how does he respond when he sees Jesus? He rends the heavens and vibrates the earth with the shout, "You are my Son, whom I love, and I am very pleased with you" (Mark 1:11).

The missionary was wrong. We don't live under the frown of God. We stir an ear-to-ear smile of joy. "He will rejoice over you with gladness, He will quiet you with His love, He will rejoice over you with singing" (Zeph. 3:17 NKJV).

Through Christ, God has accepted you. Think about what this means. I'm scooting forward and talking softly again: *You cannot keep people from rejecting you. But you can keep rejections from enraging you.*

Rejections are like speed bumps on the road. They come with the journey. Tacky purse peddlers populate the world. You're going to get cut, dished, dropped, and kicked around. You cannot keep people from rejecting you. But you can keep rejections from enraging you. How? By letting his acceptance compensate for their rejection.

Think of it this way. Suppose you dwell in a high-rise apartment. On the window sill of your room is a solitary daisy. This morning you picked the daisy and pinned it on your lapel. Since you have only one plant, this is a big event and a special daisy.

But as soon as you're out the door, people start picking petals off your daisy. Someone snags your subway seat. Petal picked. You're blamed for the bad report of a coworker. Three petals. The promotion is given to someone with less experience but USC water polo looks. More petals. By the end of the day, you're down to one. Woe be to the soul who dares to draw near it. You're only one petal-snatching away from a blowup.

What if the scenario was altered slightly? Let's add one character. The kind man in the apartment next door runs a flower shop on the corner. Every night on the way home he stops at your place with a fresh, undeserved, yet irresistible bouquet. These are not leftover flowers. They are top-of-the-line arrangements. You don't know why he thinks so highly of you, but you aren't complaining. Because of him, your apartment has a sweet fragrance, and your step has a happy bounce. Let someone mess with your flower, and you've got a basketful to replace it!

The difference is huge. And the interpretation is obvious.

God will load your world with flowers. He hand-delivers a bouquet to your door every day. Open it! Take them! Then, when rejections come, you won't be left short-petaled.

God can help you get rid of your anger. He made galaxies no one has ever seen and dug canyons we have yet to find. "The LORD . . . heals all your diseases" (Ps. 103:2–3 NIV). Do you think among those diseases might be the affliction of anger?

Do you think God could heal your angry heart?

Do you want him to? This is not a trick question. He asks the same question of you that he asked of the invalid: "Do you want to be well?" (John 5:6). Not everyone does. You may be addicted to anger. You may be a rage junkie. Anger may be part of your identity. But if you want him to, he can change your identity. Do you want him to do so?

Do you have a better option? Like moving to a rejection-free zone? If so, enjoy your life on your desert island.

Take the flowers. Receive from him so you can love or at least put up with others.

Do what T. D. Terry did. Many years ago a stressful job stirred within him daily bouts of anger. His daughter, upon hearing him describe them years later, responded with surprise. "I don't remember any anger during those years."

He asked if she remembered the tree—the one near the driveway about halfway between the gate and the house. "Remember how it used to be tall? Then lost a few limbs? And after some time was nothing more than a stump?"

She did.

"That was me," T. D. explained. "I took my anger out on the tree. I kicked it. I took an ax to it. I tore the limbs. I didn't want to come home mad, so I left my anger at the tree."[3]

Let's do the same. In fact, let's go a step farther. Rather than take out our anger on a tree in the yard, let's take our anger to the tree on the hill. Leave your anger at the tree of Calvary. When others reject you, let God accept you. He is not frowning. He is not mad. He sings over you. Take a long drink from his limitless love, and cool down.

CHAPTER

NINE

The Heart Full of Hurts

Love . . . keeps no record of wrongs.

1 Corinthians 13:4–5 NIV

Today's thoughts are tomorrow's actions.

Today's jealousy is tomorrow's temper tantrum.

Today's bigotry is tomorrow's hate crime.

Today's anger is tomorrow's abuse.

Today's lust is tomorrow's adultery.

Today's greed is tomorrow's embezzlement.

Today's guilt is tomorrow's fear.

The *Pelicano* is the world's most unwanted ship. Since 1986 she has been the hobo of the high seas. No one wants her. Sri Lanka doesn't. Bermuda doesn't. The Dominican Republic turned her away. So did the Netherlands, the Antilles, and Honduras.

The problem is not the boat. Though rusty and barnacled, the 466-foot freighter is seaworthy.

The problem is not the ownership. The owners have kept the license current and taxes paid.

The problem is not the crew. They may feel unwanted, but they aren't inefficient.

Then what is the problem? What is the reason for years of rejections? Waved away in Sri Lanka. Turned away in Indonesia. Rejected in Haiti. Why is the *Pelicano* the most unwanted ship in the world?

Simple. She is full of trash. Fifteen thousand tons of trash. Orange peelings. Beer bottles. Newspapers. Half-eaten hot dogs. Trash. The trash of Philadelphia's long summer of 1986. That's when the municipal workers went on strike. That's when the trash piled higher and higher. That's when

Georgia refused it and New Jersey declined it. No one wanted Philadelphia's trash.

That's when the *Pelicano* entered the picture. The owners thought they would turn a quick penny by transporting the rubbish. The trash was burned, and the ashes were dumped into the belly of the boat. But no one would take it. Initially it was too much. Eventually it was too old. Who wants potentially toxic trash?[1]

The plight of the *Pelicano* is proof. Trash-filled ships find few friends. The plight of the *Pelicano* is also a parable. Trash-filled hearts don't fare any better.

I wonder if you can relate to the *Pelicano.* Are you unwanted at the dock? Drifting farther from friends and family? If so, you might check your heart for garbage. Who wants to offer dock space to a smelly heart?

Life has a way of unloading her rubbish on our decks. Your husband works too much. Your wife gripes too much. Your boss expects too much. Your kids whine too much. The result? Trash. Load after load of anger. Guilt. Pessimism. Bitterness. Bigotry. Anxiety. Deceit. Impatience. It all piles up.

Trash affects us. It contaminates our relationships. It did Cain's. He had anger in his mind before he had blood on his hands. And Martha? Martha was meddlesome in her attitude before she was quarrelsome with her tongue. And what about the Pharisees? They killed Christ in their hearts before they killed him on the cross.

Mark it down. Today's thoughts are tomorrow's actions.

Today's jealousy is tomorrow's temper tantrum.

Today's bigotry is tomorrow's hate crime.

Today's anger is tomorrow's abuse.

Today's lust is tomorrow's adultery.

Today's greed is tomorrow's embezzlement.

Today's guilt is tomorrow's fear.

Today's thoughts are tomorrow's actions. Could that be why Paul writes, "Love . . . keeps no record of wrongs" (1 Cor. 13:5 NIV)? Let trash on board, and people are going to smell it. The troubles for the *Pelicano* began with the first shovelful. The crew should have turned it away at the gate. Life would have been easier for everyone on board if they had never allowed the trash to pile up.

Life will be better for you if you do the same.

Some folks don't know we have an option. To listen to our vocabulary you'd think we are the victims of our thoughts. "Don't talk to me," we say. "I'm in a bad mood." As if a mood were a place to which we were assigned ("I can't call you. I'm in Bosnia.") rather than an emotion we permit.

Or we say, "Don't mess with her. She has a bad disposition." Is a disposition something we "have"? Like a cold or the flu? Are we the victims of the emotional bacteria of the season? Or do we have a choice?

Paul says we do: "We capture every thought and make it give up and obey Christ" (2 Cor. 10:5).

Do you hear some battlefield jargon in that passage—"capture every thought," "make it give up" and "obey Christ"? You get the impression that we are the soldiers and the thoughts are the enemies. Our assignment is to protect the boat and refuse entrance to trashy thoughts. The minute they appear on the dock we go into action. "This heart belongs to God," we declare, "and you aren't getting on board until you change your allegiance."

Selfishness, step back! Envy, get lost! Find another boat, Anger! You aren't allowed on this ship. Capturing thoughts is serious business.

It was for Jesus. Remember the thoughts that came his way courtesy of the mouth of Peter? Jesus had just prophesied his death, burial, and resurrection, but Peter couldn't bear the thought of it. "Peter took Jesus aside and told him not to talk like that. . . . Jesus said to Peter, 'Go away from me, Satan! You are not helping me! You don't care about the things of God, but only about the things people think are important'" (Matt. 16:22–23).

See the decisiveness of Jesus? A trashy thought comes his way. He is tempted to entertain it. A cross-less life would be nice. But what does he do? He stands at the gangplank of the dock and says, "Get away from me." As if to say, "You are not allowed to enter my mind."

What if you did that? What if you took every thought captive? What if you refused to let any trash enter your mind? What if you took the counsel of Solomon: "Be careful what you think, because your thoughts run your life" (Prov. 4:23).

You are driving to work when the words of your coworker come to mind. He needled you about your performance. He second-guessed your efficiency. Why was he so hard on you? You begin to wonder. *I didn't deserve any of that. Who is he to criticize me? Besides, he has as much taste as a rice cake. Have you seen those shoes he wears?*

At this point you need to make a choice. *Am I going to keep a list of these wrongs?* You can. Standing on the gangplank is Self-pity and her seven sisters. They want on board. Are you going to let them? If you do, you'll be as smelly as the *Pelicano* by the time you reach your office.

Or you can do something else. You can take those thoughts captive. You can defy the culprit. Quote a verse if you have to: "Bless those who persecute you; bless and do not curse" (Rom. 12:14 NIV).

Another scene. Anger at your parents is keeping you awake. You want to sleep, but this afternoon's phone call won't let you. As always, all they did was criticize. No compliments. No applause. Just pick, pick, pick. Why aren't you married? When are you coming home? Why don't you have a good job like your cousin Homer at the bank? Grrrr. See that fellow at the bottom of the gangplank? The one wearing the dark robe? He's a judge from the court of critical attitudes. Judge Mental. Let him on board, and the two of you can spend the night passing out guilty verdicts. You can alphabetize and codify all the parents' mistakes. Are you going to let him on board? Do so at great risk, my friend. By morning you'll be smelling like a landfill.

Remember, just because there is trash on the dock, that doesn't mean there must be trash on your ship. You are not a victim of your thoughts. You have a vote. You have a voice. You can exercise thought prevention. You can also exercise thought permission.

How could you change the plight of the *Pelicano*? Change her cargo. Load the decks with flowers instead of trash, presents instead of ash, and no one would turn the ship away. Change the cargo, and you change the ship.

By the same token, change the thoughts, and you change the person. If today's thoughts are tomorrow's actions, what happens when we fill our minds with thoughts of God's love? Will standing beneath the downpour of his grace change the way we feel about others?

Paul says absolutely! It's not enough to keep the bad stuff out. We've got to let the good stuff in. It's not enough to keep no list of wrongs. We have to cultivate a list of blessings. The same verb Paul uses for *keeps* in the phrase "keeps no list of wrongs" is used for *think* in Philippians 4:8: "Whatever is true, whatever is honorable, whatever is just, whatever is pure, whatever is lovely, whatever is gracious, if there is any excellence, if there is anything worthy of praise, think about these things" (RSV). *Thinking* conveys the idea of pondering—studying and focusing, allowing what is viewed to have an impact on us.

Rather than store up the sour, store up the sweet.

You want to make a list? Then list his mercies. List the times God has forgiven you. Stand face to feet with the form of your crucified Savior and pray, "Jesus, if you can forgive me for hurting you, then I can forgive them for hurting me." You didn't deserve to be hurt by them. But neither did you deserve to be forgiven by him.

But, Max, I'm a decent person. I've never done anything to hurt Christ. Be careful now. That opinion can lead to trouble. Do you really think you haven't done things that hurt Christ?

Have you ever been dishonest with his money? That's cheating.

Has your love for flesh or fame ever turned you away from him? That's adultery.

Ever spoken an angry word with the intent to hurt? In the corpus juris of heaven, you are guilty of assault.

Have you ever been silent while he was mocked? Don't we call that treason?

Ever gone to church to be seen rather than to see him? Hypocrite.

Ever broken a promise you've made to God? Whoa. Deceit. That's serious.

Need we go further? Only six questions, just two inches of copy, and look at you. Guilty of dishonesty, adultery, assault, treason, hypocrisy, and deceit. A list worthy of indictment. Don't you deserve to be punished? And yet, here you are. Reading this book. Breathing. Still witnessing sunsets and hearing babies gurgle. Still watching the seasons change. There are no lashes on your back or hooks in your nose or shackles on your feet. Apparently God hasn't kept a list of your wrongs. Apparently David knew what he was saying: "[God] has not punished us as our sins should be punished; he has not repaid us for the evil we have done" (Ps. 103:10). And he meant it when he prayed, "LORD, if you kept a record of our sins, who, O Lord, could ever survive?" (Ps. 130:3 NLT).

Listen. You have not been sprinkled with forgiveness. You have not been spattered with grace. You have not been dusted with kindness. You have been immersed in it. You are submerged in mercy. You are a minnow in the ocean of his mercy. Let it change you! See if God's love doesn't do for you what it did for the woman in Samaria.

Talk about a woman who could make a list. Number one, discrimination. She is a Samaritan, hated by Jews. Number two, gender bias. She is a female, condescended to by the men. Third, she is a divorcée, not once, not twice. Let's see if we can count. Four? Five? Five marriages turned south, and now she's sharing a bed with a guy who won't give her a ring.

When I add this up, I envision a happy-hour stool sitter who lives with her mad at half boil. Husky voice, cigarette breath, and a dress cut low at the top and high at the bottom. Certainly not Samaria's finest. Certainly not the woman you'd put in charge of the Ladies' Bible class.

Which makes the fact that Jesus does just that all the more surprising. He doesn't just put her in charge of the class; he puts her in charge of evangelizing the whole town. Before the day is over, the entire city hears about a man who claims to be God. "He told me everything I ever did" (John 4:39), she tells them, leaving unsaid the obvious, "and he loved me anyway."

A little rain can straighten a flower stem. A little love can change a life. Who knew the last time this woman had been entrusted with anything, much less the biggest news in history! In fact, flip to the left out of John 4, and you'll make this startling discovery. She is Jesus' missionary! She precedes the more noted. The lineage of Peter and Paul, St. Patrick and St. Francis of Assisi can be traced back to a town trollop who was so overwhelmed by Christ that she had to speak.

Another *Pelicano* forever fumigated. Why?

Not just because of what Jesus did, though that was huge. But because she let him do it. She let him on board. She let him love her. She let him change her cargo. He found her full of trash and left her full of grace. She and Zacchaeus and the apostle Paul and the woman in Capernaum and millions of others invited him into the hold of their hearts.

She didn't have to.

They didn't have to.

And you don't have to.

You really don't.

You can stick with your long lists and stinky cargo. And drift from port to port.

But why would you? Let the *Pelicano* have the high seas.

Your Captain has better plans for you.

CHAPTER TEN

The Love Test

Love does not delight in evil
but rejoices with the truth.

1 Corinthians 13:6 niv

ISN'T IT GOOD TO KNOW THAT EVEN WHEN WE DON'T LOVE WITH A PERFECT LOVE, HE DOES?

A jog wasn't on my mind when we checked into the hotel. It was dark. Waco, Texas, was windy and cold. The book tour was fun but tiring—third city in three days. I was just happy to get to bed. A good night's rest changed things, however. So did the bright sun and warm morning. I laced up my shoes, waved good-bye to the desk clerk, and took off through the neighborhood.

Running through unfamiliar towns can be tricky. I once spent three hours seeing parts of Fresno that most citizens of Fresno have never seen. So, to keep my bearings, I stay on one road. Run out. Run back.

The run back to the hotel seemed longer, but I chalked it up to poor conditioning. Upon entering the lobby, I noticed a breakfast buffet. One of those free ones where you toast your own toast and heat your own oatmeal. *Fine by me,* I thought, wondering why I hadn't noticed the food when I left.

I filled a tray, ate the meal, and was going back for seconds when I heard a couple of Brazilians speaking. For five years Brazil was home to our family. I couldn't resist a good conversation. *"Bom dia,"* I greeted. We talked about the country, the economy. I shared the only Portuguese joke I remembered. They invited me to take a seat. "Let me refill my coffee cup first," I replied. I returned and took a seat, not just with coffee, but more toast.

As I left to clean up, I passed the food bar again and, believe it or not, was still hungry. *No harm,* I reasoned. Calculating in the jog, I figured I'd break even. So I filled a bowl with oatmeal and decided to eat it in my room.

I walked straight through the lobby, turned right at the first hallway, past the indoor pool (h'm, I didn't notice a pool last night), and came to the first door on the right. But something was wrong. My key card wouldn't open the door. Tried a second time. No luck. I looked up at the room number. *Wait a minute, this isn't my room!*

I retraced my steps. Back down the hall. Past the pool. (How could I not notice that pool?) Back into the lobby. Past the breakfast bar. Smile at the manager. Surely she wonders where I'm headed with the food. Out the front door. Into the parking lot. I looked up at the sign over the entrance. *This isn't my hotel! Where is my hotel?* I looked to the right. Then to the left. There it was! Next door. Well, what do you know? I'd jogged past my place and into this one. Duh! What else to do but shrug and walk across the lot and to my room? (I took the oatmeal with me. They wouldn't have wanted it back.)

I'd spent an hour in the wrong hotel. Visiting in the lobby. Chatting with the guests. Eating the food. Drinking the coffee. I even complimented the manager on the decorations. For an hour I was in the wrong hotel. And you know what?

I *felt* as though I was in the right place. Had you asked me what I was doing eating a free meal in the wrong hotel, I would have looked at you as if you were wearing hockey clothes in the Amazon. "You're crazy."

Not once did I lift my head and furrow my brow and think, *This place feels funny.* It didn't. It *felt* fine. But my feelings were wrong. My key card proved them wrong. The room number proved them wrong. The manager, had she been asked, could have proved them wrong. No matter how much I felt as though I was in the right place, I was not. And no mountain of feelings could change that.

I wonder if you've ever made the same mistake. Not with a hotel, but with love. Have you ever made decisions about your relationships based on your feelings instead of the facts? When it comes to love, feelings rule the day. Emotions guide the ship. Goose bumps call the shots. But should they? Can feelings be trusted? Can a relationship feel right but be wrong? Heads are nodding.

A single mom is nodding.

A college kid with a broken heart is nodding.

The fellow who fell in love with a figure that could cause a twelve-car pileup is nodding.

Feelings can fool you. Yesterday I spoke with a teenage girl who is puzzled by the lack of feelings she has for a guy. Before they started dating, she was wild about him. The minute he showed interest in her, however, she lost interest.

I'm thinking also of a young mom. Being a parent isn't as romantic as she anticipated. Diapers and midnight feedings aren't any fun, and she's feeling guilty because they aren't. *Am I low on love?* she wonders.

How do you answer such questions? Ever wish you had a way to assess the quality of your affection? A DNA test for love? Paul offers us one: "Love does not delight in evil but rejoices with the truth" (1 Cor. 13:6 NIV). In this verse lies a test for love.

Want to separate the fake from the factual, the counterfeit from the real thing? Want to know if what you feel is genuine love? Ask yourself this:

Do I encourage this person to do what is right? For true love "takes no pleasure in other people's sins but delights in the truth" (1 Cor. 13:6 JB).

For instance, one lady calls another and says, "We're friends, right?"

"Yeah, we're friends."

"If my husband asks, you tell him we were together at the movies last night."

"But we weren't."

"I know, but I was, well, I was with another guy and—hey, you'll do this for me, won't you? We're friends, right? Tighter than sisters, right?"

Does this person pass the test? No way. The room key doesn't work. Love doesn't ask someone to do what is wrong. How do we know? "Love does not delight in evil but rejoices with the truth" (1 Cor. 13:6 NIV).

If you find yourself prompting evil in others, heed the alarm. This is not love. And if others prompt evil in you, be alert. Check the room key.

Here's an example. A classic one. A young couple are on a date. His affection goes beyond her comfort zone. She resists. But he tries to persuade her with the oldest line in the book: "But I love you. I just want to be near you. If you loved me . . ."

That siren you hear? It's the phony-love detector. This guy doesn't love her. He may love having sex with her. He may love her body. He may love boasting to his buddies about his conquest. But he doesn't love her. True love will never ask the "beloved" to do what he or she thinks is wrong.

Love doesn't tear down the convictions of others. Quite the contrary.

"Love builds up" (1 Cor. 8:1).

"Whoever loves a brother or sister lives in the light and will not cause anyone to stumble" (1 John 2:10).

"You are sinning against Christ when you sin against other Christians by encouraging them to do something they believe is wrong" (1 Cor. 8:12 NLT).

Do you want to know if your love for someone is true? If your friendship is genuine? Check the room key. Ask yourself: Do I influence this person to do what is right?

If you answered yes, have some coffee. You're in the right hotel. If you want to be doubly sure, however, ask the next question.

Do I applaud what is right? For love "rejoices whenever the truth wins out" (1 Cor. 13:6 NLT).

The summer before my eighth-grade year I made friends with a guy named Larry. He was new to town, so I encouraged him to go out for our school football team. He could meet some guys, and being a stocky fellow, he might even make the squad. He agreed.

The result was a good news–bad news scenario. The good news? He made the cut. The bad news? He won my position. I was demoted to second string. I tried to be happy for him, but it was tough.

A few weeks into the season Larry fell off a motorcycle and broke a finger. I remember the day he stood at my front door holding up his bandaged hand. "Looks like you're going to have to play."

I tried to feel sorry for him, but it was hard. The passage was a lot easier for Paul to write than it was for me to practice. "Rejoice with those who rejoice, and weep with those who weep" (Rom. 12:15 NASB).

You want to plumb the depths of your love for someone? How do you feel when that person succeeds? Do you rejoice? Or are you jealous? And when he or she stumbles? Falls to misfortune? Are you really sorry? Or are you secretly pleased?

Love never celebrates misfortune. Never. I like the way Eugene Peterson translates the passage: "Love . . . doesn't revel when others grovel, [but] takes pleasure in the flowering of truth" (1 Cor. 13:6 MSG). J. B. Phillips is equally descriptive: "Love . . . does not . . . gloat over the wickedness of other people. On the contrary, it shares the joy of those who live by the truth."

You know your love is real when you weep with those who weep and rejoice with those who rejoice. You know your love is real when you feel for others what Catherine Lawes felt for the inmates of Sing Sing prison. When her husband, Lewis, became the warden in 1921, she was a young mother of three daughters. Everybody warned her never to step foot inside the walls. But she didn't listen to them. When the first prison basketball game was held, in she went, three girls in tow, and took a seat in the bleachers with the inmates.

She once said, "My husband and I are going to take care of these men, and I believe they will take care of me! I don't have to worry!"

When she heard that one convicted murderer was blind, she taught him Braille so he could read. Upon learning of inmates who were hearing impaired, she studied sign language so they could communicate. For sixteen years Catherine Lawes softened the hard hearts of the men of Sing Sing. In 1937 the world saw the difference real love makes.

The prisoners knew something was wrong when Lewis Lawes didn't report to work. Quickly the word spread that Catherine had been killed in a car accident. The following day her body was placed in her home, three-quarters of a mile from the prison. As the acting warden took his early morning walk, he noticed a large gathering at the main gate. Every prisoner pressed against the fence. Eyes awash with tears. Faces solemn. No one spoke or moved. They'd come to stand as close as they could to the woman who'd given them love.

The warden made a remarkable decision. "All right, men, you can go. Just be sure to check in tonight." These were America's hardest criminals. Murderers. Robbers. These were men the nation had locked away for life. But the warden unlocked the gate for them, and they walked without escort or guard to the home of Catherine Lawes to pay their last respects. And to a man, each one returned.[1]

Real love changes people.

Didn't God's love change you? Weren't you, like the prisoner, blind? You couldn't see beyond the grave. You couldn't see your purpose in life until he showed you. And you couldn't hear either. Oh, your ears functioned, but your heart didn't understand. You'd never heard of such love and kindness, and you never would have heard of it, but God spoke in your language. And, most of all, he set you free. You are free! Free to run away. Free to harden your heart. Free to duck down side streets and hide behind trash cans. But you don't. Or if you do, you come back. Why?

Because you've never been loved like this before.

God passes the test of 1 Corinthians 13:7. Does he want the best for you? "God himself does not tempt anyone" (James 1:13). Every action of heaven has one aim: that you know God. "He . . . made the earth hospitable, with plenty of time and space for living so we could seek after God, and not just grope around in the dark but actually find him" (Acts 17:26–27 MSG).

And does God rejoice when you do what is right? Certainly. "The LORD delights in those who fear him, who put their hope in his unfailing love" (Ps. 147:11 NIV). Does he weep when you do? Absolutely! He is the "God of all healing counsel! He comes alongside us when we go through hard times" (2 Cor. 1:3–4 MSG).

Do you want to know what love is? "This is what real love is: It is not our love for God; it is God's love for us in sending his Son to be the way to take away our sins" (1 John 4:10).

God passes the test. Well, he should; he drafted it.

So where does this leave us? Perhaps with a trio of reminders. When it comes to love:

Be careful. Make sure you're in the right hotel. Before you walk down the aisle, take a good long look around. Make sure this is God's intended place for you. And, if you suspect it isn't, get out. Don't force what is wrong to be right. Suppose I'd done that in the hotel. Suppose I'd demanded that the manager change the lock and the numbers on the door? I still would have been in the wrong place. Be careful.

And, until love is stirred, let God's love be enough for you. There are seasons when God allows us to feel the frailty of human love so we'll appreciate the strength of his love. Didn't he do this with David? Saul turned on him. Michal, his wife, betrayed him. Jonathan and Samuel were David's friends, but they couldn't follow him into the wilderness. Betrayal and circumstances left David alone. Alone with God. And, as David discovered, God was enough. David wrote these words in a desert: "Because your love is better than life, my lips will glorify you. . . . My soul will be satisfied as with the richest of foods" (Ps. 63:3, 5 NIV).

Be prayerful. What if it's too late? Specifically, what if you're married to someone you don't love—or who doesn't love you? Many choose to leave. That may be the step you take. But if it is, take at least a thousand others first. And bathe every one of those steps in prayer. Love is a fruit of the Spirit. Ask God to help you love as he loves. "God has given us the Holy Spirit, who fills our hearts with his love" (Rom. 5:5 CEV). Ask everyone you know to pray for you. Your friends. Your family. Your church leaders. Get your name on every prayer list available. And, most of all, pray for and, if possible, with your spouse. Ask the same God who raised the dead to resurrect the embers of your love.

Be grateful. Be grateful for those who love you. Be grateful for those who have encouraged you to do what is right and applauded when you did. Do you have people like that in your world? If so, you are doubly blessed. Be grateful for them. And be grateful for your Father in heaven. He passes the test with ease.

Isn't it good to know that even when we don't love with a perfect love, he does? God always nourishes what is right. He always applauds what is right. He has never done wrong, led one person to do wrong, or rejoiced when anyone did wrong. For he is love, and love "does not rejoice in unrighteousness, but rejoices with the truth" (1 Cor. 13:6 NASB).

CHAPTER ELEVEN

Love Is a Package Deal

Love . . . bears all things, believes all things, hopes all things, endures all things.

1 Corinthians 13:4–7 NASB

How long must I put up with you?

Jesus' actions answered his own question. . . .

Until the rooster sings and the sweat stings and the mallet rings

and a hillside of demons smirk at a dying God.

How long? Long enough for every sin to so soak my sinless soul that heaven will turn in horror

until my swollen lips pronounce the final transaction: "It is finished."

How long? Until it kills me.

My parents were not too big on restaurants. Partly because of the selection in our small town. Dairy Queen offered the gourmet selection, and everything went downhill from there. The main reason, though, was practicality. Why eat out when you can stay home? Restaurant trips were a Sunday-only, once-or-twice-a-month event. Funny, now that I am a parent, the philosophy is just the opposite. Why stay home when you can go out? (We tell our daughters it's time to eat, and they head for the garage.)

But when I was growing up, we typically ate at home. And every time we ate at home, my mom gave my brother and me the same instructions: "Put a little bit of everything on your plate."

We never had to be told to clean the plate. Eating volume was not a challenge. Variety was. Don't get me wrong, Mom was a good cook. But boiled okra? Asparagus? More like "croak-ra" and "gasp-aragus." Were they really intended for human consumption?

According to Mom, they were, and—according to Mom—they had to be eaten. "Eat some of everything." That was the rule in our house.

But that was not the rule at the cafeteria. On special occasions we made the forty-five-minute drive to the greatest culinary innovation since the gas stove: the cafeteria line. Ah, what a fine moment indeed to take a tray and gaze down the midway at the endless options. A veritable cornucopia of fine cuisine. Down the row you walk, intoxicated by the selection and liberated by the freedom. Yes to the fried fish; no to the fried tomatoes. Yes to the pecan pie; no, no, a thousand times no to the "croak-ra" and "gasp-aragus." Cafeteria lines are great.

Wouldn't it be nice if love were like a cafeteria line? What if you could look at the person with whom you live and select what you want and pass on what you don't? What if parents could do this with kids? "I'll take a plate of good grades and cute smiles, and I'm passing on the teenage identity crisis and tuition bills."

What if kids could do the same with parents? "Please give me a helping of allowances and free lodging but no rules or curfews, thank you."

And spouse with spouse? "H'm, how about a bowl of good health and good moods. But job transfers, in-laws, and laundry are not on my diet."

Wouldn't it be great if love were like a cafeteria line? It would be easier. It would be neater. It would be painless and peaceful. But you know what? It wouldn't be love. Love doesn't accept just a few things. Love is willing to accept all things.

"Love . . . bears all things, believes all things, hopes all things, endures all things" (1 Cor. 13:4–7 NKJV).

The apostle is looking for a ribbon to wrap around one of the sweetest paragraphs in Scripture. I envision the leathery-faced saint pausing in his dictation. "Let me think for a moment." Checking off his fingers, he reviews his list. "Let's see, patience, kindness, envy, arrogance. We've mentioned rudeness, selfishness, and anger, forgiveness, evil, and truth. Have I covered all things? Ah, that's it—all things. Here, write this down. Love bears all things, believes all things, hopes all things, endures all things."

Paul was never more the wordsmith than when he crafted this sentence. Listen to its rhythm as originally written: *panta stegei, panta pisteuei, panta elpigei, panta upomenei.* (Now when people ask you what you are doing, you can say, "I'm reading some Greek." Say it humbly, however, for love does not boast.) Did you notice the fourfold appearance of *panta*?

Expansions of *panta* appear in your English dictionary. *Pantheism* is the belief that God is in all things. A *pantry* is a cupboard where one can, hopefully, store all things. A *panacea* is a cure for all things. And a *panoply* is an array of all things. *Panta* means "all things."

God's view of love is like my mom's view of food. When we love someone, we take the entire package. No picking and choosing. No large helpings of the good and passing on the bad. Love is a package deal.

But how can we love those we find difficult to love?

The apostle Paul faced that same question. In fact, that's the reason we have this epistle. The church he began in southern Greece had gone wacko. When it came to unity, the members of the church in Corinth were out of step with each other. The apostle has barely placed pen on parchment before he writes:

> I appeal to you, brethren, by the name of our Lord Jesus Christ, that all of you agree and that there be no dissensions among you, but that you be united in the same mind and the same judgment. For it has been reported to me by Chloe's people that there is quarreling among you, my brethren. (1 Cor. 1:10–11 RSV)

The Greek word for *quarreling* also described battles in war. The Corinthian congregation was at war. Why? They couldn't agree on a leader. "One of you says, 'I follow Paul'; another says, 'I follow Apollos'; another says, 'I follow Peter'; and another says, 'I follow Christ'" (v. 12).

The church members had their favorite leaders. Some rallied around Paul, the church founder. Others liked Apollos, a dynamic speaker. Some preferred Peter, one of the original apostles. Some followed him, and others were happy just to follow Jesus. The congregation was divided into four groups, drawn and quartered into the Paulites, Apollosites, Peterites, and Jesusites. When it came to unity, the members were out of step.

When it came to morals, the church was out of control. Paul writes:

> I can hardly believe the report about the sexual immorality going on among you, something so evil that even the pagans don't do it. I am told that you have a man in your church who is living in sin with his father's wife. And you are so proud of yourselves! Why aren't you mourning in sorrow and shame? And why haven't you removed this man from your fellowship? (1 Cor. 5:1–2 NLT)

Paul wonders what is worse—the activity of the man or the apathy of the church?

One man was having an affair with his father's wife. Since Paul makes no mention of incest, the woman was likely his stepmother. Even the Corinthian society rebuffed such behavior. Roman law prohibited a son from marrying his father's wife, even if the father had died.[1] But smack-dab in the middle of the church, an interfamily affair was taking place, and no one was saying anything!

When it came to morals, the church was out of control. Their moral depravity likely resulted from their shallow theology, for when it came to biblical knowledge, the church was out of line.

The controversy was this: Can we eat meat that has been offered to idols? Pagan worship, like Jewish, involved the sacrifice of animals. Only a portion of the sacrifice was actually burned. The rest was divided between the priests and the public. Could Christians eat such meat?

The pro-meats said yes. After all, as Paul says, "We all know that an idol is not really a god and that there is only one God and no other" (1 Cor. 8:4 NLT). The pro-meats saw no problem with eating the meat.

The anti-meats, however, had a conscience problem. Paul uses verse 7 to put their dilemma in words: "Some are accustomed to thinking of idols as being real, so when they eat food that has been offered to idols, they think of it as the worship of real gods, and their weak consciences are violated" (NLT).

Some members felt that eating idol-offered meat endorsed idol worship. The anti-meats had a hard time making the break. And the pro-meats had a hard time being patient. They felt free in Christ and couldn't understand why others didn't feel the same.

Paul agrees with their conviction: "We don't miss out on anything if we don't eat it, and we don't gain anything if we do" (8:8 NLT). He had no trouble with the belief of the pro-meaters. But he had a lot of trouble with their arrogance. It's hard to miss the sarcasm of verse 2: "You think that everyone should agree with your perfect knowledge. While knowledge may make us feel important, it is love that really builds up the church. Anyone who claims to know all the answers doesn't really know very much" (8:1–2 NLT).

Ouch. The people had the right information but the wrong approach. They were too sophisticated for their own good.

Let's tally up the Corinthian confusion. Regarding unity, they were out of step. In terms of morality, they were out of control. Theologically, they were out of line.

But there's more! In the area of worship the church was way out of order. Just as their newfound freedom got them in trouble with morals and meat, it caused problems in the assembly.

Veils were a problem. Some of the women were coming to church without one. In Corinth, a veil was a sign of modesty and virtue. To appear unveiled in public was nothing short of immoral. The "enlightened" believers wanted to chuck the veils and "face" the future. Others, however, said, "Not so fast." Paul was one of them. The unveiled woman might as well shave her head, he argues (11:5). As long as she is going to attract attention to herself, why hold back?

And then there was the matter of the Lord's Supper. In Corinth the meal was more than crackers and juice; it was an extended time of food, fellowship, and worship. But some of the members were missing the point. They liked the food but disregarded the fellowship and worship. They arrived early and ate heartily, leaving nothing for the others but an empty table.

The women were missing the point with the veil. The others were missing the point with communion. And all of them were missing the point with the gifts of the Spirit. Some were proud of their gifts; others felt shortchanged. There was too much tongue speaking and preaching and not enough interpretation and listening, resulting in pandemonium (14:23).

Oh, Corinth. You have a problem on every pew! Territorially selfish. Morally shameless. Theologically reckless. And corporately thoughtless. How do you help a congregation like that?

You can correct them. Paul does. You can instruct them, which Paul does. You can reason with them; Paul does. But at some point, you stop talking to the head and start appealing to the heart.

And Paul does that: "Love . . . bears all things, believes all things, hopes all things, endures all things" (13:4–7 NKJV).

You parents can relate to Paul's problem. You've been there. From your daughter's bedroom comes a bloodcurdling cry. You rush to find your eight-year-old son yelling and his six-year-old sister tear streaked. You sigh, "What happened?" You never should have asked.

"He threw my Baby-Don't-Potty out the window."

"Well, she stepped on my WWF Nintendo game."

And off they go. He did. She did. She did. He did. You shake your head and wonder why your kids couldn't have been blessed with more traits from your side of the family.

Finally you make a "T" with your hands and shout, "Time out!" Forget the problems. You're going to the heart of the matter. You speak to your kids about something higher than toys, something grander than games. You speak to them about love. You speak to them about family. You dry her tears and stroke his head and wax eloquent on the topic of families' sticking together and looking out for each other. You tell them that life is too short for fights, and people are too precious for anger, and in the end the only thing that really solves it all is love.

They listen. They nod. And you are flooded with a fine feeling of satisfaction. You stand and then leave. The fighting could start again. But at least you planted the seed.

Paul could say the same. For twelve chapters, he's wrestled to untie the knots of disunity. For three more chapters, he'll try to make sense out of their conflicts. But chapter thirteen is his "Time out!" He sees only one solution. And that solution is a five-letter Greek word: A-G-A-P-E. *Agape.*

Paul could have used the Greek word *eros.* But he's not speaking of sexual love. He could have used the term *phileo,* but he presents far more than friendship. Or he could have used *storge,* a tender term for the love of family. But Paul has more in mind than domestic peace.

He envisions an *agape* love. *Agape* love cares for others because God has cared for us. *Agape* love goes beyond sentiment and good wishes. Because God loved first, *agape* love responds. Because God was gracious, *agape* love forgives the mistake when the offense is high. *Agape* offers patience when stress is abundant and extends kindness when kindness is rare. Why? Because God offered both to us.

Agape love "bears all things, believes all things, hopes all things, endures all things" (13:7 NKJV).

This is the type of love that Paul prescribes for the church in Corinth. Don't we need the same prescription today? Don't groups still fight with each other? Don't we flirt with those we shouldn't? Aren't we sometimes quiet when we should speak? And don't those who have found freedom still have the hardest time with those who haven't? Someday there will be a community where everyone behaves and no one complains. But it won't be this side of heaven.

So till then what do we do? We reason. We confront. We teach. But most of all we love.

Such love isn't easy. Not for you. Not for me. Not even for Jesus. Want proof? Listen to his frustration: "You people have no faith. How long must I stay with you? How long must I put up with you?" (Mark 9:19).

Even the Son of God was handed plates of "croak-ra" and "gasp-aragus." To know Jesus asked such a question reassures us. But to hear how he answered it will change us. *How long must I put up with you?*

"Long enough to be called crazy by my brothers and a liar by my neighbors. Long enough to be run out of my town and my Temple. Long enough to be laughed at, cursed, slapped, hit, blindfolded, and mocked. Long enough to feel warm spit and sharp whips and see my own blood puddle at my feet."

How long? "Until the rooster sings and the sweat stings and the mallet rings and a hillside of demons smirk at a dying God."

How long? "Long enough for every sin to so soak my sinless soul that heaven will turn in horror until my swollen lips pronounce the final transaction: 'It is finished.'"

How long? "Until it kills me."

Jesus bore all things, believed all things, hoped all things, and endured all things. Every single one.

CHAPTER TWELVE

A Cloak of Love

Love . . . always protects.

1 Corinthians 13:6–7 niv

We hide. He seeks.

We bring sin. He brings a sacrifice.

We try fig leaves. He brings the robe of righteousness.

And we are left to sing the song of the prophet:

"He has covered me with clothes of salvation
    and wrapped me with a coat of goodness,
like a bridegroom dressed for his wedding,
    like a bride dressed in jewels" (Isa. 61:10).

In the 1930s, Joe Wise was a young, single resident at Cook Hospital in Fort Worth, Texas. Patients called him the "doctor with the rose." He made them smile by pinning a flower from bedside bouquets on his lab coat.

Madge, however, needed more than a smile. The automobile accident had left her leg nearly severed at the knee. She was young, beautiful, and very much afraid. When Joe spotted her in the ER, he did something he'd never done before.

Joe took his lab coat, bejeweled with the rose, and placed it gently over the young woman. As she was wheeled into the operating room, the coat was removed, but she asked to keep the flower. When she awoke from surgery, it was still in her hand.

When I tell you that Madge never forgot Joe, you won't be surprised. When I tell you how she thanked him, you very well may be.

But before we finish the story of Joe's cloak, could I ask you to think about your own? Do you own a cloak of love? Do you know anyone who needs one? When you cover someone with concern, you are fulfilling what

Paul had in mind when he wrote the phrase "love . . . always protects" (1 Cor. 13:4–7 NIV).

Paul employed a rich word here. Its root meaning is "to cover or conceal." Its cousins on the noun side of the family are *roof* and *shelter.* When Paul said, "Love always protects," he might have been thinking of the shade of a tree or the refuge of a house. He might even have been thinking of a coat. One scholar thinks he was. The *Theological Dictionary of the New Testament* is known for its word study, not its poetry. But the scholar sounds poetic as he explains the meaning of *protect* as used in 1 Corinthians 13:7. The word conveys, he says, "the idea of covering with a cloak of love."[1]

Remember receiving one? You were nervous about the test, but the teacher stayed late to help you. You were far from home and afraid, but your mother phoned to comfort you. You were innocent and accused, so your friend stood to defend you. Covered with encouragement. Covered with tender-hearted care. Covered with protection. *Covered with a cloak of love.*

Your finest cloak of love, however, came from God. Never thought of your Creator as a clothier? Adam and Eve did.

Every clothing store in the world owes its existence to Adam and Eve. Ironing boards, closets, hangers—all trace their ancestry back to the Garden of Eden. Before Adam and Eve sinned, they needed no clothing; after they sinned, they couldn't get dressed fast enough. They hid in the bushes and set about the task of making a wardrobe out of fig leaves.

They craved protection. Well they should have. They knew the consequences of their mistake. God had warned them, "You must not eat fruit from the tree that is in the middle of the garden. You must not even touch it, or you will die" (Gen. 3:3).

Of course the one tree they were told not to touch was the one they couldn't resist, and the fruit of the tree became a doorknob that, once pulled, permitted a slew of unwanted consequences to enter.

One of which was shame. Adam and Eve had felt no shame. Then they felt nothing but. Hence they hid, and hence they sewed, but the covering was insufficient. What is a grove of trees to the eyes of God? What protection is found in a fig leaf?

Adam and Eve found themselves, like Madge, vulnerable on a gurney—wounded, not by a car, but by their own sin.

But what would God do? Had he not announced his judgment? Hadn't his law been broken? Didn't justice demand their death? Is he not righteous?

But, we are quick to counter, is God not love? And weren't Adam and Eve his children? Could his mercy override his justice? Is there some way that righteousness can coexist with kindness?

According to Genesis 3:21 it can. The verse has been called the first gospel sermon. Preached not by preachers, but by God himself. Not with words, but with symbol and action. You want to see how God responds to our sin?

"The Lord God made clothes from animal skins for the man and his wife and dressed them" (Gen. 3:21).

The mystery behind those words! Read them again, and try to envision the moment.

"The Lord God made clothes from animal skins for the man and his wife and dressed them."

That simple sentence suggests three powerful scenes.

Scene 1: God slays an animal. For the first time in the history of the earth, dirt is stained with blood. Innocent blood. The beast committed no sin. The creature did not deserve to die.

Adam and Eve did. The couple deserve to die, but they live. The animal deserves to live, but it dies. In scene 1, innocent blood is shed.

Scene 2: Clothing is made. The shaper of the stars now becomes a tailor.

And in Scene 3: God dresses them. "The Lord . . . dressed them."

Oh, for a glimpse of that moment. Adam and Eve are on their way out of the garden. They've been told to leave, but now God tells them to stop. "Those fig leaves," he says, shaking his head, "will never do." And he produces some clothing. But he doesn't throw the garments at their feet and tell them to get dressed. He dresses them himself. "Hold still, Adam. Let's see how this fits." As a mother would dress a toddler. As a father would zip up the jacket of a preschooler. As a physician would place a lab coat over a frightened girl. God covers them. He protects them.

Love always protects.

Hasn't he done the same for us? We eat our share of forbidden fruit. We say what we shouldn't say. Go where we shouldn't go. Pluck fruit from trees we shouldn't touch.

And when we do, the door opens, and the shame tumbles in. And we hide. We sew fig leaves. Flimsy excuses. See-through justifications. We cover ourselves in good works and good deeds, but one gust of the wind of truth, and we are naked again—stark naked in our own failure.

So what does God do? Exactly what he did for our parents in the garden. He sheds innocent blood. He offers the life of his Son. And from the scene of the sacrifice the Father takes a robe—not the skin of an animal—but the robe of righteousness. And does he throw it in our direction and tell us to shape up? No, he dresses us himself. He dresses us *with* himself. "You were all baptized into Christ, and so you were all clothed with Christ" (Gal. 3:26–27).

The robing is his work, not ours. Did you note the inactivity of Adam and Eve? They did nothing. Absolutely nothing. They didn't request the sacrifice; they didn't think of the sacrifice; they didn't even dress themselves. They were passive in the process. So are we. "You have been saved by grace through believing. You did not save yourselves; it was a gift from God. It was not the result of your own efforts, so you cannot brag about it. God has made us what we are" (Eph. 2:8–10).

We hide. He seeks. We bring sin. He brings a sacrifice. We try fig leaves. He brings the robe of righteousness. And we are left to sing the song of the prophet: "He has covered me with clothes of salvation and wrapped me with a coat of goodness, like a bridegroom dressed for his wedding, like a bride dressed in jewels" (Isa. 61:10).

God has clothed us. He protects us with a cloak of love. Can you look back over your life and see instances of God's protection? I can too. My junior year in college I was fascinated by a movement of Christians several thousand miles from my campus. Some of my friends decided to spend the summer at the movement's largest church and be discipled. When I tried to do the same, every door closed. Problem after problem with finances, logistics, and travel.

A second opportunity surfaced: spending a summer in Brazil. In this case, every door I knocked on swung open. Two and one half decades later I see how God protected me. The movement has become a cult—dangerous and oppressive. Time in Brazil introduced me to grace—freeing and joyful. Did God protect me? Does God protect us?

Does he do for us what he did for the woman caught in adultery? He protected her from the stones. And his disciples? He protected them from the storm. And the demoniac? He protected him from hell itself. Why, Jesus even protected Peter from the tax collectors by providing a tax payment.[2]

And you? Did he keep you from a bad relationship? Protect you from the wrong job? Insulate you from ______________ (you fill in the blank)? "Like hovering birds, so will [the LORD Almighty] protect Jerusalem" (Isa. 31:5 JB). "He will strengthen and protect you" (2 Thess. 3:3 NIV). "He will command his angels . . . to guard you" (Ps. 91:11 NIV). God protects you with a cloak of love.

Wouldn't you love to do the same for him? What if you were given the privilege of Mary? What if God himself were placed in your arms as a naked baby? Would you not do what she did? "She wrapped the baby with pieces of cloth" (Luke 2:7).

The baby Jesus, still wet from the womb, was cold and chilled. So this mother did what any mother would do; she did what love does: She covered him.

Three decades later another lover of Christ did the same. This time the body of Jesus wasn't cold from the chill; it was cold from death. Joseph of Arimathea had it lowered from the cross. Just as Mary cleansed the child from the womb, Joseph prepared the Savior for the tomb. He washed the spit from the face and sponged the blood from the beard. "Then Joseph took the body and wrapped it in a clean linen cloth" (Matt. 27:59).

Mary dressed the baby. Joseph cleansed the body.

Wouldn't you cherish an opportunity to do the same? You have one. Such opportunities come your way every day. Jesus said,

> "I was without clothes, and you gave me something to wear." . . .
>
> "When," [the people asked,] "did we see you without clothes and give you something to wear?" . . .
>
> "I tell you the truth, anything you did for even the least of my people here, you also did for me." (Matt. 25:36, 38, 40)

Do you know anyone, like Madge, who is wounded and afraid? Do you know anyone, like Adam and Eve, who is guilty and embarrassed? Do you know anyone who needs a cloak of love?

Have you ever had a teenager in trouble? You hear the garage door open after the curfew hour. You climb out of bed and march to the kitchen, and there you find him at the counter. The smell of beer is on his breath. The flush of alcohol is on his cheeks. This is serious. He has been drinking. He has been driving. You have a problem, and I have a question. What are you going to give your son?

Are you going to give him a lecture? He deserves one. Are you going to give him three months with no keys? That may be wise. Are you going to give him a life sentence with no parole? That may be understandable, considering your worry—but don't forget to give your child a cloak of love. At some point over the next few hours he desperately needs to feel your arm around his shoulders. He needs to be cloaked, covered, blanketed in your love. Love always protects.

Know anyone who needs a cloak of love?

Have you ever heard anyone gossip about someone you know? Ever seen human jackals make a meal out of a fallen friend? "Well, I heard that she . . ." "Oh, but didn't you know that she . . ." "Let me tell you what a friend told me about him . . ." Then all of a sudden it's your turn. Everybody is picking your friend apart. What do you have to say?

Here is what love says: Love says nothing. Love stays silent. "Love covers a multitude of sins" (1 Pet. 4:8 NASB). Love doesn't expose. It doesn't gossip. If love says anything, love speaks words of defense. Words of kindness. Words of protection.

Know anyone in need of a cloak of love?

A few years back I offered one to my daughters. The whirlwind of adolescence was making regular runs through our house, bringing with it more than our share of doubts, pimples, and peer pressure. I couldn't protect the girls from the winds, but I could give them an anchor to hold in the midst. On Valentine's Day, 1997, I wrote the following and had it framed for each daughter:

I have a special gift for you. My gift is warmth at night and sunlit afternoons, chuckles and giggles and happy Saturdays.

But how do I give this gift? Is there a store which sells laughter? A catalog that offers kisses? No. Such a treasure can't be bought. But it can be given. And here is how I give it to you.

Your Valentine's Day gift is a promise, a promise that I will always love your mother. With God as my helper, I will never leave her. You'll never come home to find me gone. You'll never wake up and find that I have run away. You'll always have two parents. I will love your mother. I will honor your mother. I will cherish your mother. That is my promise. That is my gift.

Love, Dad

Know anyone who could use some protection? Of course you do. Then give some.

Pay a gas bill for a struggling elderly couple.

Promise your kids that, God being your helper, they'll never know a hungry day or a homeless night.

Tell your husband that you'd do it all over again and invite him on a honeymoon.

Make sure your divorced friends are invited to your parties.

And when you see a wounded soul, shivering and shaken on a gurney of life, offer a lab coat and leave the rose.

That's what Dr. Wise did. And he didn't stop there. As Madge recovered, he paid visits to her room. Many visits. When he learned that she was engaged, he hung a "No Visitors" sign on her door so her fiancé couldn't enter. Madge didn't object. Her diary reads, "I hope that handsome young doctor comes by to visit today." He did, that day and many others, always with a rose. One a day until she was dismissed from the hospital.

And Madge never forgot. Her response? She gave him a rose in return. The next day she gave another. Then the next, another. As they started dating, the daily roses still came. When they married, she didn't stop giving them. Madge convinced the Colonial Golf Course across the street from her house to plant roses so she could give the doctor his daily gift. For nearly forty years, every day—a rose. Their younger son, Harold, says he can't remember a time when there wasn't a glass in the refrigerator containing roses for his dad.[3]

A cloak of love. A rose of gratitude.

Have you been given the first? Then take time to give the second.

CHAPTER THIRTEEN

THE RING OF BELIEF

Love . . . believes all things.

1 CORINTHIANS 13:4–7 NASB

When you speak truth, you are God's ambassador.

As you steward the money he gives, you are his business manager.

When you declare forgiveness, you are his priest.

As you stir the healing of the body or the soul, you are his physician.

And when you pray, he listens to you as a father listens to a son.

You have a voice in the household of God. He has given you his ring.

By all rules, Skinner was a dead man." With these words Arthur Bressi begins his retelling of the day he found his best friend in a World War II Japanese concentration camp. The two were high-school buddies. They grew up together in Mount Carmel, Pennsylvania—playing ball, skipping school, double-dating. Arthur and Skinner were inseparable. It made sense, then, that when one joined the army, the other would as well. They rode the same troopship to the Philippines. That's where they were separated. Skinner was on Bataan when it fell to the Japanese in 1942. Arthur Bressi was captured a month later.

Through the prison grapevine, Arthur learned the whereabouts of his friend. Skinner was near death in a nearby camp. Arthur volunteered for work detail in the hope that his company might pass through the other camp. One day they did.

Arthur requested and was given five minutes to find and speak to his friend. He knew to go to the sick side of the camp. It was divided into two sections—one for those expected to recover, the other for those given no hope. Those expected to die lived in a barracks called "zero ward." That's where Arthur found Skinner. He called his name, and out of the barracks walked the seventy-nine-pound shadow of the friend he had once known. As he writes:

> I stood at the wire fence of the Japanese prisoner-of-war camp on Luzon and watched my childhood buddy, caked in filth and racked with the pain of multiple diseases, totter toward me. He was dead; only his boisterous spirit hadn't left his body. I wanted to look away, but couldn't. His blue eyes, watery and dulled, locked on me and wouldn't let go.[1]

Malaria. Amebic dysentery. Pellagra. Scurvy. Beriberi. Skinner's body was a dormitory for tropical diseases. He couldn't eat. He couldn't drink. He was nearly gone.

Arthur didn't know what to do or say. His five minutes were nearly up. He began to finger the heavy knot of the handkerchief tied around his neck. In it was his high-school class ring. At the risk of punishment, he'd smuggled the ring into camp. Knowing the imminence of disease and the scarcity of treatment, he had been saving it to barter for medicine or food for himself. But one look at Skinner, and he knew he couldn't save it any longer.

As he told his friend good-bye, he slipped the ring through the fence into Skinner's frail hand and told him to "wheel and deal" with it. Skinner objected, but Arthur insisted. He turned and left, not knowing if he would ever see his friend alive again.

What kind of love would do something like that? It's one thing to give a gift to the healthy. It's one thing to share a treasure with the strong. But to give your best to the weak, to entrust your treasure to the dying—that's saying something. Indeed, that's saying something to them. "I believe in you," the gesture declares. "Don't despair. Don't give up. I believe in you." It's no wonder Paul included this phrase in his definition of love. "[Love] believes all things" (1 Cor. 13:7 NASB).

Do you know anyone who is standing on Skinner's side of the fence? If your child is having trouble in school, you do. If your husband struggles with depression or your wife has been laid off, you do. If you have a friend with cancer, if the class mocks your classmate, if your son doesn't make the squad, if you know anyone who is afraid or has failed or is frail, then you know someone who needs a ring of belief.

And, what's more, you can give them one. You may, by virtue of your words or ways, change that person's life forever.

Arthur did. Want to know what happened to Skinner? He took the ring and buried it in the barracks floor. The next day he took the biggest risk of his life. He approached the "kindest" of the guards and passed him the ring through the fence. *"Takai?"* the guard asked. "Is it valuable?" Skinner assured him that it was. The soldier smiled and slipped the ring into a pocket and left. A couple of days later he walked past Skinner and let a packet drop at his feet. Sulfanilamide tablets. A day later he returned with limes to combat the scurvy. Then came a new pair of pants and some canned beef. Within three weeks Skinner was on his feet. Within three months he was taken to the healthy side of the sick camp. In time he was able to work. As far as Skinner knew, he was the only American ever to leave the zero ward alive.

All because of a ring. All because someone believed in him.

I know what some of you are thinking. You're looking at Arthur and Skinner and wishing your situation were so easy. Skinner was a dying man but a good man, a good friend. How do you believe in someone who isn't? How do you believe in a man who cheats on you or an employee who swindles you? Does love ignore all things? I don't think so. This passage is not a call to naiveté or blindness. It is, however, a call for us to give to others what God has given us.

Skinner is not the only person to be given a ring, you know. You have one on your finger as well. Your heavenly Father placed it there. Jesus described the moment when he told the story of the prodigal son.

The tale involves a wealthy father and a willful son. The boy prematurely takes his inheritance and moves to Las Vegas and there wastes the money on slot machines and call girls. As fast as you can say "blackjack," he is broke. Too proud to go home, he gets a job sweeping horse stables at the racetrack. When he finds himself tasting some of their oats and thinking, *H'm, a dash of salt and this wouldn't be too bad,* he realizes enough is enough. It's time to go home. The gardener at his father's house does better than this. So off he goes, rehearsing his repentance speech every step of the way.

But the father has other ideas. "When he was still a great way off, his father saw him." The dad was looking for the boy, always craning his neck, ever hoping the boy would show, and when he did, when the father saw the familiar figure on the trail, he "had compassion, and ran and fell on his neck and kissed him."

We don't expect such a response. We expect crossed arms and a furrowed brow. At best a guarded handshake. At least a stern lecture. But the father gives none of these. Instead he gives gifts. "Bring out the best robe . . . a ring . . . sandals. . . . And bring the fatted calf . . . and let us eat and be merry" (Luke 15:11–23 NKJV). Robe, sandals, calf, and . . . Did you see it? A ring.

Before the boy has a chance to wash his hands, he has a ring to put on his finger. In Christ's day rings were more than gifts; they were symbols of delegated sovereignty. The bearer of the ring could speak on behalf of the giver. It was used to press a seal into soft wax to validate a transaction. The one who wore the ring conducted business in the name of the one who gave it.

Would you have done this? Would you have given this prodigal son power-of-attorney privileges over your affairs? Would you have entrusted him with a credit card? Would you have given him this ring?

Before you start questioning the wisdom of the father, remember, in this story you are the boy. When you came home to God, you were given authority to conduct business in your heavenly Father's name.

When you speak truth, you are God's ambassador.

As you steward the money he gives, you are his business manager.

When you declare forgiveness, you are his priest.

As you stir the healing of the body or the soul, you are his physician.

And when you pray, he listens to you as a father listens to a son. You have a voice in the household of God. He has given you his ring.

The only thing more remarkable than the giving of the ring is the fact that he hasn't taken it back! Weren't there times when he could have?

When you promoted your cause and forgot his. When you spoke lies and not truth. When you took his gifts and used them for personal gain. When you took the bus back to Las Vegas and found yourself seduced into the world of lights, luck, and long nights. Couldn't he have taken the ring? Absolutely. But did he? Do you still have a Bible? Are you still allowed to pray? Do you still have a dollar to manage or a skill to use? Then it appears that he still wants you to have the ring. It appears that he still believes in you!

He hasn't given up on you. He hasn't turned away. He hasn't walked out. He could have. Others would have. But he hasn't. God believes in you. And, I wonder, could you take some of the belief that he has in you and share it with someone else? Could you believe in someone?

There is such power in belief. Robert Schuller said, "I am not who I think I am. I am not who you think I am. I am who I think you think I am."[2] (You might want to read that twice.) Right or wrong, we define ourselves through other people's eyes. Tell me enough times that I'm stupid, and I'll believe you. Tell me enough times that I'm bright, and I might agree. Or as the German poet Goethe stated, "Treat a man as he appears to be, and you make him worse. But treat a man as if he were what he potentially could be, and you make him what he should be."

Robert Rosenthal demonstrated this in a famous classroom study. He and an elementary-school principal tested a group of students. They then mentioned to the students' teachers that some of the kids had done extremely well on the tests. The teachers were led to believe that five or six of the students had exceptional learning ability.

What the teachers did not know was that the names of the "exceptional" students had been chosen entirely at random. They were no different from the others, but since the teachers thought they were, the teachers treated them differently. By the end of the year the ones the teachers thought were brighter actually were! They scored ahead of their peers and gained as much as fifteen to twenty-seven IQ points. The teachers described the students as happier, more curious, more affectionate than the average, and having a better chance of success later in life. This was all due to the attitude of the teachers! The teachers thought the students were special, and the students lived up to their treatment. Rosenthal wrote:

> The explanation probably lies in the subtle interaction between teachers and pupils; tone of voice, facial expressions, touch and posture may be the means by which—often unwittingly—teachers communicate their expectations to their pupils. Such communication may help a child by changing his perception of himself.[3]

Arthur gave Skinner much more than a ring; he gave him a proclamation, a judgment that said, "You are worth this much to me! Your life is worth saving. Your life is worth living." He believed in him and, as a result, gave Skinner the means and the courage to save himself.

You and I have the privilege to do for others what Arthur did for Skinner and what God does for us. How do we show people that we believe in them?

Show up. Nothing takes the place of your presence. Letters are nice. Phone calls are special, but being there in the flesh sends a message.

After Albert Einstein's wife died, his sister, Maja, moved in to assist with the household affairs. For fourteen years she cared for him, allowing his valuable research to continue. In 1950 she suffered a stroke and lapsed into a coma. Thereafter, Einstein spent two hours every afternoon reading aloud to her from Plato.[4] She gave no sign of understanding his words, but he read anyway. If she understood anything by his gesture, she understood this—he believed that she was worth his time.

Do you believe in your kids? Then show up. Show up at their games. Show up at their plays. Show up at their recitals. It may not be possible to make each one, but it's sure worth the effort. An elder in our church supports me with his presence. Whenever I speak at an area congregation, he'll show up. Does nothing. Says little. Just takes a seat in a pew and smiles when we make eye contact. It means a lot to me. In fact, as I write the final draft of this book, he is one room away. Made the ninety-minute drive from his house to my hideout just to pray for me. Do you believe in your friends? Then show up. Show up at their graduations and weddings. Spend time with them. You want to bring out the best in someone? Then show up.

Listen up. You don't have to speak to encourage. The Bible says, "It is best to listen much, speak little" (James 1:19 TLB). We tend to speak much and listen little. There is a time to speak. But there is also a time to be quiet. That's what my father did. Dropping a fly ball may not be a big deal to most people, but if you are thirteen years old and have aspirations of the big leagues, it is a big deal. Not only was it my second error of the game, it allowed the winning run to score.

I didn't even go back to the dugout. I turned around in the middle of left field and climbed over the fence. I was halfway home when my dad found me. He didn't say a word. Just pulled over to the side of the road, leaned across the seat, and opened the passenger door. We didn't speak. We didn't need to. We both knew the world had come to an end. When we got home, I went straight to my room, and he went straight to the kitchen. Presently he appeared in front of me with cookies and milk. He took a seat on the bed, and we broke bread together. Somewhere in the dunking of the cookies I began to realize that life and my father's love would go on. In the economy of male adolescence, if you love the guy who drops the ball, then you really love him. My skill as a baseball player didn't improve, but my confidence in Dad's love did. Dad never said a word. But he did show up. He did listen up. To bring out the best in others, do the same, and then, when appropriate:

Speak up. Nathaniel Hawthorne came home heartbroken. He'd just been fired from his job in the custom house. His wife, rather than responding with anxiety, surprised him with joy. "Now you can write your book!"

He wasn't so positive. "And what shall we live on while I'm writing it?"

To his amazement she opened a drawer and revealed a wad of money she'd saved out of her housekeeping budget. "I always knew you were a man of genius," she told him. "I always knew you'd write a masterpiece."

She believed in her husband. And because she did, he wrote. And because he wrote, every library in America has a copy of *The Scarlet Letter* by Nathaniel Hawthorne.[5]

You have the power to change someone's life simply by the words that you speak. "Death and life are in the power of the tongue" (Prov. 18:21 NKJV). That's why Paul urges you and me to be careful. "When you talk, do not say harmful things, but say what people need—words that will help others become stronger" (Eph. 4:29).

Earlier I gave you a test for love. There's also a test for the tongue. Before you speak, ask: Will what I'm about to say help others become stronger? You have the ability, with your words, to make a person stronger. Your words are to their soul what a vitamin is to their body. If you had food and saw someone starving, would you not share it? If you had water and saw someone dying of thirst, would you not give it? Of course you would. Then won't you do the same for their hearts? Your words are food and water! Do not withhold encouragement from the discouraged. Do not keep affirmation from the beaten down! Speak words that make people stronger. Believe in them as God has believed in you.

You may save someone's life.

Arthur did. His friend Skinner survived. Both men returned home to Mount Carmel. One day, soon after their arrival, Skinner came over for a visit. He had a gift with him. A small box. Arthur knew immediately what it was. It was an exact copy of the high-school ring. After a lame attempt at humor—"Don't lose that; it cost me eighteen dollars"—he gave his friend a warm smile and said, "That ring, Artie . . . it saved my life."[6]

May someone say the same to you.

May you say the same to God.

CHAPTER
FOURTEEN

When You're Low on Hope

Love . . . always hopes.

1 Corinthians 13:7 NIV

Hope is an olive leaf—evidence of dry land after a flood. Proof to the dreamer that dreaming is worth the risk.

Water. All Noah can see is water. The evening sun sinks into it. The clouds are reflected in it. His boat is surrounded by it. Water. Water to the north. Water to the south. Water to the east. Water to the west. Water.

All Noah can see is water.

He can't remember when he's seen anything but. He and the boys had barely pushed the last hippo up the ramp when heaven opened a thousand fire hydrants. Within moments the boat was rocking, and for days the rain was pouring, and for weeks Noah has been wondering, *How long is this going to last?* For forty days it rained. For months they have floated. For months they have eaten the same food, smelled the same smell, and looked at the same faces. After a certain point you run out of things to say to each other.

Finally the boat bumped, and the rocking stopped. Mrs. Noah gave Mr. Noah a look, and Noah gave the hatch a shove and poked his head through. The hull of the ark was resting on ground, but the ground was still surrounded by water. "Noah," she yelled up at him, "what do you see?"

"Water."

He sent a raven on a scouting mission; it never returned. He sent a dove. It came back shivering and spent, having found no place to roost. Then, just this morning, he tried again. He pulled a dove out of the bowels of the ark and ascended the ladder. The morning sun caused them both to squint. As he kissed the breast of the bird, he felt a pounding heart. Had he put a hand on his chest, he would have felt another. With a prayer he let it go and watched until the bird was no bigger than a speck on a window.

All day he looked for the dove's return. In between chores he opened the hatch and searched. The boys wanted him to play a little pin the tail on the donkey, but he passed. He chose instead to climb into the crow's-nest and look. The wind lifted his gray hair. The sun warmed his weather-beaten face. But nothing lifted his heavy heart. He had seen nothing. Not in the morning. Not after lunch. Not later.

Now the sun is setting, and the sky is darkening, and he has come to look one final time, but all he sees is water. Water to the north. Water to the south. Water to the east. Water to the . . .

You know the feeling. You have stood where Noah stood. You've known your share of floods. Flooded by sorrow at the cemetery, stress at the office, anger at the disability in your body or the inability of your spouse. You've seen the floodwater rise, and you've likely seen the sun set on your hopes as well. You've been on Noah's boat.

And you've needed what Noah needed; you've needed some hope. You're not asking for a helicopter rescue, but the sound of one would be nice. Hope doesn't promise an instant solution but rather the possibility of an eventual one. Sometimes all we need is a little hope.

That's all Noah needed. And that's all Noah received.

The old sailor stares at the sun bisected by the horizon. Could hardly imagine a more beautiful sight. But he'd give this one and a hundred more for an acre of dry ground and a grove of grapes. Mrs. Noah's voice reminds him that dinner is on the table and he should lock the hatch, and he's just about to call it a day when he hears the cooing of the dove. Here is how the Bible describes the moment: "When the dove returned to him in the evening, there in its beak was a freshly plucked olive leaf!" (Gen. 8:11 NIV).

An olive leaf. Noah would have been happy to have the bird but to have the leaf! This leaf was more than foliage; this was promise. The bird brought more than a piece of a tree; it brought hope. For isn't that what hope is? Hope is an olive leaf—evidence of dry land after a flood. Proof to the dreamer that dreaming is worth the risk.

Don't we love the olive leaves of life?

"It appears the cancer may be in remission."

"I can help you with those finances."

"We'll get through this together."

What's more, don't we love the doves that bring them? When the father walks his son through his first broken heart, he gives him an olive leaf. When the wife of many years consoles the wife of a few months, when she tells her that conflicts come and all husbands are moody and these storms pass, you know what she is doing? She is giving an olive leaf.

We love olive leaves. And we love those who give them.

Perhaps that's the reason so many loved Jesus.

He stands near a woman who was yanked from a bed of promiscuity. She's still dizzy from the raid. A door slammed open, covers were pulled back, and the fraternity of moral police barged in. And now here she stands. Noah could see nothing but water. She can see nothing but anger. She has no hope.

But then Jesus speaks, "If any one of you is without sin, let him be the first to throw a stone at her" (John 8:7 NIV). Silence. Both the eyes and the rocks of the accusers hit the ground. Within moments they have left, and Jesus is alone with the woman. The dove of heaven offers her a leaf.

> "Woman, where are they? Has no one condemned you?"
>
> "No one, sir," she said.
>
> "Then neither do I condemn you," Jesus declared. "Go now and leave your life of sin." (vv. 10–11 NIV)

Into her shame-flooded world he brings a leaf of hope.

He does something similar for Martha. She is bobbing in a sea of sorrow. Her brother is dead. His body has been buried. And Jesus, well, Jesus is late. "If you had been here, my brother would not have died." Then I think she might have paused. "But I know that even now God will give you whatever you ask" (John 11:21–22 NIV). As Noah opened his hatch, so Martha opens her heart. As the dove brought a leaf, so Christ brings the same.

> "I am the resurrection and the life. He who believes in me will live, even though he dies; and whoever lives and believes in me will never die. Do you believe this?"
>
> "Yes, Lord," she told him, "I believe that you are the Christ, the Son of God, who was to come into the world." (John 11:25–27 NIV)

How could he get by with such words? Who was he to make such a claim? What qualified him to offer grace to one woman and a promise of resurrection to another? Simple. He had done what the dove did. He'd crossed the shoreline of the future land and journeyed among the trees. And from the grove of grace he plucked a leaf for the woman. And from the tree of life he pulled a sprig for Martha.

And from both he brings leaves to you. Grace and life. Forgiveness of sin. The defeat of death. This is the hope he gives. This is the hope we need.

In his book *The Grand Essentials,* Ben Patterson tells of an S-4 submarine that sank off the coast of Massachusetts. The entire crew was trapped.

Every effort was made to rescue the sailors, but every effort failed. Near the end of the ordeal, a deep-sea diver heard tapping on the steel wall of the sunken sub. As he placed his helmet against the vessel, he realized he was hearing a sailor tap out this question in Morse code: "Is there any hope?"[1]

To the guilty that ask that question, Jesus says, "Yes!"

To the death-struck that ask that question, Jesus answers, "Yes!"

To all the Noahs of the world, to all who search the horizon for a fleck of hope, he proclaims, "Yes!" And he comes. He comes as a dove. He comes bearing fruit from a distant land, from our future home. He comes with a leaf of hope.

Have you received yours? Don't think your ark is too isolated. Don't think your flood is too wide. Your toughest challenge is nothing more than bobby pins and rubber bands to God. *Bobby pins and rubber bands?*

My older sister used to give them to me when I was a child. I would ride my tricycle up and down the sidewalk, pretending that the bobby pins were keys and my trike was a truck. But one day I lost the "keys." Crisis! What was I going to do? My search yielded nothing but tears and fear. But when I confessed my mistake to my sister, she just smiled. Being a decade older, she had a better perspective.

God has a better perspective as well. With all due respect, our severest struggles are, in his view, nothing worse than lost bobby pins and rubber bands. He is not confounded, confused, or discouraged.

Receive his hope, won't you? Receive it because you need it. Receive it so you can share it.

What do you suppose Noah did with his? What do you think he did with the leaf? Did he throw it overboard and forget about it? Do you suppose he stuck it in his pocket and saved it for a scrapbook? Or do you think he let out a whoop and assembled the troops and passed it around like the Hope Diamond it was?

Certainly he whooped. That's what you do with hope. What do you do with olive leaves? You pass them around. You don't stick them in your pocket. You give them to the ones you love. Love always hopes. "Love . . . bears all things, believes all things, *hopes* all things, endures all things" (1 Cor. 13:4–7 NKJV, emphasis mine).

Love has hope in you.

The aspiring young author was in need of hope. More than one person had told him to give up. "Getting published is impossible," one mentor said. "Unless you are a national celebrity, publishers won't talk to you." Another warned, "Writing takes too much time. Besides, you don't want all your thoughts on paper."

Initially he listened. He agreed that writing was a waste of effort and turned his attention to other projects. But somehow the pen and pad were bourbon and Coke to the wordaholic. He'd rather write than read. So he wrote. How many nights did he pass on that couch in the corner of the apartment reshuffling his deck of verbs and nouns? And how many hours did his wife sit with him? He wordsmithing. She cross-stitching. Finally a manuscript was finished. Crude and laden with mistakes but finished.

She gave him the shove. "Send it out. What's the harm?"

So out it went. Mailed to fifteen different publishers. While the couple waited, he wrote. While he wrote, she stitched. Neither expecting much, both hoping everything. Responses began to fill the mailbox. "I'm sorry, but we don't accept unsolicited manuscripts." "We must return your work. Best of luck." "Our catalog doesn't have room for unpublished authors."

I still have those letters. Somewhere in a file. Finding them would take some time. Finding Denalyn's cross-stitch, however, would take none. To see it, all I do is lift my eyes from this monitor and look on the wall. "Of all those arts in which the wise excel, nature's chief masterpiece is writing well."

She gave it to me about the time the fifteenth letter arrived. A publisher had said yes. That letter is also framed. Which of the two is more meaningful? The gift from my wife or the letter from the publisher? The gift, hands down. For in giving the gift, Denalyn gave hope.

Love does that. Love extends an olive leaf to the loved one and says, "I have hope in you."

Love is just as quick to say, "I have hope *for* you."

You can say those words. You are a flood survivor. By God's grace you have found your way to dry land. You know what it's like to see the waters subside. And since you do, since you passed through a flood and lived to tell about it, you are qualified to give hope to someone else.

What? Can't think of any floods in your past? Let me jog your memory.

How about adolescence? Remember the torrent of the teenage years? Remember the hormones and hemlines? The puberty and pimples? Those were tough times. *Yeah,* you're thinking, *but you get through them.* That's exactly what teenagers need to hear you say. They need an olive leaf from a survivor.

So do young couples. It happens in every marriage. The honeymoon ends, and the river of romance becomes the river of reality, and they wonder if they will survive. You can tell them they will. You've been through it. Wasn't easy, but you survived. You and your spouse found dry land. Why don't you pluck an olive leaf and take it to an ark?

Are you a cancer survivor? Someone in the cancer ward needs to hear from you. Have you buried a spouse and lived to smile again? Then find the recently widowed and walk with them. Your experiences have deputized you into the dove brigade. You have an opportunity—yea, verily an obligation—to give hope to the arkbound.

Remember Paul's admonition?

> What a wonderful God we have—he is the Father of our Lord Jesus Christ, the source of every mercy, and the one who so wonderfully

> comforts and strengthens us in our hardships and trials. And why does he do this? So that when others are troubled, needing our sympathy and encouragement, we can pass on to them this same help and comfort God has given us. (2 Cor. 1:3–4 TLB)

Encourage those who are struggling. Don't know what to say? Then open your Bible. The olive leaf for the Christian is a verse of Scripture. "For everything that was written in the past was written to teach us, so that through endurance and the encouragement of the Scriptures we might have hope" (Rom. 15:4 NIV).

Do you have a Bible? Do you know a Noah? Then start passing out the leaves.

To the grief stricken: "God has said, 'Never will I leave you; never will I forsake you'" (Heb. 13:5 NIV).

To the guilt ridden: "There is now no condemnation for those who are in Christ Jesus" (Rom. 8:1 NIV).

To the jobless: "In all things God works for the good of those who love him" (Rom. 8:28 NIV).

To those who feel beyond God's grace: "Whoever believes in him shall not perish but have eternal life" (John 3:16 NIV).

Your Bible is a basket of leaves. Won't you share one? They have amazing impact. After receiving his, Noah was a changed man. "Then Noah knew that the water had receded from the earth" (Gen. 8:11 NIV). He went up the ladder with questions and came down the ladder with confidence.

What a difference one leaf makes.

CHAPTER FIFTEEN

He Could Have Given Up

Love . . . endures all things.

1 Corinthians 13:4–7 nasb

At any step along the way he could have called it quits. . . .

When he saw the dirt floor of his Nazareth house.

When Joseph gave him a chore to do.

When his fellow students were dozing off

during the reading of the Torah, his Torah.

When the neighbor took his name in vain.

When the lazy farmer blamed his poor crop on God.

At any point Jesus could have said, "That's it! That's enough!

I'm going home." But he didn't.

He didn't, because he is love.

He could have given up. No one would have known otherwise. Jesus could have given up.

One look at the womb could have discouraged him. God is as unbridled as the air and limitless as the sky. Would he reduce his world to the belly of a girl for nine months?

And nine months? There is another reason to quit. Heaven has no months. Heaven has no time. Or, perhaps better said, heaven has all the time. It's we who are running out. Ours passes so quickly that we measure it by the second. Wouldn't Christ rather stay on the other side of the ridge of time?

He could have. He could have given up. If not, at least he could have stopped short. Did he have to become *flesh*? How about becoming light? Here is an idea. Heaven could open, and Christ could fall on the earth in the form of a white light. And then in the light there could be a voice, a booming, thundering, teeth-shaking voice. Toss in a gust of wind and the angels for background vocals, and the whole world notices!

As things turned out, when he came, hardly anyone noticed. Bethlehem held no parade. The village offered no banquet. You'd think a holiday would have been appropriate. At least a few streamers for the stable.

And the stable. Is that not yet another reason for Christ to back out? Stables are smelly, dirty. Stables have no linoleum floors or oxygen tanks. How are they going to cut the umbilical cord? And who is going to cut the umbilical cord? Joseph? A small-time carpenter from a one-camel town? Is there not a better father for God? Someone with an education, a pedigree. Someone with a bit of clout? This fellow couldn't even swing a room at the hotel. You think he's got what it takes to be the father to the Maker of the universe?

Jesus could have given up. Imagine the change he had to make, the distance he had to travel. What would it be like to become flesh?

This question surfaced as I was golfing recently. Waiting my turn to putt, I squatted down to clean my ball and noticed a mountain of ants beside it. Must have been dozens of them, all over each other. A pyramid of motion at least half an inch tall.

I don't know what you think when you see ants on a green as you are waiting to putt. But here is what I thought: *Why are you guys all bunched up? You have the whole green. Why, the entire golf course is yours to spread out in.* Then it occurred to me. These ants are nervous. Who could blame them? They live under a constant meteor shower. Every few minutes a dimpled orb comes crashing into their world. *Bam! Bam! Bam!* Just when the bombing stops, the mallet-swinging giants arrive. If you survive their feet and sticks, they roll a meteor at you. A golf green is no place for an ant.

So I tried to help them. Leaning down where they could hear me, I invited, "Come on, follow me. We'll find a nice spot in the rough. I know it well." Not one looked in my direction. "Hey, ants!" Still no reply. Then I realized, *I don't speak their language.* I don't speak Ant. Pretty fluent in the idiom of Uncle, but I don't speak Ant.

So what could I do to reach them? Only one thing. I needed to become an ant. Go from six feet two inches to teeny-weeny. From 200-plus pounds to tenths of an ounce. Swap my big world for their tiny one. Give up burgers and start eating grass. "No thanks," I said. Besides, it was my turn to putt.

Love goes the distance . . . and Christ traveled from limitless eternity to be confined by time in order to become one of us. He didn't have to. He could have given up. At any step along the way he could have called it quits.

When he saw the size of the womb, he could have stopped.

When he saw how tiny his hand would be, how soft his voice would be, how hungry his tummy would be, he could have stopped. At the first whiff of the stinky stable, at the first gust of cold air. The first time he scraped his knee or blew his nose or tasted burnt bagels, he could have turned and walked out.

When he saw the dirt floor of his Nazareth house. When Joseph gave him a chore to do. When his fellow students were dozing off during the reading of the Torah, his Torah. When the neighbor took his name in vain. When the lazy farmer blamed his poor crop on God. At any point Jesus could have said, "That's it! That's enough! I'm going home." But he didn't.

He didn't, because he is love. And "love . . . endures all things" (1 Cor. 13:4–7 NKJV). He endured the distance. What's more, he endured the resistance.

"The Word became flesh and made his dwelling among us. We have seen his glory" (John 1:14 NIV).

"We have seen his glory." What did John mean by those words? Could it be that he saw in Christ flashes of heaven? Occasional, yet unforgettable, gasoline-on-the-fire flashes. Could it be that Christ would occasionally open his cape of humanity and allow a ray of glory to spill forth?

One of the regular attendees of our congregation is David Robinson. David is a big man. He stands seven feet two inches and weighs 235 pounds. His body fat is 6 percent. (I have that much in one thigh.) He is an NBA MVP, an NBA champion, and an NBA All-Star. But David is much more. He is a lover of God and a lover of kids. For that reason, the following scene won't be hard to imagine.

Let's say big-hearted David agrees to a game of one-on-one with a six-year-old girl. Just for the fun of it. She asks. He agrees. The two are on the same court, playing with the same ball, playing the same game, but everyone knows this isn't the same David. This is a mild David. A restrained David. A reserved David. How he plays against Shaq and how he plays against the girl are not the same.

Suppose some bully starts making fun of the little girl. He even comes out of the stands and taunts her. Calls her names and steals the ball from her. He throws it back so hard she falls over. You know what David might do? David might be David for a few moments. He might just take the dare and take the bully and dunk him like a donut.

For just a moment, the real David might take over.[1]

There were moments when the real Jesus did. Most of the time he was restrained. But then there were moments when he opened the cape. There were moments when he had all he could take of the bully from hell.

When the storm scared his followers, he stood and opened the cape: "Be still!" When death broke the hearts of his friends, he stepped into the cemetery and opened the cape: "Come forth!" When disease stole the joy of his children, he touched the leper with power: "Be healed!"

"For a moment"—John must have sighed when he wrote the words—"we beheld his glory."

A few, like John, were stunned by the sight. Others, however, missed it. They missed the glory of God. For whatever reason, they missed it. How did they react to his presence?

"They laughed at him" (Matt. 9:24 NIV).

"Many of them said, 'He is demon-possessed and raving mad. Why listen to him?'" (John 10:20 NIV).

They "hurled insults at him, shaking their heads" (Mark 15:29 NIV).

"The Pharisees, who loved money, heard all this and were sneering at Jesus" (Luke 16:14 NIV).

Isaiah prophesied the reception like this: "He was despised and rejected by men" (Isa. 53:3 NIV).

John summarized the rejection with these words: "He was in the world, and though the world was made through him, the world did not recognize him. He came to that which was his own, but his own did not receive him" (John 1:10–11 NIV).

How did Christ endure treatment like that? At any point he could have said, "I quit. I've had enough." Why didn't he? What kept him from giving up?

I wonder if Lee Ielpi understands the answer. He is a retired firefighter, a New York City firefighter. He gave twenty-six years to the city. But on September 11, 2001, he gave much more. He gave his son. Jonathan Ielpi was a fireman as well. When the Twin Towers fell, he was there.

Firefighters are a loyal clan. When one perishes in the line of duty, the body is left where it is until a firefighter who knows the person can come and quite literally pick it up. Lee made the discovery of his son's body his personal mission. He dug daily with dozens of others at the sixteen-acre graveyard. On Tuesday, December 11, three months after the disaster, his son was found. And Lee was there to carry him out.[2]

He didn't give up. The father didn't quit. He refused to turn and leave. Why? Because his love for his son was greater than the pain of the search. Can't the same be said about Christ? Why didn't he quit? Because the love for his children was greater than the pain of the journey. He came to pull you out. Your world had collapsed. That's why he came. You were dead, dead in sin. That's why he came. He loves you. That's why he came.

That's why he endured the distance between us. "Love . . . endures *all things.*"

That's why he endured the resistance from us. "Love . . . endures *all things.*"

That's why he went the final step of the incarnation: "God made him who had no sin to be sin for us, so that in him we might become the righteousness of God" (2 Cor. 5:21 NIV).

Why did Jesus do that? There is only one answer. And that answer has one word. Love. And the love of Christ "bears all things, believes all things, hopes all things, endures all things" (1 Cor. 13:7 NKJV).

Think about that for a moment. Drink from that for a moment. Drink deeply. Don't just sip or nip. It's time to gulp. It's time to let his love cover all things in your life. All secrets. All hurts. All hours of evil, minutes of worry.

The mornings you awoke in the bed of a stranger? His love will cover that. The years you peddled prejudice and pride? His love will cover that. Every promise broken, drug taken, penny stolen. Every cross word, cuss word, and harsh word. His love covers all things.

Let it. Discover along with the psalmist: "He . . . loads me with love and mercy" (Ps. 103:4). Picture a giant dump truck full of love. There you are behind it. God lifts the bed until the love starts to slide. Slowly at first, then down, down, down until you are hidden, buried, covered in his love.

"Hey, where are you?" someone asks.

"In here, covered in love."

Let his love cover all things.

Do it for his sake. To the glory of his name.

Do it for your sake. For the peace of your heart.

And do it for their sake. For the people in your life. Let his love fall on you so yours can fall on them.

CHAPTER SIXTEEN

UNFAILING LOVE

Love never fails.

1 CORINTHIANS 13:8 NIV

God loves you simply because He has chosen to do so.

He loves you when you don't feel lovely.

He loves you when no one else loves you.

Others may abandon you, divorce you, and ignore you,

but God will love you.

Always.

No matter what.

My friend Mike tells how his three-year-old daughter, Rachel, lost her balance and hit her head against the corner of an electric space heater. After a short cry, she blacked out. Her parents rushed her to the hospital, where the tests revealed a skull fracture.

Pretty traumatic for a child. Pretty traumatic for Mom and Dad. Rachel was kept overnight for observation and then sent home. She spent a couple of days understandably quiet. But Mike knew she was okay the morning he heard her talking to herself. He was still in bed, and she was down the hall in her room. "Bear? Doggie? Sheep? Baby? Ruff-ruff?" Mike smiled. She was calling roll in her crib, making sure her friends were all present. After all, she'd been through quite an ordeal, and she wanted to make sure things were in order.

A few moments of silence passed before she continued. "Eyes? Nose? Hair? Hand? Piggy?" Having verified the presence of her friends, Rachel was now taking inventory of herself.

Suppose we follow her lead? Before bringing this book to a close, let's take inventory. Let's take stock of our relationships. Think for a moment about the people in your world. If you want to write a few names in the margin, go ahead. Your husband, wife, kids, teachers, friends, parents, carpool buddies, coworkers. Give it some thought. Who populates your circle of the world?

As names surface, let me whisper a reminder. Aren't they valuable? Aren't they essential? Aren't those relationships worth whatever it takes to keep them healthy? Granted, people can be difficult. But still, what's more important than people?

Think of it this way. When you are in the final days of your life, what will you want? When death extends its hands to you, where will you turn for comfort? Will you hug that college degree in the walnut frame? Will you ask to be carried to the garage so you can sit in your car? Will you find comfort in rereading your financial statement? Of course not. What will matter then will be people. If relationships will matter most then, shouldn't they matter most now?

So what can you do to strengthen them? Following Rachel's example would be a good start. She inventoried her hands and hair; let's take inventory of our hearts. Am I living in the overflow of God's love? How well do I love the people in my life? Does the way I treat people reflect the way God has treated me?

Loving people isn't always easy. In fact, this book has been a challenging one for some of you. You've been forced to think again about some of the people in your life whom you find hard to love. This is serious business. It's not easy to love those who have been the source of heartache, abuse, rejection, or loneliness. Some of you wonder how you could ever love the people who have caused you such pain. So what can you do?

Conventional wisdom says that a lack of love implies a lack of effort, so we try harder, dig deeper, strain more.

But could a lack of love imply something else? Could we be skipping a step? An essential step? Could it be that we are trying to give what we don't have? Are we forgetting to receive first?

The woman in Capernaum didn't forget. Remember her from the first chapter? Remember how she lavished love on Christ? Bathing his feet with tears. Drying his feet with her hair. If love were a waterfall, she'd be a Niagara.

And Simon, well, Simon was a Sahara. Dry. Parched. Hard. His arid heart surprises us. He was the churchgoer, the pastor, the seminarian. She, on the other hand, was the town slut. He'd forgotten more Bible than she ever knew. But she'd discovered one truth Simon had somehow missed: God's love has no limits.

God's love meets the standard of our final passage. "Love," Paul says, "never fails" (1 Cor. 13:8 NIV).

The verb Paul uses for the word *fail* is used elsewhere to describe the demise of a flower as it falls to the ground, withers, and decays. It carries the meaning of death and abolishment. God's love, says the apostle, will never fall to the ground, wither, and decay. By its nature, it is permanent. It is never abolished.

Love "will last forever" (NLT).

It "never dies" (MSG).

It "never ends" (RSV).

Love "is eternal" (TEV).

God's love "will never come to an end" (NEB).

Love never fails.

Governments will fail, but God's love will last. Crowns are temporary, but love is eternal. Your money will run out, but his love never will.

How could God have a love like this? No one has unfailing love. No person can love with perfection. You're right. No person can. But God is not a person. Unlike our love, his never fails. His love is immensely different from ours.

Our love depends on the receiver of the love. Let a thousand people pass before us, and we will not feel the same about each. Our love will be regulated by their appearance, by their personalities. Even when we find a few people we like, our feelings will fluctuate. How they treat us will affect how we love them. The receiver regulates our love.

Not so with the love of God. We have no thermostatic impact on his love for us. The love of God is born from within him, not from what he finds in us. His love is uncaused and spontaneous. As Charles Wesley said, "He hath loved us. He hath loved us. Because he would love."[1]

Does he love us because of our goodness? Because of our kindness? Because of our great faith? No, he loves us because of *his* goodness, kindness, and great faith. John says it like this: "This is love: not that we loved God, but that he loved us" (1 John 4:10 NIV).

Doesn't this thought comfort you? God's love does not hinge on yours. The abundance of your love does not increase his. The lack of your love does not diminish his. Your goodness does not enhance his love, nor does your weakness dilute it. What Moses said to Israel is what God says to us:

> The LORD did not choose you and lavish his love on you because you were larger or greater than other nations, for you were the smallest of all nations! It was simply because the LORD loves you. (Deut. 7:7–8 NLT)

God loves you simply because he has chosen to do so.

He loves you when you don't feel lovely.

He loves you when no one else loves you. Others may abandon you, divorce you, and ignore you, but God will love you. Always. No matter what.

This is his sentiment: "I'll call nobodies and make them somebodies; I'll call the unloved and make them beloved" (Rom. 9:25 MSG).

This is his promise. "I have loved you, my people, with an everlasting love. With unfailing love I have drawn you to myself" (Jer. 31:3 NLT).

Do you know what else that means? You have a deep aquifer of love from which to draw. When you find it hard to love, then you need a drink! Drink deeply! Drink daily!

Don't forget, love is a fruit. Step into the orchard of God's work, and what is the first fruit you see? "*Love,* joy, peace, patience, kindness, goodness, faithfulness, gentleness and self-control" (Gal. 5:22 NIV, emphasis mine).

Love is a fruit. A fruit of whom? Of your hard work? Of your deep faith? Of your rigorous resolve? No. Love is a fruit of the Spirit of God. "The Spirit produces the fruit" (Gal. 5:22).

And, this is so important, you are a branch on the vine of God. "I am the vine, and you are the branches" (John 15:5). Need a refresher course on how vines function? What is the role of the branch in the bearing of fruit? Branches don't exert a lot of energy. You never hear of gardeners treating branches for exhaustion. Branches don't attend clinics on stress management. Nor do they groan and grunt: "I've got to get this grape out. I've got to get this grape out. I'm going to bear this grape if it kills me!"

No, the branch does none of that. The branch has one job—to receive nourishment from the vine. And you have one job—to receive nourishment from Jesus. "I am the Vine, you are the branches. When you're joined with me and I with you, the relation intimate and organic, the harvest is sure to be abundant. Separated, you can't produce a thing" (John 15:5 MSG).

Our Lord gets no argument from us on that last line, does he? We have learned the hard way—apart from him we can't produce a thing. Don't you think it's time we learn what happens if we stay attached?

His job is to bear fruit. Our job is to stay put. The more tightly we are attached to Jesus, the more purely his love can pass through us. And oh, what a love it is! Patient. Kind. Does not envy. Does not boast. Is not proud.

Let's rewrite 1 Corinthians 13:4–8 one more time. Not with your name or Jesus' name but with both. Read it aloud with your name in the blank, and see what you think.

> Christ in _______ is patient, Christ in ______ is kind. Christ in ____ does not envy, Christ in _____ does not boast, Christ in _____ is not proud. Christ in _____ is not rude, Christ in _____ is not self-seeking, Christ in _____ is not easily angered, Christ in _____ keeps no record of wrongs. Christ in ______ does not delight in evil but rejoices with the truth. Christ in _____ always protects, always trusts, always hopes, always perseveres. Christ in _____ never fails.

Will we ever love like that? Will we ever love perfectly? No. This side of heaven only God will. But we will love better than we have.

When kindness comes grudgingly, we'll remember his kindness to us and ask him to make us more kind. When patience is scarce, we'll thank him for his and ask him to make us more patient. When it's hard to forgive, we won't list all the times we've been given grief. Rather, we'll list all the times we've been given grace and pray to become more forgiving. We will receive first so we can give later. We will drink deeply from heaven's endless love. And when we do, we will discover a love worth giving.

Discussion Guide

A Love Worth Giving

by Steve Halliday

CHAPTER ONE

THE 7:47 PRINCIPLE

Love Remembered

1. We can't give what we've never received. If we've never received love, how can we love others?
   - A. Do you agree that we can't give what we haven't received? Explain.
   - B. How does someone "receive" love? How does someone "refuse" love?
   - C. Have you received God's love? Explain.

2. Our relationships need more than a social gesture. Some of our spouses need a foot washing. A few of our friends need a flood of tears. Our children need to be covered in the oil of our love.
   - A. If you are married, what does your spouse need today? What does your closest friend need? If you have children, what do they need?
   - B. How can you cover others "in the oil" of your love?
   - C. How do you need to be covered "in the oil" of others' love?

3. How can we love as God loves? We want to. We long to. But how can we? By living loved. By following the 7:47 Principle: Receive first, love second.
   - A. How does God love *you?*
   - B. What does the phrase "living loved" mean to you? Are you living loved? Explain.
   - C. How do you receive God's love on a day-to-day basis?

Love Deepened

1. Read Luke 7:36–50.
   A. In your own words, describe the scene depicted here. What happened?
   B. What lesson did Jesus want Simon to learn? How did he communicate this lesson?
   C. What principle did Jesus develop in verse 47? How does this principle relate to you? Explain.

2. Read 1 John 4:9–11.
   A. What does God's love look like?
   B. How is our love supposed to take its cue from God?
   C. Why did God love us? Why are we supposed to love others?

3. Read Ephesians 4:32–5:2.
   A. What three commands does God give us in verse 32? What example does he provide to show *how* we are to obey these commands?
   B. What command does God give us in verse 1? In what way can we obey this command? What gives us the ability to obey this command, according to the second part of the verse?
   C. What command does God give us in verse 2? What example are we given? How can we practically follow this example?

Love Given

1. Think of the person closest to you (whether spouse, friend, child, parent, etc.). Periodically throughout one entire day, take a little notepad, and list the reasons why this person is so close to you. Why do you love him or her? Then at the end of the day, make another list

by responding to the question "How can I do a better job of showing love to this person?" Last, before the end of the week, begin doing at least one of the things you wrote on the second list.

2. What volunteer opportunities are available in your neighborhood or city? Carve out some time in the next month to serve others in an arena unfamiliar to you. How can you show these people the love of God?

CHAPTER TWO

LOVE'S FLAGSHIP

Love Remembered

1. Paul presents patience as the premiere expression of love. Positioned at the head of the apostle's Love Armada—a boat-length or two in front of kindness, courtesy, and forgiveness—is the flagship known as patience.
   A. Have you ever thought of patience as "the premiere expression of love"? Explain.
   B. Why do you think Paul positioned patience at the head of his Love Armada? What is it about patience that best shows love?
   C. Do you consider yourself a patient person? Explain.
   D. How does God try to build your patience?

2. Patience is more than a virtue for long lines and slow waiters. Patience is the red carpet upon which God's grace approaches us.
   A. In what way is patience the red carpet upon which God's grace approaches us?
   B. How is God patient with us? How is God patient with *you*?
   C. How are grace and patience related? How do they play off of one another?

3. How infiltrated are you with God's patience? You've heard about it. Read about it. Perhaps underlined Bible passages regarding it. But have you received it? The proof is in your patience.

A. What does it mean to "receive" God's patience? Have you received it? Explain.
B. Thus far in your life, what have you learned in God's Word about patience? Do you struggle with any of these lessons? Explain.
C. Would others say that you are a patient person? Explain.

Love Deepened

1. Read Romans 2:1–4.
   A. How does a tendency to judge others reveal a lack of understanding about God's patience? Do you struggle with judging others? Explain.
   B. How is it possible to show contempt for the riches of God's kindness (v. 4)?
   C. How does God's patience lead us toward repentance?
   D. Where would you be if God were not patient with you? Why is it important to remember this when you deal with others?

2. Read 2 Peter 3:8–9.
   A. What does Peter want to make sure we don't forget (v. 8)? Why is this so important?
   B. Why do we sometimes think the Lord is slow in keeping his promise?
   C. Why is God patient with us (v. 9)? What is his motivation?
   D. How can we model God's patience in dealing with others?

3. Read Matthew 18:21–35.
   A. What prompted Jesus to tell this story? What do you think was behind the question to Jesus?
   B. Retell the story in your own words.

C. What was the first servant's problem? What was the second servant's problem?

D. What is the main point of Jesus' story? How does it affect you? Explain.

E. How does Jesus' story answer Peter's question in verse 21? How does this relate to patience?

Love Given

1. Sit down with a sheet of paper and a pen or pencil, and write out your answers to the following questions: How has God shown you patience in the past week? How has he shown you patience in the past year? Did he show patience in bringing you to salvation? If so, how? How have you responded to his patience?

2. With whom are you most likely to display impatience? A spouse? A son or a daughter? A coworker? A neighbor? Spend some protracted time this week praying about your impatience toward this person. Ask God to show you specifically what you can do to show patience to this person. Then monitor your behavior over the next month, and invite God to encourage and discipline you as needed.

CHAPTER THREE

Your Kindness Quotient

Love Remembered

1. The kindness of Jesus. We are quick to think of his power, his passion, and his devotion. But those near him knew and know God comes cloaked in kindness.
   A. Do you usually think of kindness when you ponder Jesus? Explain.
   B. What does kindness mean to you? How have people shown you kindness?
   C. What does it mean to be "cloaked" in kindness? What does this image suggest to you?

2. Isn't kindness good *and* good for you? Pleasant *and* practical? Kindness not only says good morning, kindness makes the coffee.
   A. How has the kindness of others ministered to you?
   B. How is kindness both pleasant and practical?
   C. Why can genuine kindness never be inactive? Why must it always be doing *something*?

3. How kind are you? What is your kindness quotient? When was the last time you did something kind for someone in your family—e.g., got a blanket, cleaned off the table, prepared the coffee—without being asked?
   A. How would you answer each of these questions?

B. Would others use the word *kind* to describe you? Explain, especially if they see you differently than you see yourself.

Love Deepened

1. Read Titus 3:3–7.
   A. How does Paul describe those who haven't yet received God's love (v. 3)?
   B. In what way did the kindness of God appear (v. 4)? What form did this kindness take?
   C. How does God's kindness connect to our salvation? What part did God's kindness play in his offer of salvation?
   D. What concrete images does Paul give us of God's kindness in this passage? What did God's kindness *do*?

2. Read Luke 6:27–36.
   A. List the various commands Jesus gives us in this passage.
   B. How does kindness relate to all of these commands?
   C. Why does Jesus tell us that God "is kind to the ungrateful and wicked" (v. 35 NIV)? What effect is that statement supposed to have upon us?
   D. In what way does Jesus connect God's kindness to the mercy we are to show others (vv. 34–35)?

3. Read Colossians 3:12–14.
   A. With what are we told to clothe ourselves?
   B. List the practical ways in which this passage fleshes out kindness. What does kindness do? What does it not do?

Love Given

1. Read through the Gospel of your choice, noting instances in which

Jesus did something kind. How did the Master show God's kindness? How can we imitate his work?

2. Jesus tells us to be kind even to those who mistreat us. Who in your sphere of influence has been unkind to you? What act of kindness could you show this person this week? Plan such an act, and then follow through with it. Pray that God will use it to touch this person, but even if the person doesn't respond in kind, determine that you will continue to reflect God's kindness regardless.

CHAPTER FOUR

INFLAMED

Love Remembered

1. What is born in innocence is deadly in adolescence. Left untended, fire consumes all that is consumable.
   A. What does envy look like in innocence? How is it deadly in adolescence?
   B. How does envy consume those it touches?
   C. In what situations are you most likely to struggle with envy? How do you deal with it?

2. God withholds what we desire in order to give us what we need.
   A. What desires has God so far withheld from you? Why do you think he has done so?
   B. Describe a time when God withheld a personal desire in order to meet a personal need.
   C. What do you think you most need today? Explain.

3. Your Father . . . offers authentic love. His devotion is the real deal. But he won't give you the genuine until you surrender the imitations.
   A. How would you describe God's authentic love, the "real deal"? How have you experienced it?
   B. What imitations have you held on to in the past?
   C. How can you surrender the imitations? What does this entail?

Love Deepened

1. Read Psalm 37:1–3.
   A. Why are we tempted to fret because of evil men and to grow envious because of those who do wrong?
   B. In this passage how does David suggest we fight envy? Of what are we to remind ourselves?
   C. In what way is trust an antidote to envy?

2. Read Proverbs 14:30.
   A. Describe a heart at peace. What does it look like? How does such a heart give "life to the body"?
   B. How does envy "rot the bones"? What does this mean?
   C. How does one get a heart at peace and avoid envy-rotted bones?

3. Read James 4:1–6.
   A. According to James, what causes fights and quarrels among us (v. 1)?
   B. Describe a time you witnessed the destructive power of envy in a relationship.
   C. What is the antidote to envy and the quarrels it produces?
   D. James says the Spirit envies intensely (v. 5)—and this is a good thing. In what sense does he envy? How can this kind of divine envy be good but our kind of envy be bad?

Love Given

1. Try to come at envy from another direction. What things do you have (talents, resources, possessions, relationships) that others might envy? Be as honest as possible: Have you ever flaunted these things to inflame the envy of others? If so, what can you do to lessen the possibility that you might make others envious?

CHAPTER FIVE

God's "No Pecking" Zone

Love Remembered

1. Would you do what Jesus did? He swapped a spotless castle for a grimy stable. He exchanged the worship of angels for the company of killers. He could hold the universe in his palm but gave it up to float in the womb of a maiden.
   A. Answer the previous question, then explain your answer.
   B. What do you think was hardest for Jesus to give up? Why?
   C. If you had been Jesus, what do you think you would have done differently? Explain.

2. What's more important to you—that the work be done or that you be seen? When a brother or sister is honored, are you joyful or jealous?
   A. Answer the previous questions. Why did you answer as you did?
   B. Describe the last time you did an excellent job but kept completely silent about it.
   C. Would you consider yourself a humble person? Explain.

3. True humility is not thinking lowly of yourself but thinking accurately of yourself. The humble heart does not say, "I can't do anything." But rather, "I can't do everything. I know my part and am happy to do it."
   A. Do you know your strengths as well as your weaknesses? Explain.
   B. Are you happy to do your part? Explain.

   C. Who is the most humble person you know? Describe him or her. What makes him or her so humble?

Love Deepened

1. Read Matthew 23:5–12.
   A. How do verses 5–7 paint a picture of showboating? What's so wrong with this picture?
   B. How does Jesus tell us to combat such showboating (vv. 8–11)?
   C. How can a servant be great?
   D. What does Jesus promise to do for the humble? What does he promise to do for those who exalt themselves (v. 12)?

2. Read Philippians 2:3–11.
   A. What general principle does Paul give us in verse 3? How is this principle to be lived out practically?
   B. How does verse 4 give us a practical way to show humility? How could you put this into practice to a greater degree in your own life?
   C. How did Jesus exemplify a lifestyle of humility?
   D. How will God reward Jesus for his humility? In what way does this provide an incentive for us?

3. Read Romans 12:3–10.
   A. How are we to think of ourselves (v. 3)? What does this mean?
   B. How does remembering the Christian body help us to remain humble (vv. 4–8)?
   C. How are we to honor one another above ourselves (v. 10)? What might this entail for you personally?

Love Given

1. Plan an "Honor Day." Give your time to someone else: an older person, a child, an invalid. Demonstrate Christlike love to that person by helping him or her feel special. At the end of the day, journal all you've learned about serving and loving.

2. Hold a little foot-washing ceremony. Go to a relative or friend, read John 13:1–17 aloud, and then reenact the scene. And be sure your servanthood stays with you beyond the reenactment!

CHAPTER SIX

A Call to Common Courtesy

Love Remembered

1. When defining what love is not, Paul put rudeness on the list.
   A. What's the rudest thing anyone has ever done to you?
   B. Describe the rudest thing you've ever done to someone else.
   C. How do you feel when someone is rude to you? How do you usually respond?

2. God calls us to a higher, more noble concern. Not "What are my rights?" but "What is loving?"
   A. Be honest: Do you usually think first about your rights or about what is most loving?
   B. What does courtesy have to do with love?
   C. Describe the most loving thing you did this week.

3. Does not the groom cherish the bride? Respect the bride? Honor the bride? Let Christ do what he longs to do. For as you receive his love, you'll find it easier to give yours.
   A. Why are a bride and groom almost never rude to one another during the wedding ceremony? What changes in the marriage?
   B. In what environments are you most tempted to be rude? How can you overcome the temptation?

Love Deepened

1. Read Luke 4:22.
   A. Why did everyone (at first) speak well of Jesus?
   B. What kind of words came from Jesus' lips?
   C. How are such words the opposite of rude?

2. Read Colossians 4:6.
   A. How can our conversation be full of grace?
   B. What does it mean to "season" our words "with salt"?
   C. What is the purpose of this grace and seasoning in our speech?

3. Read Romans 12:16.
   A. What does "living in harmony" say about God's people?
   B. What is the relationship between pride and rudeness?
   C. Why should we be willing to associate with people of low position?
   D. How can we keep from becoming conceited?

Love Given

1. Sit down with a loved one, and watch a favorite movie. Watch especially for scenes where someone is rude. What happened in the story because of the rude behavior? What might have happened had the behavior not occurred? How would a humble spirit have changed things?

2. All of us will, at some point, be subjected to rude behavior. Be proactive and think ahead of time how you will react to it. What stock phrases might you use to defuse the situation? How can you prepare yourself to infuse the incident with God's grace?

CHAPTER SEVEN

GETTING THE "I" OUT OF YOUR EYE

Love Remembered

1. Selfishness is an obsession with self that excludes others, hurting everyone.
   A. How would you describe selfishness?
   B. Describe a time when someone's selfishness hurt you badly.
   C. Describe a time when your selfishness hurt someone else.

2. Desire success? Fine. Just don't hurt others in achieving it. Wish to look nice? That's okay. Just don't do so by making others look bad.
   A. How do we sometimes hurt others in trying to achieve success? How is this selfish?
   B. How do we try to make ourselves look nice by making others look bad?
   C. How would you respond to someone who said, "Well, if I don't take care of myself, who will?"

3. What's the cure for selfishness? Get your self out of your eye by getting your eye off your self. Quit staring at that little self, and focus on your great Savior.
   A. What do you think of this cure for selfishness?
   B. How can one put this cure into action, practically speaking? How can it become more than a nice set of words?

Love Deepened

1. Read James 3:13–16.
   A. How would James define "selfish ambition"?
   B. What does it accomplish? To what does it lead? From where does it come?
   C. How can we combat selfish ambition?

2. Read Psalm 119:36.
   A. What prayer does the psalmist offer in this verse?
   B. How can God's Word help to turn us away from selfish gain?
   C. How do you use the Bible to combat selfishness?

3. Read Romans 2:7–8.
   A. To what group of people will God give eternal life (v. 7)?
   B. What awaits those who are self-seeking (v. 8)?
   C. Why is there such a difference between these two groups?

Love Given

1. In what area of life are you tempted to be most selfish? Since selfishness never goes away by itself, you need to put together a plan to kill it. How can you most effectively confront your self-seeking tendencies? Think about this on your own, then discuss your plan with the person closest to you. Together try to put your plan into action.

2. A good way to combat selfishness is to get into the habit of giving to others. Rather than giving something you don't need or use, select something personal and meaningful to share with someone who is lonely or overlooked.

CHAPTER EIGHT

THE HEADWATERS OF ANGER

Love Remembered

1. The fire of anger has many logs, but according to biblical accounts, the thickest and the hottest block of wood is rejection.
   A. What makes you angry?
   B. Does rejection make you angry? Explain.
   C. Why does rejection anger most of us?

2. If rejection causes anger, wouldn't acceptance cure it? If rejection by heaven makes you mad at others, wouldn't acceptance from heaven stir your love for them?
   A. Does acceptance always cure anger? Explain.
   B. How does heaven's acceptance prompt us to show love toward others?
   C. If this statement is true, then why do many Christians seem to be so angry? Why are many believers lacking in love?

3. Rejections are like speed bumps on the road. They come with the journey. . . . You cannot keep people from rejecting you. But you can keep rejections from enraging you.
   A. Can we keep rejections from injuring us? Explain.
   B. How can we keep rejections from enraging us?
   C. How have you learned to best deal with rejection?

Love Deepened

1. Read Genesis 4:2–8.
   A. What caused Cain's anger in this account?
   B. How did God respond to Cain's anger (vv. 6–7)?
   C. How did Cain deal with his anger (v. 8)?
   D. What can we learn from Cain about how *not* to deal with anger?

2. Read Romans 9:1–5.
   A. How did Paul feel toward his countrymen? Why did he feel this way?
   B. Paul had great cause to oppose his Jewish brothers, but he didn't. Why not?
   C. Upon what did Paul focus in order to maintain his love for his estranged brothers and sisters (v. 5)? How can we follow his example?

3. Read John 5:6.
   A. What question did Jesus ask of the invalid?
   B. Why would Jesus ask the man such a question? Wouldn't the answer be obvious?
   C. If Jesus were to ask you this question regarding your anger, what would you say? Explain.

Love Given

1. Make a detailed study of Ephesians 4:26. Read this verse in several translations, research what commentators say about it, and meditate on it in your quiet times for several weeks. At the end of your study, try to bring to life what you've learned. What can you do in your home to better comply with God's command? What can you do at work? In church? In your neighborhood?

CHAPTER NINE

The Heart Full of Hurts

Love Remembered

1. Our assignment is to protect the boat and refuse entrance to trashy thoughts. The minute they appear on the dock we go into action. "This heart belongs to God," we declare, "and you aren't getting on board until you change your allegiance."
   A. How vigilant have you been in refusing entrance to trashy thoughts?
   B. Describe some strategies that either you or your acquaintances have used to police the thought life.
   C. How can you get a wicked thought out of your mind once it's entered? Is it possible to drive it away? Explain.

2. You have not been sprinkled with forgiveness. You have not been spattered with grace. You have not been dusted with kindness. You have been immersed in it. You are submerged in mercy. You are a minnow in the ocean of his mercy.
   A. What does it mean to you to be immersed in God's grace?
   B. Why is it important to know that God has not merely sprinkled us with his goodness?
   C. Describe someone you know who thinks God is a miser with his kindness and mercy. How does this person move through life?

3. You can stick with your long lists and stinky cargo. And drift from port to port. But why would you? Let the *Pelicano* have the high seas. Your Captain has better plans for you.
   A. To what "long lists" and "stinky cargo" does Max refer?
   B. Why would anyone choose to stick with such loathsome cargo? Have you ever chosen to stick with it? Explain.
   C. What plans does your Captain have for you? How does your knowledge of these plans change the way you move through life?

Love Deepened

1. Read Colossians 2:13–15.
   A. What kind of "trash" does Paul speak of in this passage?
   B. How did Christ deal with it? What did he nail to the cross?
   C. How did Christ triumph through the cross? How can we share in this triumph?

2. Read 2 Corinthians 10:4–5.
   A. What kind of weapons does Paul have in mind here?
   B. What kind of strongholds does Paul have in mind here?
   C. How do these weapons demolish these strongholds?

3. Read Philippians 4:8.
   A. Paul lists several characteristics of the kinds of thoughts we are to entertain. Name them.
   B. How can we fill our minds with such thoughts?
   C. Why do we sometimes disobey this instruction?

Love Given

1. How can you help the members of your family to "take captive every

thought" to Christ (2 Cor. 10:5 NIV)? Do you allow any stumbling blocks to trip up your loved ones, whether they come in the form of trashy entertainment, inappropriate magazines, or other unhelpful media offerings? Do an inventory of your home. Physically walk through every room in the house, and ask yourself, "Is there anything in this room that better belongs on the *Pelicano*?"

CHAPTER TEN

THE LOVE TEST

Love Remembered

1. Feelings can fool you.
   A. Describe a time when your feelings fooled you.
   B. How do feelings fool us? How do they manage to deceive us?
   C. How does our culture encourage us to do whatever we feel? How can we resist its unwise urgings?

2. True love will never ask the "beloved" to do what he or she thinks is wrong. Love doesn't tear down the convictions of others. Quite the contrary.
   A. Describe a time when someone tried to use "love" to get you to do something you considered wrong. What happened?
   B. Why will genuine love never encourage someone to do something he or she considers wrong? What if the person's convictions are themselves wrong?
   C. How does true love attempt to persuade its beloved to take a certain course of action?

3. You want to plumb the depths of your love for someone? How do you feel when that person succeeds? Do you rejoice? Or are you jealous? And when he or she stumbles? Falls to misfortune? Are you really sorry? Or are you secretly pleased? Love never celebrates misfortune. Never.

A. Answer the previous questions, then explain your answers.

B. Why does love never celebrate misfortune?

C. How does love react to a *deserved* misfortune?

Love Deepened

1. Read 1 Corinthians 8:1–13.

   A. What relationship does Paul see between knowledge and love (vv. 1–3)? Which ought to take the lead? Why?

   B. How did love control Paul's use of his knowledge about idols (vv. 9–11)?

   C. What general principle does Paul develop out of this discussion (vv. 12–13)?

2. Read Luke 13:34–35.

   A. What truth did Jesus know about the future of Jerusalem?

   B. How did this truth affect him?

   C. Did Jesus rejoice over the judgment of his enemies? Why or why not?

3. Read Psalm 147:10–11.

   A. In what things does the Lord *not* take pleasure (v. 10)? Why not?

   B. In what *does* the Lord take pleasure (v. 11)? Why?

   C. What kind of love does the Lord express toward us? Why should this give us hope?

Love Given

1. Celebrate an unexpected success enjoyed by someone in your family. Make it fun, memorable, and significant. Make sure the person whose success you celebrate knows how much joy you take in him or her, not just because of the success, but because of who he or she is.

2. Take stock of how you react when a believing brother or sister enjoys some success. Can you truly rejoice with that person, or do you feel a little envious? Also consider how you react when a rival takes a stumble. Do you enjoy it? Ask the Lord to show you your heart, and then ask him to help you become more like Christ.

CHAPTER ELEVEN

Love Is a Package Deal

Love Remembered

1. Wouldn't it be great if love were like a cafeteria line? It would be easier. It would be neater. It would be painless and peaceful. But you know what? It wouldn't be love. Love doesn't accept just a few things. Love is willing to accept all things.
   A. Have you ever known someone who treated love like a cafeteria line? If so, how did this person treat others?
   B. Does the fact that love is willing to accept all things mean that love never tries to change some of those things? Explain.
   C. What kinds of things in a loved one are hardest for you to accept? Explain.

2. God's view of love is like my mom's view of food. When we love someone, we take the entire package.
   A. Describe some of the ways we try *not* to take the entire package.
   B. What part of your entire package have others had a hard time accepting? Explain.
   C. How can we accept someone's whole person when there are parts of his or her personality that we dislike?

3. Jesus bore all things, believed all things, hoped all things, and endured all things. Every single one.

A. Why is it important for us to remember that Jesus himself endured all things? How can this knowledge change our behavior toward others?

B. What might have happened if Jesus had refused to endure all things? What would have happened to you?

C. How can we learn to imitate Jesus' example of enduring all things?

Love Deepened

1. Read 1 Corinthians 1:10–17.

   A. What church problem does Paul discuss in this passage? Is such a problem common today? Explain.

   B. How did Paul want the church to behave (v. 10)? Is such a hope realistic? Explain.

   C. What might have happened in Corinth had the church learned to bear all things among its membership? Explain.

2. Read 1 Corinthians 5:1–13.

   A. Does this passage fit with the idea that love bears all things? Explain.

   B. How does this passage illustrate the difference between the judgment of behavior and the judgment of motivation?

   C. How is it possible to love a brother or sister who sins and yet refuse to tolerate the sin? Why is this so hard to put into practice?

3. Read Romans 12:18.

   A. What command are we given in this verse?

   B. How does the idea of bearing all things help us to obey this command?

Love Given

1. Here's an exercise to try only if you're feeling pretty satisfied with yourself. Make a list of what you believe to be your most annoying habits or traits. Be brutally honest. As you think about this list, which habits or traits can you realistically do something about? How can you work on them to make it easier for those around you to bear all things?

2. Identify the person in your sphere of influence who you believe best exemplifies the loving trait of bearing all things. Make an appointment to interview this person. What can you learn that might help you to better bear all things?

CHAPTER TWELVE

A Cloak of Love

Love Remembered

1. The scholar sounds poetic as he explains the meaning of *protect* as used in 1 Corinthians 13:7. The word conveys, he says, "the idea of covering with a cloak of love."
   A. Describe someone you know who is good at covering with a cloak of love.
   B. Describe a time when someone covered you with a cloak of love.
   C. Try to come up with several other images that convey this idea of protecting in love. What pictures convey loving protection to you?

2. We hide. He seeks. We bring sin. He brings a sacrifice. We try fig leaves. He brings the robe of righteousness.
   A. How do we try to hide when we sin? How do *you* try to hide?
   B. What motivates God to bring a sacrifice for our sin?
   C. How does one put on a robe of righteousness? Have you put on such a robe? Explain.

3. Do you know anyone, like Madge, who is wounded and afraid? Do you know anyone, like Adam and Eve, who is guilty and embarrassed? Do you know anyone who needs a cloak of love?
   A. Answer the previous questions.
   B. How can you help those you identified to put on a cloak of love?

C. Who has been a protector for you? Describe the person.

Love Deepened

1. Read Matthew 25:31–46.
   A. What scene is depicted in verses 31–33?
   B. How does the king describe the blessed ones in verses 34–36? What had they done?
   C. Why are the blessed ones surprised at the king's statement (vv. 37–39)?
   D. How does the king respond to their surprise (v. 40)?
   E. What does this suggest to us about our responsibility to protect the less fortunate?

2. Read 2 Thessalonians 3:1–3.
   A. What request did Paul make of his Thessalonian friends (v. 1)? Why did he make this request?
   B. What additional request did Paul make (v. 2)? How does this prayer relate to protection?
   C. What promise does God make through the apostle in verse 3? Can we take advantage of this promise? Explain.

3. Read Matthew 14:22–33.
   A. Recount in your own words what happened in this story.
   B. In how many ways did Jesus protect his disciples in this incident?
   C. How can this story give us hope? What can we learn from it?

Love Given

1. Using a good concordance, do a word study on the term *protect,* along with related words such as *protects, protected,* and *protection.* What do

you learn about how God protects his children? What does this do for your sense of security? How can you use this knowledge to help others build their trust in God?

2. Matthew 25 makes it plain that Christ wants us to protect and help the less fortunate among us. What are *you* currently doing to feed the hungry, give drink to the thirsty, house the homeless, clothe the naked, care for the sick, and visit those in prison? If you want to take Christ's words seriously, what *can* you do?

CHAPTER THIRTEEN

The Ring of Belief

Love Remembered

1. God believes in you. And, I wonder, could you take some of the belief that he has in you and share it with someone else? Could you believe in someone?
   A. Do you agree that God believes in you? Explain.
   B. How can we share God's belief in us with others?
   C. How has someone shown that he or she believed in you? What did this belief do for you?

2. Right or wrong, we define ourselves through other people's eyes. Tell me enough times that I'm stupid, and I'll believe you. Tell me enough times that I'm bright, and I might agree.
   A. Do you tend to define yourself through the eyes of others? Explain.
   B. Describe a time when someone's comments about you affected your self-image or behavior.
   C. How do you try to show people that you believe in them? What do you say to them?

3. How do we show people that we believe in them? *Show up. . . . Listen up. . . . Speak up.*
   A. How do you show up in the lives of others? How do they show up in yours?

B. How do you listen up in the lives of others? How do they listen up in yours?

C. How do you speak up in the lives of others? How do they speak up in yours?

Love Deepened

1. Read Luke 15:11–23.

   A. Describe the main characters in this story. What are they like?

   B. What is the main point of this story? What are we to take away from it?

   C. In what way is the father in the story a picture of God? How does God act like the father?

   D. How did the father show his belief in his son? How did this belief affect his son?

2. Read Proverbs 18:21; 12:18; 15:2, 4.

   A. What powers are attributed to the tongue in these verses?

   B. How does the tongue of the wise bring healing?

   C. How can you teach your own tongue to bring life and healing? What may have to change to make that happen?

3. Read Ephesians 4:29.

   A. What is prohibited in this verse?

   B. What is commended in this verse?

   C. What good result is described in this verse?

   D. Are you complying with this verse? Explain.

Love Given

1. Try your hand as an author. Write an account of how someone

showed his or her belief in you, including as many details as possible. Tell what he or she did, as well as what happened in your life as a result. Then share your story with a friend or loved one.

2. How can you show someone else that you believe in him or her? This week pick someone at home or in the office who needs to hear that you believe in him or her, and think of a creative way to express your belief. Send a card, make a call, arrange a lunch, plan a special outing—but don't let this week go by without expressing your belief in this individual.

CHAPTER FOURTEEN

When You're Low on Hope

Love Remembered

1. Hope is an olive leaf—evidence of dry land after a flood. Proof to the dreamer that dreaming is worth the risk.
   A. In what areas of your life do you most need hope right now?
   B. How has hope rescued you from a "flood" in the past?
   C. What dreams do you hold dear? Do you believe they are worth the risk? Explain.

2. With all due respect, our severest struggles are, in God's view, nothing worse than lost bobby pins and rubber bands. He is not confounded, confused, or discouraged. Receive his hope, won't you? Receive it because you need it. Receive it so you can share it.
   A. How big is your God? Can he handle your problems? Explain.
   B. How would you feel if God *could* be confused or discouraged?
   C. How do you receive God's hope? How can you share it?

3. Love extends an olive leaf to the loved one and says, "I have hope in you." Love is just as quick to say, "I have hope *for* you."
   A. What does it mean to say that love declares, "I have hope in you"?
   B. What does it mean to say that love declares, "I have hope *for* you"?
   C. How can you declare to those nearest to you that you have hope in

them and for them? What do you think such a declaration would mean to them?

Love Deepened

1. Read Romans 8:18–25.
   A. Why did Paul not grumble about his present sufferings (v. 18)?
   B. To what did Paul look forward (vv. 19–21)? How did this expectation change his outlook?
   C. Did Paul downplay his troubles (vv. 22–23)? How did he forbid them from bringing him down?
   D. How did Paul understand hope (vv. 24–25)? How can his understanding help us in our difficult times?

2. Read Romans 15:4.
   A. Why was the Bible written, according to this verse?
   B. How do we receive hope, according to this verse?
   C. Why do we need hope?

3. Read Hebrews 13:5–6.
   A. Why can we be content with what we have (v. 5)?
   B. What promise does God make to us in this passage?
   C. How can this promise give us hope?
   D. How can this hope change the way we live (v. 6)?

Love Given

1. Read a good book on the topic of hope. How has God designed our faith to give us hope, even in trying times?

2. Pretend you're a journalist for a while, and do some investigative

reporting. Ask several of your coworkers or neighbors to talk about hope: whether they have it, what they think it is, how it changes things, where it comes from, etc. Is hope a common or a rare commodity these days? How can you give people hope?

CHAPTER FIFTEEN

He Could Have Given Up

Love Remembered

1. Jesus could have given up.
   - A. If you had been the devil, how would you have tempted Jesus to give up?
   - B. Why do you think Jesus *didn't* give up? What kept him on track?
   - C. What would have happened had Jesus given up? How would history have changed?

2. Love goes the distance . . . and Christ traveled from limitless eternity to be confined by time in order to become one of us.
   - A. In what ways does love go the distance? How has it gone the distance in your own life?
   - B. How did love cause Jesus to relocate from heaven to earth?

3. Why didn't he quit? Because the love for his children was greater than the pain of the journey. He came to pull you out. Your world had collapsed. That's why he came. You were dead, dead in sin. That's why he came.
   - A. How did love overcome pain in Jesus' life? How can it do the same in your life?
   - B. How did Jesus pull you out of your collapsed world?
   - C. What does it mean to be dead in sin? How did Jesus' coming rescue us from sin and death?

Love Deepened

1. Read Hebrews 12:2–3.
   A. What guidance does the writer give us in verse 2? What is the reason for this guidance?
   B. How did Jesus endure the Cross, according to the writer? To what joy does he refer (v. 2)?
   C. In what way can we follow Jesus' example here (v. 3)? What happens when we do follow his example?

2. Read 2 Corinthians 4:7–18.
   A. Why does Paul call our bodies "jars of clay" (v. 7)? What is God's purpose in giving us such bodies?
   B. How does Paul describe his challenges and hardships (vv. 8–10)? How did he endure them?
   C. What hope drove Paul and gave him such endurance (v. 14)? Do you share this hope? Explain.
   D. What is one secret to not losing heart (v. 16)?
   E. What is the key to endurance (v. 18)? Have you found this key? Explain.

3. Read Revelation 1:9.
   A. What is "ours in Jesus," according to Revelation 1:9 (NIV)? Why is it ours?
   B. How might Colossians 1:3–12 give insight into John's statement?

Love Given

1. Read a good biography of a missionary, looking especially for the ways in which the missionary endured and persevered despite hardship. What can you learn for your own Christian life from this person's experience?

2. Be on the lookout this week for someone in your life who desperately needs encouragement. What can you do to help this person endure? Invite him or her to breakfast or lunch, and gently probe how you might offer hope and assistance.

CHAPTER SIXTEEN

Unfailing Love

Love Remembered

1. When you are in the final days of your life, what will you want? When death extends its hands to you, where will you turn for comfort?
   A. Answer the previous questions.
   B. Describe someone in your life who exemplifies unfailing love. What is this person like?

2. Let's take inventory of our hearts. Am I living in the overflow of God's love? How well do I love the people in my life? Does the way I treat people reflect the way God has treated me?
   A. Answer the previous questions.
   B. How does one live in the overflow of God's love? What does this mean?
   C. List ten ways God has shown you his love. How have you passed on this love to others?

3. God's love does not hinge on yours. The abundance of your love does not increase his. The lack of your love does not diminish his. Your goodness does not enhance his love, nor does your weakness dilute it.
   A. Why does God's love not hinge on yours?
   B. How does it make you feel that God's love is unchanging?
   C. How do we know that God's love is unchanging?

4. Let's rewrite 1 Corinthians 13:4–8 one more time. Not with your name or Jesus' name but with both. Read it aloud with your name in the blank, and see what you think.

> Christ in _______ is patient, Christ in ______ is kind. Christ in ____ does not envy, Christ in _____ does not boast, Christ in ____ is not proud. Christ in _____ is not rude, Christ in ____ is not self-seeking, Christ in ____ is not easily angered, Christ in ____ keeps no record of wrongs. Christ in ______ does not delight in evil but rejoices with the truth. Christ in _____ always protects, always trusts, always hopes, always perseveres. Christ in _____ never fails.

A. How did this passage sound, with both your name and Christ's in it? Explain.

B. What changes does such a reading urge you to make in your Christian walk? Explain.

Love Deepened

1. Read Deuteronomy 7:7–9.

A. What were *not* factors in God's setting his affection on Israel (v. 7)?

B. Why *did* God set his affection on Israel (v. 8)?

C. In what way is this principle the same for all believers in Christ today?

2. Read 1 Corinthians 13:8–13.

A. Why will prophecies, tongues, and knowledge cease? Why will love never cease?

B. To what day does Paul refer when he speaks of perfection coming (v. 10)? When will we see God "face to face" (v. 12)? When will we know fully, even as we are fully known (v. 12)?

C. Why is love greater than faith and hope?

3. Read John 15:5–12.
   A. In what way is Jesus the vine? In what way are we the branches?
   B. What promise is given to those who remain in Jesus (v. 7)?
   C. What happens to the branch that remains in Jesus (v. 8)? Why is this to God's glory?
   D. How do we remain in Christ's love (v. 10)?
   E. What is the result of remaining in Christ's love (v. 11)?
   F. What command does Jesus give those who remain in his love (v. 12)?

Love Given

1. Make a list of the ways others have blessed you through their love. How can you pass along this love to others?

2. In your quiet time, thank God for the many ways he has shown you his love over the years. Be as specific as possible, naming his individual expressions of love. Then ask him to show you how you can better pass along his love to others. Do not conclude your prayer until the Lord has revealed to you several ways in which you can practically show his love to specific individuals in your life.

NOTES

Chapter 2: Love's Flagship

1. David Aikman, *Great Souls: Six Who Changed the Century* (Nashville: Word Publishing, 1998), 341–42.
2. Ibid., 338–44.

Chapter 3: Your Kindness Quotient

1. John 2:1–11; Luke 19:1–10; Mark 5:21–34; Matthew 9:22 NKJV.
2. Gerhard Kittel and Gerhard Friedrich, eds., *Theological Dictionary of the New Testament,* trans. Geoffrey W. Bromiley (Grand Rapids: Eerdmans Publishing Co., 1971), 9:483.

Chapter 4: Inflamed

1. Paul Lee Tan, *Encyclopedia of 7,700 Illustrations* (Rockville, Md.: Assurance Publishers, 1979), 274.
2. Linda Dillow and Lorraine Pintus, *Gift-Wrapped by God: Secret Answers to the Question "Why Wait?"* (Colorado Springs, Colo.: WaterBrook Press, 2002).
3. Hank Hanegraaff, *The Prayer of Jesus* (Nashville, Tenn.: W Publishing Group, 2001), 13–14.
4. My appreciation to Jim Barker for relating this fictional piece.

Chapter 5: God's "No Pecking" Zone

1. Dan McCarney, "Courage to Quit," *San Antonio Express News,* 13 July 2000, sec. 4C.

2. Gerald F. Hawthorne, *Philippians,* vol. 43 of *Word Biblical Commentary* (Waco, Tex.: Word Publishing, 1983), 70.
3. William Barclay, *The Letter to the Romans,* rev. ed. (Philadelphia: Westminster Press, 1975), 164.

Chapter 6: A Call to Common Courtesy

1. King Duncan, *Lively Illustrations for Effective Preaching* (Knoxville, Tenn.: Seven World's Publishing, 1987), 61.

Chapter 7: Getting the "I" Out of Your Eye

1. Gerhard Kittel and Gerhard Friedrich, eds., *Theological Dictionary of the New Testament,* trans. Geoffrey W. Bromiley (Grand Rapids: Eerdmans Publishing Co., 1971), 2:660.

Chapter 8: The Headwaters of Anger

1. Dwight Edwards, *Revolution Within* (Colorado Springs, Colo.: WaterBrook Press, 2001), 57–58.
2. Ibid., 58.
3. Robert Emmit, *Anger Management,* audiotape from a sermon at the Community Bible Church, 2477 East 1604, San Antonio, TX 78232 on 14 January 2001.

Chapter 9: The Heart Full of Hurts

1. Jerry Schwartz, "Where Does One Stash That Trash Ash?" *San Antonio Express News,* 3 September 2000, sec. 29A.

Chapter 10: The Love Test

1. Tim Kimmel, quoted in Stu Weber, *Tender Warrior* (Sisters, Oreg.: Multnomah Books, 1993), excerpted as "Changed Lives," in *A 4th*

Course of Chicken Soup for the Soul (Deerfield, Fla.: Health Communications, 1997), 60–61.

Chapter 11: Love Is a Package Deal

1. Robert J. Dean, *First Corinthians for Today* (Nashville, Tenn.: Broadman Press, 1972), 60.

Chapter 12: A Cloak of Love

1. Gerhard Kittel and Gerhard Friedrich, eds., *Theological Dictionary of the New Testament,* trans. Geoffrey W. Bromiley (Grand Rapids: Eerdmans Publishing Co., 1971), 7:587.
2. John 8:1–11; Matt. 14:22–33; Mark 5:1–20; Matt. 17:24–27.
3. My appreciation to Dr. Harold Wise and Dr. Joe Bob Wise for allowing me to tell their parents' story.

Chapter 13: The Ring of Belief

1. Barbara Bressi-Donahue, "Friends of the Ring," *Reader's Digest,* June 1999, 154.
2. Robert H. Schuller, *The Peak to Peek Principle* (Garden City, N.Y.: Doubleday and Co., 1980), 107.
3. Alan Loy McGinnis, *Bringing Out the Best in People: How to Enjoy Helping Others Excel* (Minneapolis: Augsburg Books, 1985), 32–33.
4. Alan Loy McGinnis, *The Friendship Factor* (Minneapolis: Augsburg Publishing House, 1979), 51–52.
5. David Jeremiah, *Acts of Love* (Gresham, Oreg.: Vision House Publishing, Inc., 1994), 92.
6. Bressi-Donahue, op. cit., 153–60.

Chapter 14: When You're Low on Hope

1. Charles Swindoll, *The Tale of the Tardy Oxcart and 1,501 Other Stories* (Nashville, Tenn.: Word Publishing, 1998), 275.

Chapter 15: He Could Have Given Up

1. My appreciation to J. R. Vassar for this parallel and to David Robinson for allowing me to share it.
2. Deborah Hastings, "Firefighters' Reward: Carrying Son's Body," *San Antonio Express News,* 14 December 2001, sec. 17A.

Chapter 16: Unfailing Love

1. J. I. Packer, *Knowing God* (Downers Grove, Ill.: InterVarsity Press, 1973), 112.

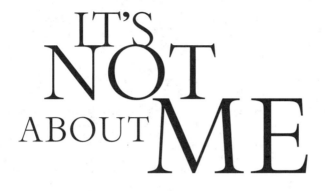

IT'S NOT ABOUT ME

Rescue from the Life
We Thought Would
Make Us Happy

IT'S NOT ABOUT ME

Published in Nashville, Tennessee, by Thomas Nelson. Thomas Nelson is a trademark of Thomas Nelson, Inc.

Thomas Nelson, Inc. titles may be purchased in bulk for educational, business, fund-raising, or sales promotional use. For information, please e-mail SpecialMarkets@ThomasNelson.com.

Cover Design: UDG Designworks

Interior Design: Susan Browne Design/Nashville, TN

Library of Congress Cataloging-in-Publication Data

Lucado, Max.
  It's not about me : rescue from the life we thought would make us happy / Max Lucado.
    p. cm.
ISBN 9781591450429
ISBN 9781591451693 (IE)
  1. Man (Christian theology) I. Title.
  BT701.3.L83 2004
  248.4—dc22

2003021164

Printed in the United States of America

To Kenny and Sharon Wilson

There may be a finer couple on this earth,
but I haven't met them.
For your friendship, faith, and
far too few hamburgers,
Denalyn and I say thank you.
We gladly dedicate this book to you:
two people who, because you already live it,
don't need to read it.

Acknowledgments

On a summer day in the late nineties I ran into a friend in a hotel lobby. Our last visit had occurred a year earlier. He had a few minutes. I had an empty stomach. So we bought deli sandwiches, found a table, and took a seat. "What has God been teaching you this year?" My question was expectation-free. But his answer gave me more than a sandwich to chew on.

"What has he been teaching me this year?" he reflected. "He's been teaching me that: It's not about me."

The phrase stirred enough reflections to become a series of messages and, eventually, this book. So it's only right for me to pause and salute Sealy Yates. Thanks for sharing the line. More important, thanks for modeling it.

Sealy is not the only one who made this work possible. Here are some others:

Liz Heaney and Karen Hill—You so skillfully and gently recraft, clarify. Thanks to you, this book, and the one who wrote it, are in better shape.

Steve and Cheryl Green—Thanks for superintending my life and being our friends. Your comradeship means more to me than I can say.

Byron Williamson, Joey Paul, and the entire Integrity team—Congratulations on the launch. Honored to be aboard.

My Peak of the Week family—You let me guinea pig this material on you. How kind you were to stay awake.

Carol Bartley—No one does it better. Your penchant for grammatical precision astounds us all.

Dwight Edwards—*Revolution Within* connected the dots for me.

John Piper—Reading *The Supremacy of God in Preaching* was like seeing a map of the solar system for the first time. Thanks for reminding me of my place.

Dean Merrill—Thanks for graciously squaring the facts.

Rick Atchley—Thanks for the great messages, for being a great friend.

Charles Prince—Thanks for untangling theological knots and sharing a lifetime of knowledge.

Jenna, Andrea, and Sara—my daughters, my treasures.

Denalyn, my wife—Vienna had Mozart. I have you. What music you bring into my life.

And most of all to you, Author of life. What a great God you are. It's all about you. Period.

But all of us who are Christians . . .
reflect like mirrors the glory of the Lord.

2 Corinthians 3:18 PHILLIPS

FOREWORD

NBA championship teams have something in common: they play with one goal in mind. Each player contributes his own gifts and efforts so that the greater goal—winning—can be reached. But players who seek their own glory at the sacrifice of the team's glory drive the team away from success. So it is with life. The goal is not our own glory. In fact, trying to make life "all about us" pushes happiness further out of reach.

Our society is not wired for this kind of thinking. It's a "me-centric" world out there, which destroys much of what should be good. Marriages are ruined because one or both partners are focused on their own happiness. Successful men and women are ruined by their own success, believing they don't need anyone else's input. And for some, life's troubles are magnified because they believe life is all about them.

The Bible is full of men and women who struggled with "me-centric" thinking, so our generation is not alone. If we would learn from them, we could live in freedom. We would be able to enjoy our successes without taking the credit, like King David. We could bear up under troubles with confidence in God, like Job. By letting go of our own agendas and timetables, as Moses finally did, we would discover that God's plans are mind-blowing. In the end, a "God-centric" lifestyle would free us to live life to the fullest!

My friend Max Lucado has years of experience in following God, which is why I am happy to recommend this book. If you want a great meal, I'll send you to a great chef. But if you want to learn about God's ways, I'll send you to someone who has walked with him for a long while.

Max is such a man; the Lord has prepared him for just this purpose. I encourage you to read with an open heart as Max shares the joy of a God-centered life.

May God free us all from "me-centric" living. All the glory is His!

—David Robinson
Former NBA Player

CHAPTER ONE

Bumping Life off Self-Center

1

Blame the bump on Copernicus.

Until Copernicus came along in 1543, we earthlings enjoyed center stage. Fathers could place an arm around their children, point to the night sky, and proclaim, "The universe revolves around us."

Ah, the hub of the planetary wheel, the navel of the heavenly body, the 1600 Pennsylvania Avenue of the cosmos. Ptolemy's second-century finding convinced us. Stick a pin in the center of the stellar map, and you've found the earth. Dead center.

And, what's more, dead still! Let the other planets vagabond through the skies. Not us. No sir. We stay put. As predictable as Christmas. No orbiting. No rotating. Some fickle planets revolve 180 degrees from one day to the next. Not ours. As budgeless as the Rock of Gibraltar. Let's hear loud applause for the earth, the anchor of the universe.

But then came Nicolaus. Nicolaus Copernicus with his

maps, drawings, bony nose, Polish accent, and pestering questions. Oh, those questions he asked.

"Ahem, can anyone tell me what causes the seasons to change?"

"Why do some stars appear in the day and others at night?"

"Does anyone know exactly how far ships can sail before falling off the edge of the earth?"

"Trivialities!" people scoffed. "Who has time for such problems? Smile and wave, everyone. Heaven's homecoming queen has more pressing matters to which to attend."

But Copernicus persisted. He tapped our collective shoulders and cleared his throat. "Forgive my proclamation, but," and pointing a lone finger toward the sun, he announced, "behold the center of the solar system."

People denied the facts for over half a century. When like-minded Galileo came along, the throne locked him up, and the church kicked him out. You'd have thought he had called the king a stepchild or the pope a Baptist.

People didn't take well to demotions back then.

We still don't.

What Copernicus did for the earth, God does for our souls. Tapping the collective shoulder of humanity, he points to the Son—his Son—and says, "Behold the center of it all."

"God raised him [Christ] from death and set him on a

throne in deep heaven, in charge of running the universe, everything from galaxies to governments, no name and no power exempt from his rule. And not just for the time being but *forever.* He is in charge of it all, has the final word on everything. At the center of all this, Christ rules the church" (Ephesians 1:20–22 MSG).

When God looks at the center of the universe, he doesn't look at you. When heaven's stagehands direct the spotlight toward the star of the show, I need no sunglasses. No light falls on me.

Lesser orbs, that's us. Appreciated. Valued. Loved dearly. But central? Essential? Pivotal? Nope. Sorry. Contrary to the Ptolemy within us, the world does not revolve around us. Our comfort is not God's priority. If it is, something's gone awry. If we are the marquee event, how do we explain flat-earth challenges like death, disease, slumping economies, or rumbling earthquakes? If God exists to please us, then shouldn't we always be pleased?

WHAT COPERNICUS DID FOR THE EARTH, GOD DOES FOR OUR SOULS.

Could a Copernican shift be in order? Perhaps our place is

not at the center of the universe. God does not exist to make a big deal out of us. We exist to make a big deal out of him. It's not about you. It's not about me. It's all about him.

The moon models our role.

What does the moon do? She generates no light. Contrary to the lyrics of the song, this harvest moon cannot shine on. Apart from the sun, the moon is nothing more than a pitch-black, pockmarked rock. But properly positioned, the moon beams. Let her do what she was made to do, and a clod of dirt becomes a source of inspiration, yea, verily, romance. The moon reflects the greater light.

And she's happy to do so! You never hear the moon complaining. She makes no waves about making waves. Let the cow jump over her or astronauts step on her; she never objects. Even though sunning is accepted while mooning is the butt of bad jokes, you won't hear ol' Cheeseface grumble. The moon is at peace in her place. And because she is, soft light touches a dark earth.

What would happen if we accepted our place as Son reflectors?

Such a shift comes so stubbornly, however. We've been demanding our way and stamping our feet since infancy. Aren't we all born with a default drive set on selfishness? *I want a spouse who makes me happy and coworkers who always ask my opin-*

ion. I want weather that suits me and traffic that helps me and a government that serves me. It is all about me. We relate to the advertisement that headlined, "For the man who thinks the world revolves around him." A prominent actress justified her appearance in a porn magazine by saying, "I wanted to express myself."

Self-promotion. Self-preservation. Selfcenteredness. It's all about me!

They all told us it was, didn't they? Weren't we urged to look out for number one? Find our place in the sun? Make a name for ourselves? We thought self-celebration would make us happy . . .

But what chaos this philosophy creates. What if a symphony orchestra followed such an approach? Can you imagine an orchestra with an "It's all about me" outlook? Each artist clamoring for self-expression. Tubas blasting nonstop. Percussionists pounding to get attention. The cellist shoving the flutist out of the center-stage chair. The trumpeter standing atop the conductor's stool tooting his horn. Sheet music disregarded. Conductor ignored. What do you have but an endless tune-up session!

Harmony? Hardly.

Happiness? Are the musicians happy to be in the group? Not at all. Who enjoys contributing to a cacophony?

You don't. We don't. We were not made to live this way. But aren't we guilty of doing just that?

No wonder our homes are so noisy, businesses so stress-filled, government so cutthroat, and harmony so rare. If you think it's all about you, and I think it's all about me, we have no hope for a melody. We've chased so many skinny rabbits that we've missed the fat one: the God-centered life.

The God-centered life works. And it rescues us from a life that doesn't.

What would happen if we took our places and played our parts? If we played the music the Maestro gave us to play? If we made his song our highest priority?

Would we see a change in families? We'd certainly *hear* a change. Less "Here is what I want!" More "What do you suppose God wants?"

What if a businessman took that approach? Goals of money and name making, he'd shelve. God-reflecting would dominate.

And your body? Ptolemaic thinking says, "It's mine; I'm going to enjoy it." God-centered thinking acknowledges, "It's God's; I have to respect it."

We'd see our suffering differently. "My pain proves God's absence" would be replaced with "My pain expands God's purpose."

Talk about a Copernican shift. Talk about a healthy shift.

Life makes sense when we accept our place. The gift of pleasures, the purpose of problems—all for him. The God-centered life works. And it rescues us from a life that doesn't.

But how do we make the shift? How can we be bumped off self-center? Attend a seminar, howl at the moon, read a Lucado book? None of these (though the author appreciates that last idea). We move from me-focus to God-focus by pondering him. Witnessing him. Following the counsel of the apostle Paul: "Beholding as in a glass the glory of the Lord, [we] are changed into the same image from glory to glory, even as by the Spirit of the Lord" (2 Corinthians 3:18 KJV).

Beholding him changes us. Couldn't we use a change? Let's give it a go. Who knows? We might just discover our place in the universe.

PART ONE

God-Pondering

CHAPTER TWO

SHOW ME YOUR GLORY

2

An anxious Moses pleads for help. "[God], you tell me, 'Lead this people,' but you don't let me know whom you're going to send with me. . . . Are you traveling with us or not?" (Exodus 33:12, 16 MSG).

You can hardly fault his fears. Encircled first by Israelites who long for Egypt, and second by a desert of hot winds and blazing boulders, the ex-shepherd needs assurance. His Maker offers it. "I myself will go with you. . . . I will do what you ask, because I know you very well, and I am pleased with you" (vv. 14, 17 NCV).

You'd think that would have been enough for Moses, but he lingers. Thinking, perhaps, of that last sentence, "I will do what you ask . . ." Perhaps God will indulge one more request. So he swallows, sighs, and requests . . .

For what do you think he will ask? He has God's attention. God seems willing to hear his prayer. "The LORD spoke to Moses face to face as a man speaks with his friend" (v. 11 NCV).

The patriarch senses an opportunity to ask for anything. What request will he make?

So many requests he could make. How about a million requests? That's how many adults are in Moses' rearview mirror (Exodus 12:37). A million stiff-necked, unappreciative, cow-worshiping ex-slaves who grumble with every step. Had Moses prayed, "Could you turn these people into sheep?" who would have blamed him?

Sheep. Only a few months before, Moses was in this same desert, near this same mountain, keeping an eye on a flock. What a difference this time around. Sheep don't make demands in a desert or a mess out of blessings. And they certainly don't make calves out of gold or ask to go back to Egypt.

And what about Israel's enemies? Battlefields lie ahead. Combat with Hittites, Jebusites . . . Termites, and Cellulites. They infest the land. Can Moses mold an army out of pyramid-building Hebrews?

I will do what you ask . . .

"Could you just beam us to Canaan?"

Moses knew what God could do. The entire Ancient East knew. They were still talking about Aaron's staff becoming a snake and the Nile becoming blood. Air so thick with gnats you breathed them. Ground so layered with locusts you crunched them. Noonday blackness. Hail-pounded crops.

Flesh landscaped with boils. Funerals for the firstborn.

God turned the Red Sea into a red carpet. Manna fell. Quail ran. Water bubbled from within a rock. God can move mountains.

In fact, he moved the very mountain of Sinai on which Moses stood. When God spoke, Sinai shook, and Moses' knees followed suit. Moses knew what God could do.

Worse, he knew what these people were prone to do.

Moses found them dancing around a golden calf, their memories of God as stale as yesterday's manna. He carried the handwriting of God on a stone, and the Israelites were worshiping a heartless farm animal.

WHEN OUR DEEPEST DESIRE IS NOT THE THINGS OF GOD, OR A FAVOR FROM GOD, BUT GOD HIMSELF, WE CROSS A THRESHOLD.

It was more than Moses could take. He melted the metal cow and pounded the gold into dust and forced the worshipers to drink up.

God was ready to be done with them and start over with Moses as he had done with Noah. But twice Moses pleads for mercy, and twice mercy is extended (Exodus 32:11–14, 31–32).

And God, touched by Moses' heart, hears Moses' prayer. "My presence will go with you. I'll see the journey to the end" (Exodus 33:14 MSG).

But Moses needs more. One more request. Glory. "Show me your glory" (33:18 NCV).

We cross a line when we make such a request. When our deepest desire is not the things of God, or a favor from God, but God himself, we cross a threshold. Less self-focus, more God-focus. Less about me, more about him.

"Show me your radiance," Moses is praying. "Flex your biceps. Let me see the *S* on your chest. Your preeminence. Your heart-stopping, ground-shaking extraspectacularness. Forget the money and the power. Bypass the youth. I can live with an aging body, but I can't live without you. I want more God, please. I'd like to see more of your glory."

Why did Moses want to see God's greatness?

Ask yourself a similar question. Why do you stare at sunsets and ponder the summer night sky? Why do you search for a rainbow in the mist or gaze at the Grand Canyon? Why do you allow the Pacific surf to mesmerize and Niagara to hypnotize? How do we explain our fascination with such sights?

Beauty? Yes. But doesn't the beauty point to a beautiful Someone? Doesn't the immensity of the ocean suggest an immense Creator? Doesn't the rhythm of migrating cranes and beluga whales hint of a brilliant mind? And isn't that what we desire? A beautiful Maker? An immense Creator? A God so mighty that he can commission the birds and command the fish?

"Show me your glory, God," Moses begs. Forget a bank; he wants to see Fort Knox. He needs a walk in the vault of God's wealth. *Would you stun me with your strength? Numb me with your wisdom? Steal my breath with a brush of yours? A moment in the spray of the cataract of grace, a glimpse of your glory, God*. This is the prayer of Moses.

And God answers it. He places his servant in the cleft of a rock, telling Moses: "You cannot see My face; for no man shall see Me, and live. . . . I . . . will cover you with My hand while I pass by. Then I will take away My hand, and you shall see My back; but My face shall not be seen" (Exodus 33:20, 22–23 NKJV).

And so Moses, cowering beneath the umbrella of God's palm, waits, surely with face bowed, eyes covered, and pulse racing, until God gives the signal. When the hand lifts, Moses' eyes do the same and catch a distant, disappearing glance of the back parts of God. The heart and center of the Maker is too much for Moses to bear. A fading glimpse will have to do. I'm seeing the long gray hair of Moses wind-whipped forward and his leathery hand grabbing a rock in the wall lest he fall. And as the gust settles and his locks rest again on his shoulders, we see the impact. His face. Gleaming. Bright as if backlit by a thousand torches. Unknown to Moses, but undeniable to the Hebrews, is his shimmering face. When he descended the mountain, "the sons of Israel could not look intently at the face of Moses because of the glory of his face" (2 Corinthians 3:7).

Witnesses saw, not anger in his jaw, or worry in his eyes, or a scowl on his lips; they saw God's glory in his face.

Did he have reason for anger? Cause for worry? Of course. Challenges await him. A desert and forty years of great challenges. But now, having seen God's face, he can face them.

Forgive my effrontery, but shouldn't Moses' request be yours? You've got problems. Look at you. Living in a dying body, walking on a decaying planet, surrounded by a self-centered society. Some saved by grace; others fueled by narcissism. Many of us by both. Cancer. War. Disease.

These are no small issues. A small god? No thanks. You and I need what Moses needed—a glimpse of God's glory. Such a sighting can change you forever.

In the early pages of my childhood memory, I see this picture. My father and I sit side by side in a chapel. We both wear our only suits. The shirt collar rubs my neck; the pew feels hard to my bottom; the sight of my dead uncle leaves us all silent. This is my first funeral. My nine years of life have not prepared me for death. What I see unnerves me. Aunts, typically jovial and talkative, weep loudly. Uncles, commonly quick with a word and joke, stare wide eyed at the casket. And Buck, my big uncle with meaty hands, big belly, and booming voice, lies whitish and waxy in the coffin.

I remember my palms moistening and my heart bouncing in my chest like tennis sneakers in a clothes dryer. Fear had me in her talons. What other emotion could I feel? Where do I look? The weeping ladies frighten me. Glassy-eyed men puzzle me. My dead uncle spooks me. But then I look up. I see my father.

YOU AND I NEED WHAT MOSES NEEDED—A GLIMPSE OF GOD'S GLORY.

He turns his face toward me and smiles softly. "It's okay, son," he assures, laying a large hand on my leg. Somehow I know it is. Why it is, I don't know. My family still wails. Uncle Buck is still dead. But if Dad, in the midst of it all, says it's okay, then that's enough.

At that moment I realized something. I could look around and find fear, or look at my father and find faith.

I chose my father's face.

So did Moses.

So can you.

CHAPTER THREE

Divine Self-Promotion

3

Moses asked to see it on Sinai.

It billowed through the temple, leaving priests too stunned to minister.

When Ezekiel saw it, he had to bow.

It encircled the angels and starstruck the shepherds in the Bethlehem pasture.

Jesus radiates it.

John beheld it.

Peter witnessed it on Transfiguration Hill.

Christ will return enthroned in it.

Heaven will be illuminated by it.[1]

It gulfstreams the Atlantic of Scripture, touching every person with the potential of changing every life. Including yours. One glimpse, one taste, one sampling, and your faith will never be the same . . .

Glory.

God's glory.

To seek God's glory is to pray, "Thicken the air with your presence; make it misty with your majesty. Part heaven's drapes, and let your nature spill forth. God, show us God."

To seek God's glory is to pray, "Let your nature spill forth. God, show us God."

What the word *Alps* does for the mountains of Europe, *glory* does for God's nature. *Alps* encompasses a host of beauties: creeks, peaks, falling leaves, running elk. To ask to see the Alps is to ask to see it all. To ask to see God's glory is to ask to see all of God. God's glory carries the full weight of his attributes: his love, his character, his strength, and on and on.

David celebrated God's glory.

Bravo, God, bravo!
Gods and all angels shout, "Encore!"
In awe before the glory,
in awe before God's visible power.
Stand at attention!
Dress your best to honor him!

God thunders across the waters,
Brilliant, his voice and his face, streaming brightness—
God, across the flood waters.

God's thunder tympanic,
God's thunder symphonic.

God's thunder smashes cedars,
God topples the northern cedars.

The mountain ranges skip like spring colts,
The high ridges jump like wild kid goats.

God's thunder spits fire.
God thunders, the wilderness quakes;
He makes the desert of Kadesh shake.

God's thunder sets the oak trees dancing
A wild dance, whirling; the pelting rain strips their branches.
We fall to our knees—we call out, "Glory!"
(Psalm 29:1–9 MSG)

The word signals high honor. The Hebrew term for *glory* descends from a root word meaning heavy, weighty, or important. God's glory, then, celebrates his significance, his uniqueness, his one-of-a-kindness. As Moses prayed, "Who among the gods is like you, O Lord? Who is like you—majestic in holiness, awesome in glory, working wonders?" (Exodus 15:11 NIV).

When you think "God's glory," think "preeminence." And, when you think "preeminence," think "priority." For God's glory is God's priority.

God's staff meetings, if he had them, would revolve around one question: "How can we reveal my glory today?" God's to-do list consists of one item: "Reveal my glory." Heaven's framed and mounted purpose statement hangs in the angels' break room just above the angel food cake. It reads: "Declare God's glory."

God exists to showcase God.

He told Moses: "By those who come near Me I must be regarded as holy; and before all the people I must be glorified" (Leviticus 10:3 NKJV).

Why did he harden Pharaoh's heart? "I will harden Pharaoh's heart, and he will pursue them [the Israelites]. But I will gain glory for myself through Pharaoh and all his army, and the Egyptians will know that I am the Lord" (Exodus 14:4 NIV).

Why do the heavens exist? The heavens exist to "declare the glory of God" (Psalm 19:1 NIV).

Why did God choose the Israelites? Through Isaiah he called out to "everyone who is called by My name, whom I have created for My glory" (Isaiah 43:7 NKJV).

Why do people struggle? God answers, "I have tested you in the furnace of affliction. For My own sake, for My own sake, I will act" (Isaiah 48:10–11). "Trust me in your times of trouble, and I will rescue you, and you will give me glory" (Psalm 50:15 NLT).

EVERY ACT OF HEAVEN REVEALS GOD'S GLORY. EVERY ACT OF JESUS DID THE SAME.

He spoke of "this people I have formed for Myself; they shall declare My praise" (Isaiah 43:21 NKJV).

The prophet Isaiah proclaimed, "You lead Your people, to make Yourself a glorious name" (Isaiah 63:14 NKJV).

Christ taught us to make God's reputation our priority in prayer: "Our Father who is in heaven, hallowed be Your name" (Matthew 6:9).

Every act of heaven reveals God's glory. Every act of Jesus did the same. Indeed, "The Son reflects the glory of God" (Hebrews 1:3 NCV). The night before his crucifixion, Jesus declared, "Now my heart is troubled, and what shall I say? 'Father, save me from this hour'? No, it was for this very reason

I came to this hour. Father, glorify your name!" (John 12:27–28 NIV). Paul explains that "Christ has become a servant of the Jews . . . so that the Gentiles may glorify God for his mercy" (Romans 15:8–9 NIV).

And Jesus declared his mission a success by saying, "I have brought you glory on earth by completing the work you gave me to do" (John 17:4 NIV).

God has one goal: God. "I have my reputation to keep up" (Isaiah 48:11 MSG).

Surprised? Isn't such an attitude, dare we ask, self-centered? Don't we deem this behavior "self-promotion"? Why does God broadcast himself?

For the same reason the pilot of the lifeboat does. Think of it this way. You're floundering neck-deep in a dark, cold sea. Ship sinking. Life jacket deflating. Strength waning. Through the inky night comes the voice of a lifeboat pilot. But you cannot see him. What do you want the driver of the lifeboat to do?

Be quiet? Say nothing? Stealth his way through the drowning passengers? By no means! You need volume! Amp it up, buddy! In biblical jargon, you want him to show his glory. You need to hear him say, "I am here. I am strong. I have room for you. I can save you!" Drowning passengers want the pilot to reveal his preeminence.

Don't we want God to do the same? Look around. People

thrash about in seas of guilt, anger, despair. Life isn't working. We are going down fast. But God can rescue us. And only one message matters. His! We need to see God's glory.

Make no mistake. God has no ego problem. *He does not reveal his glory for his good. We need to witness it for ours.* We need a strong hand to pull us into a safe boat. And, once aboard, what becomes our priority?

He does not reveal his glory for his good. We need to witness it for ours.

Simple. Promote God. We declare his preeminence. "Hey! Strong boat over here! Able pilot! He can pull you out!"

Passengers promote the pilot. "Not to us, O Lord, not to us, but to Your name give glory because of Your loving-kindness, because of Your truth" (Psalm 115:1). If we boast at all, we "boast in the Lord" (2 Corinthians 10:17).

The breath you took as you read that last sentence was given to you for one reason, that you might for another moment "reflect the Lord's glory" (2 Corinthians 3:18 NIV). God awoke you and me this morning for one purpose: "Declare his glory among the nations, his marvelous deeds among all peoples" (1 Chronicles 16:24 NIV).

"God made all things, and everything continues through

him and *for* him. To him be the glory forever" (Romans 11:36 NCV, emphasis mine). "There is only one God, the Father, who created everything, and *we exist for him*" (1 Corinthians 8:6 NLT, emphasis mine).

Why does the earth spin? For him.

Why do you have talents and abilities? For him.

Why do you have money or poverty? For him.

Strength or struggles? For him.

Everything and everyone exists to reveal his glory.

Including you.

CHAPTER FOUR

HOLY DIFFERENT

4

John Hanning Speke stands on the river edge and stares at the wall of water. He has dedicated the better part of 1858 to getting here. For weeks he and his party slashed through African brush and forded deep rivers. Natives bearing iron-headed spears pursued them. Crocodiles and sterns kept an eye on them. But finally, after miles of jungle marching and grass plodding, they found the falls.

Only a Britisher could so clearly understate the sight. "We were well rewarded," he wrote in his journal.

> The roar of the waters, the thousands of passenger fish, leaping at the falls with all their might, the Wasoga and Waganda fishermen coming out in boats and taking post on all the rocks with rod and hook, hippopotami and crocodiles lying sleepily on the water . . . made in all, as interesting a picture as one would want to see.[1]

Speke could not leave. He sketched the sight over and over. He dedicated an entire day to simply staring at the majesty of the falls at the upper Nile. Not hard to understand why. No region of England boasted any such sight. Rarely do eyes fall on a hitherto unseen image. Speke's did. And he was stunned by what he saw.

Fourteen years later, halfway around the globe, Frederick Dellenbaugh was equally impressed. He was only eighteen when he joined Major Powell on his pioneering river voyages through the Grand Canyon. Led by the one-armed Powell, the explorers floated on leaky boats and faced high waters. It's a wonder they survived. It's every bit as much a wonder what they saw. Dellenbaugh described the scene:

> My back being towards the fall I could not see it. . . . Nearer and nearer came the angry tumult; the Major shouted "Back water!" there was a sudden dropping away of all support; then the mighty wavers [*sic*] smote us. The boat rose to them well, but we were flying at twenty-five miles an hour and at every leap the breakers rolled over us. "Bail!" shouted the Major,—"Bail for your lives!" and we dropped the oars to bail, though bailing was almost useless. . . . The boat rolled and pitched like a ship in a tornado.

> ... canopies of foam pour[ed] over gigantic black boulders, first on one side, then on the other. . . . If you will take a watch and count by it ninety seconds, you will probably have about the time we were in this chaos, though it seemed much longer to me. Then we were through.[2]

Young Dellenbaugh knew rapids. Rivers and raging water were not new to him. But something about this river was. The sudden immensity, stark intensity—something stole the oarsman's breath. He knew rapids. But none like this.

Speke, speechless. Dellenbaugh, drenched and awestruck.

And Isaiah, facefirst on the temple floor. Arms crossed above his head, muffled voice crying for mercy. Like the explorers, he's just seen the unseen. But unlike the explorers, he's seen more than creation—he's seen the Creator. He's seen God.

Seven and one-half centuries before Christ, Isaiah was ancient Israel's version of a Senate chaplain or court priest. His family, aristocratic. His Hebrew, impeccable. Polished, professional, and successful. But the day he saw God only one response seemed appropriate: "Woe is me, for I am ruined." What caused such a confession? What stirred such a reply? The answer is found in the thrice-repeated words of the seraphim: "Holy, holy, holy."

> Seraphim stood above Him, each having six wings: with two he covered his face, and with two he covered his feet, and with two he flew. And one called out to another and said,
>
> "Holy, Holy, Holy, is the LORD of hosts,
> The whole earth is full of His glory."
>
> And the foundations of the thresholds trembled at the voice of him who called out, while the temple was filling with smoke. Then I said,
>
> "Woe is me, for I am ruined!
> Because I am a man of unclean lips,
> And I live among a people of unclean lips;
> For my eyes have seen the King, the LORD of hosts."
> (Isaiah 6:2–5)

On the one occasion seraphim appear in Scripture, they endlessly trilogize the same word. "Holy, holy, holy is the LORD Almighty" (NIV). Repetition, in Hebrew, performs the work of our highlighter. A tool of emphasis. God, proclaims the six-winged angels, is not holy. He is not holy, holy. He is holy, holy, holy.

What other attribute receives such enforcement? No verse describes God as "wise, wise, wise" or "strong, strong, strong." Only as "holy, holy, holy." God's holiness commands headline attention. The adjective qualifies his name more than all others combined.[3] The first and final songs of the Bible magnify the holiness of God. Having crossed the Red Sea, Moses and the Israelites sang, "Who among the gods is like you, O LORD? Who is like you—majestic in holiness, awesome in glory, working wonders?" (Exodus 15:11 NIV). In Revelation those who had been victorious over the beast sang, "Who will not fear you, O Lord, and bring glory to your name? For you alone are holy" (15:4 NIV).

The Hebrew word for *holy* is *qadosh*, which means cut off or separate. Holiness, then, speaks of the "otherness" of God. His total uniqueness. Everything about God is different from the world he has made.

GOD IS NOT HOLY.
HE IS NOT HOLY, HOLY.
HE IS HOLY, HOLY, HOLY.

What you are to a paper airplane, God is to you. Take a sheet of paper and make one. Contrast yourself with your creation. Challenge it to a spelling contest. Who will win? Dare it to race you around the block. Who is faster? Invite the airplane to a game of one-on-one basketball. Will you not dominate the court?

And well you should. The thing has no brainwaves, no

pulse. It exists only because you formed it and flies only when someone throws it. Multiply the contrasts between you and the paper plane by infinity, and you will begin to catch a glimpse of the disparity between God and us.

To what can we compare God? "Who in the skies is comparable to the LORD? Who among the sons of the mighty is like the LORD?" (Psalm 89:6). "To whom then will you liken God? Or what likeness will you compare with Him?" (Isaiah 40:18).

Even God asks, "To whom will you compare me? Who is my equal?" (Isaiah 40:25 NLT). As if his question needed an answer, he gives one:

> I am God—I alone! I am God, and there is no one else like me. Only I can tell you what is going to happen even before it happens. Everything I plan will come to pass, for I do whatever I wish. I will call a swift bird of prey from the east—a leader from a distant land who will come and do my bidding. I have said I would do it, and I will. (Isaiah 46:9–11 NLT)

Any pursuit of God's counterpart is vain. Any search for a godlike person or position on earth is futile. No one and nothing compares with him. No one advises him. No one helps him. It is he who "executes judgment, putting down one and lifting up another" (Psalm 75:7 ESV).

You and I may have power. But God *is* power. We may be a lightning bug, but he is lightning itself. "Wisdom and power are his" (Daniel 2:20 NIV).

Consider the universe around us. Unlike the potter who takes something and reshapes it, God took nothing and created something. God created everything that exists by divine fiat *ex nihilo* (out of nothing). He did not rely on material that was preexistent or coeternal. Prior to creation the universe was not a dark space. The universe did not exist. God even created the darkness. "I am the one who creates the light and makes the darkness" (Isaiah 45:7 NLT). John proclaimed, "You created everything, and it is for your pleasure that they exist and were created" (Revelation 4:11 NLT).

TRACE THE UNIVERSE BACK TO GOD'S POWER, AND FOLLOW HIS POWER UPSTREAM TO HIS WISDOM.

Trace the universe back to God's power, and follow his power upstream to his wisdom. God's omniscience governs his omnipotence. Infinite knowledge rules infinite strength. "He is wise in heart, and mighty in strength" (Job 9:4 KJV). "With him is wisdom and strength" (Job 12:13 KJV). "He is mighty in strength and wisdom" (Job 36:5 KJV).

His power is not capricious or careless. Quite the contrary. His wisdom manages and equals his strength. Paul announced, "Oh, the depths of the riches of the wisdom and knowledge of God! How unsearchable his judgments, and his paths beyond tracing out" (Romans 11:33 NIV).

His knowledge about you is as complete as his knowledge about the universe. "Even before a word is on my tongue, behold, O Lord, you know it altogether. . . . Your eyes saw my unformed substance; in your book were written, every one of them, the days that were formed for me, when as yet there were none of them" (Psalm 139:4, 16 ESV).

The veils that block your vision and mine do not block God's. Unspoken words are as if uttered. Unrevealed thoughts are as if proclaimed. Unoccurred moments are as if they were history. He knows the future, the past, the hidden, and the untold. Nothing is concealed from God. He is all-powerful, all-knowing, and all-present.

King David marveled, "Where can I go from Your Spirit? Or where can I flee from Your presence?" (Psalm 139:7). God reminds us, "I am everywhere—both near and far, in heaven and on earth" (Jeremiah 23:23–24 CEV).

See the "holy otherness" of God? In Isaiah's encounter, those who see him most clearly regard him most highly. He is so holy that sinless seraphim cannot bear to look at him! They cover their faces with their wings. They also, oddly, cover their feet. Why? In Hebrew the word for *feet* and the word for *genitalia* are the same.[4] Forgive the thought, but the confession of the angels is that they are absolutely impotent in the presence of God.

INFINITE KNOWLEDGE RULES INFINITE STRENGTH.

Isaiah could relate. When he sees the holiness of God, Isaiah does not boast or swagger. He takes no notes, plans no sermon series, launches no seminar tours. Instead, he falls on his face and begs for mercy. "Woe is me, for I am ruined! Because I am a man of unclean lips, and I live among a people of unclean lips; for my eyes have seen the King, the LORD of hosts" (Isaiah 6:5).

The God-given vision was not about Isaiah but about God and his glory. Isaiah gets the point. "It's not about me. It's all about him." He finds humility, not through seeking it, but through seeking him. One glimpse and the prophet claims citizenship among the infected and diseased—the "unclean," a term used to describe those with leprosy. God's holiness silences human boasting.

And God's mercy makes us holy. Look what happens next.

GOD'S HOLINESS SILENCES HUMAN BOASTING.

> Then one of the seraphim flew to me with a burning coal in his hand, which he had taken from the altar with tongs. He touched my mouth with it and said, "Behold, this has touched your lips; and your iniquity is taken away and your sin is forgiven." (Isaiah 6:6–7)

Isaiah makes no request. He asks for no grace. Indeed, he likely assumed mercy was impossible. But God, who is quick to pardon and full of mercy, purges Isaiah of his sin and redirects his life.

God solicits a spokesman. "Whom shall I send, and who will go for Us?" (6:8).

Isaiah's heart and hand shoot skyward. "Here am I. Send me!" (6:8). A glimpse of God's holiness and Isaiah had to speak. As if he'd found the source of the river, ridden the rage of the canyon. As if he'd seen what Moses had seen—God himself.

Albeit a glimpse, but a God-glimpse nonetheless.

And he was different as a result.

Holy different.

CHAPTER FIVE

JUST A MOMENT

5

Young parents typically rejoice when their children learn new phrases.

"Honey, little Bobby just said bye-bye!"

"Mom, you'll never believe what your granddaughter just did. She counted to five."

Or, "Ernie, tell your uncle what the bird says."

We applaud such moments. I did too.

With one exception.

One phrase my daughter learned gave me pause. Jenna was nearly or barely two years of age, just learning to speak well. With her little hand lost in my big one, we walked through the lobby of our apartment building. Suddenly she stopped. Spotting a ball, she looked up at me and requested, "Just a moment." Sliding her hand from mine, she walked away.

A moment? Who had told her about moments? To date, her existence had been time-free. Toddlers know no beginning or end or hurry or slow or late or soon. The small world of a child amplifies present tense and diminishes future and past. But Jenna's phrase, "Just a moment," announced that time had entered her world.

In his autobiography, *The Sacred Journey,* Frederick Buechner divides his life into three parts: "once below a time," "once above a time," and "beyond time." The childhood years, he says, are lived "once below a time. . . . What child, while summer is happening, bothers to think that summer will end? What child, when snow is on the ground, stops to remember that not long ago the ground was snowless?"[1]

Is childhood for us what life in the Garden was like for Adam and Eve? Before the couple swallowed the line of Satan and the fruit of the tree, no one printed calendars or wore watches or needed cemeteries. They indwelt a time-free world. Minutes passed equally unmeasured in Jenna's two-year-old world. No thought of life being anything different than daily walks and naps and music and Mom and Dad. But "just a moment" belied the intrusion of pirates on her innocent island. Time had invaded her world.

Life, she was discovering, is a cache of moments: measurable and countable increments, like change in a pocket or buttons in a can. Your pocket may be full of decades, my pocket may be down to a few years, but everyone has a certain number of moments.

NOT EVEN GOD MADE GOD.

Everyone, that is, except God. As we list the mind-stretching claims of Christ, let's include this one near the top. "Before Abraham was born, I am" (John 8:58). If the mob didn't want to kill Jesus before that sentence, they did afterward. Jesus claimed to be God, the Eternal Being. He identified himself as "the High and Lofty One Who inhabits eternity" (Isaiah 57:15 NKJV).

Scripture broadcasts this attribute in surround-sound. God is "from everlasting" (Psalm 93:2 NKJV) and the "everlasting King" (Jeremiah 10:10 NKJV), "incorruptible" (Romans 1:23 NKJV), "who alone has immortality" (1 Timothy 6:16 NKJV). The heavens and the earth will perish, "but You [O God] are the same, and Your years will have no end" (Psalm 102:27 NKJV). You'll more quickly measure the salt of the ocean than measure the existence of God because "the number of His years is unsearchable" (Job 36:26).

Trace the tree back to a seed. Trace the dress back to a factory. Trace the baby back to a mommy. Trace God back to . . . to . . . to . . .

No one. Not even God made God. "From eternity I am He" (Isaiah 43:13). For that reason we have Jesus making statements such as, "Before Abraham was born, I am" (John 8:58). He didn't say, "Before Abraham was born, *I was*." God never says, "I was," because he still is. He is—right now—in the days of Abraham and in the end of time. He is eternal. He does not live sequential moments, laid out on a time line, one following the other. His world is one moment or, better stated, momentless.

HE KNOWS YOUR BEGINNING AND YOUR END, BECAUSE HE HAS NEITHER.

He doesn't view history as a progression of centuries but as a single photo. He captures your life, your entire life, in one glance. He sees your birth and burial in one frame. He knows your beginning and your end, because he has neither.

Doesn't make sense, does it? Eternity makes no sense to us, the timebound. You might as well be handed a book written in kanji (unless, of course, you are Japanese). You look at the characters, and all you see is zigzagged lines. You shake your head. This language finds no home in your mind.

But what if someone taught you how to read and write the language? Suppose a native speaker had the time and you had the will so that day by day the symbols that meant nothing to you began to mean something?

With God's help, the same is happening to you and me regarding eternity. He is teaching us the language. "He has also set eternity in their heart" (Ecclesiastes 3:11). Tucked away in each of us is a hunch that we were made for forever and a hope that the hunch is true.

Remember the story of the eagle who was raised by chickens? From the floor of the barnyard she spots an eagle in the clouds, and her heart stirs. "I can do that!" she whispers. The other chickens laugh, but she knows better. She was born different. Born with a belief.

You were too. Your world extends beyond the barnyard of time. A foreverness woos you. Your heavenly life Everests the pebbles of your earthly life. If grains of sand measured the two, how would they stack up? Heaven would be every grain of sand on every beach on earth, plus more. Earthly life, by contrast, would be one hundredth of one grain of sand. Need a phrase to summarize the length of your life on earth? Try Jenna's: "Just a moment."

Wasn't this the phrase of choice for Paul? "Our light affliction, which is *but for a moment,* is working for us a far more exceeding and eternal weight of glory" (2 Corinthians 4:17 NKJV, emphasis mine).

What if we had a glimpse of the apostle as he wrote those words? By this time he had been "beaten times without number, often in danger of death. Five times," he writes, "I received from the Jews thirty-nine lashes. Three times I was beaten with rods, once I was stoned, three times I was shipwrecked, a night and a day I have spent in the deep" (2 Corinthians 11:23–25). He goes on to refer to life-threatening river trips, wilderness wanderings, and exposure to cold, attacks, hunger, and thirst. These, in Paul's words, are light afflictions to be endured for just a moment.

What if we took the same attitude toward life? What if we saw our tough times as a grain of sand scarcely worthy of contrast with the forever dunes?

What if the woman who stopped me the other day would do that? She spoke of seventeen years of a bad marriage. His mistakes, her mistakes. His drinking, her impatience. And now she wants out. After all, her life is blitzing past. If she is going to live, she'd best get busy! Besides, who can assure her that the marriage will work? How does she know that she's not in for two more decades of tough times? She doesn't.

"All about me," counsel says. "Life is short—get out."

God's wisdom, however, says, "Life is short—stay in."

The brevity of life grants power to abide, not an excuse to bail. Fleeting days don't justify fleeing problems. Fleeting days strengthen us to endure problems. Will your problems pass? No guarantee they will. Will your pain cease? Perhaps. Perhaps not. But heaven gives this promise: "our light affliction, which is but for a moment, is working for us a far more exceeding and eternal weight of glory" (2 Corinthians 4:17 NKJV).

The words "weight of glory" conjure up images of the ancient pan scale. Remember the blindfolded lady of justice? She holds a pan scale—two pans, one on either side of the needle. The weight of a purchase would be determined by placing weights on one side and the purchase on the other.

THE BREVITY OF LIFE GRANTS POWER TO ABIDE, NOT AN EXCUSE TO BAIL.

God does the same with your struggles. On one side he stacks all your burdens. Famines. Firings. Parents who forgot you. Bosses who ignored you. Bad breaks, bad health, bad days. Stack them up, and watch one side of the pan scale plummet.

Now witness God's response. Does he remove them? Eliminate the burdens? No, rather than take them, he offsets them. He places an eternal weight of glory on the other side. Endless joy. Measureless peace. An eternity of him. Watch what happens as he sets eternity on your scale.

Everything changes! The burdens lift. The heavy becomes

light when weighed against eternity. If life is "just a moment," can't we endure any challenge for a moment?

We can be sick for *just a moment.*

We can be lonely for *just a moment.*

We can be persecuted for *just a moment.*

We can struggle for *just a moment.*

Can't we?

Can't we wait for our peace? It's not about us anyway. And it's certainly not about now.

CHAPTER SIX

HIS UNCHANGING HAND

6

1966. Lyndon Johnson was president. The voices of Goldwater and Dirksen dominated the Senate. Watergate was a D.C. apartment building, and the best known Bush was the one that spoke to Moses. Vietnam rumbled. Hippies rocked. Woodstock was a dairy farm, and the Lucados were moving into a new home.

LBJ soon moved back to Texas, and Watergate snakebit Nixon. Goldwater and Dirksen stepped down, and the Bushes stepped up. Vietnam, hippies, and Woodstock faded like tie-dyed T-shirts, but the Lucado family stayed in that yellow-brick house. For thirty-five years we stayed.

The Beatles came and went. The economy rose and fell and rose again. Much changed, but there was always a Lucado living in the three-bedroom house just off Avenue G.

Until today. As I write, movers load three decades of family life into a truck. The mailman is peeling "Lucado" off the mailbox and stenciling on "Hernandez."

The vacating was bound to happen. It had to happen. But

it's hard to see it happen. Change, like taxes, is necessary but unwelcome.

Change? a few of you are thinking. *You want to talk about change? Let me tell you about change . . .*

Let me tell you about my changing body—Chemotherapists treat my body like a pincushion.

My changing family—We're "Surprise! Pregnant." I'll wear maternity clothes to the high school graduation of my firstborn.

The changing economy—If my investments don't improve, I'll spend my retirement eating macaroni and cheese.

Our changing business—I'm jobless. Mailing resumés pays no bills.

Change. Had more than your share? Wishing you could freeze-frame the video of your world? Would it help to stand in Saint Peter's Square and tell the fellow on the balcony, "Stop! No more change!"?

Save your breath. He can't help. If you're looking for a place with no change, try a soda machine. With life comes change.

With change comes fear, insecurity, sorrow, stress. So what do you do? Hibernate? Take no risks for fear of failing? Give no love for fear of losing? Some opt to. They hold back.

A better idea is to look up. Set your bearings on the one and only North Star in the universe—God. For though life changes, he never does. Scripture makes pupil-popping claims about his permanence.

Consider his strength. Unending. According to Paul, God's power lasts forever (Romans 1:20). His strength never diminishes. Yours and mine will and has. Our energy ebbs and flows more than the Thames River. You aren't as alert in the evening as in the morning. You can't run as fast when you are eighty as when you are twenty. Even the strongest among us must eventually rest. Lance Armstrong can maintain a bike speed of thirty-two mph for a solid hour. Healthy college males last forty-five seconds at that pace. I'd make thirty before wanting to throw up. Armstrong lives up to the last half of his last name. He is strong. But at some point he must rest. His head seeks the pillow, and his body seeks sleep.[1]

Call Jim Eubank strong. Swimming seventy laps a day and holding half a dozen endurance swim records would be proof alone. But still logging a daily mile in the pool and winning races at age eighty-five?[2] Don the Speedo and flex those lats, Mr. Eubank. You are strong, but you won't be strong forever.

God will. The words "I'm feeling strong today" he has never said. He feels equally strong every day.

Daniel calls him "the living God, enduring forever" (Daniel 6:26 ESV). The psalmist tells him, "I will sing of your strength. . . . For you have been to me a fortress and a refuge in the day of my distress. O my Strength, I will sing praises to you, for you, O God, are my fortress, the God who shows me steadfast love" (Psalm 59:16–17 ESV).

Think about it. God never pauses to eat or asks the angels to cover for him while he naps. He never signals a time-out or puts the prayer requests from Russia on hold while he handles South Africa. He "never tires and never sleeps" (Psalm 121:4 NLT). Need a strong hand to hold? You'll always find one in his. His strength never changes.

Need unchanging truth to trust? Try God's. His truth never wavers.

Would that we could say the same. We've learned to season our words with salt, we eat them so often. Our opinions change like Rodeo Drive fashion trends. (Weren't your convictions about child rearing stronger before you had kids? Do you know any Republicans who used to be Democrats and vice versa?) Our convictions tend to change.

He never signals a time-out or puts the prayer requests from Russia on hold while he handles South Africa.

Good to know God's don't. His view of right and wrong is the same with you and me as it was with Adam and Eve.

"The word of our God shall stand for ever" (Isaiah 40:8 KJV). "For ever, O Lord, thy word is settled in heaven. . . . All thy commandments are truth. . . . Thou hast founded them for ever" (Psalm 119:89, 151–152 KJV).

Your outlook may change. My convictions may sway, but "the Scripture cannot be broken" (John 10:35 NKJV). And since it can't, since his truth will not waver, God's ways will never alter.

He will always hate sin and love sinners, despise the proud and exalt the humble. He will always convict the evildoer and comfort the heavy-hearted. He never changes direction midstream, recalibrates the course midway home, or amends the heavenly Constitution. God will always be the same.

No one else will. Lovers call you today and scorn you tomorrow. Companies follow pay raises with pink slips. Friends applaud you when you drive a classic and dismiss you when you drive a dud. Not God. God is "always the same" (Psalm 102:27 ESV). With him "there is no variation or shadow due to change" (James 1:17 ESV).

Catch God in a bad mood? Won't happen. Fear exhausting his grace? A sardine will swallow the Atlantic first. Think he's given up on you? Wrong. Did he not make a promise to you? "God is not a human being, and he will not lie. He is not a human, and he does not change his mind. What he says he will do, he does. What he promises, he makes come true" (Numbers 23:19 NCV). He's never sullen or sour, sulking or stressed. His strength, truth, ways, and love never change. He is "the same yesterday and today and forever" (Hebrews 13:8 ESV). And because he is, the Lord "will be the stability of your times" (Isaiah 33:6 NKJV).

And couldn't we use some stability? For twenty-seven years the citizens of South Padre trusted the stability of the Queen Isabella Causeway, the longest bridge in Texas. Every day 19,000 motorists used her to travel between Port Isabel and South Padre Island. Secured by tons of concrete, the two-and-a-quarter-mile bridge was the only connection between the mainland and the island. Buttressed by deep pilings, approved by the best engineers. No one questioned the Queen Isabella.

Until September 15, 2001. At two o'clock in the morning four barges and a tugboat crashed into the support system and brought the bridge down, plunging cars and people into the Laguna Madre eighty-five feet below. Eight people died when 240 feet of the bridge collapsed.[3]

You need never fear the same will happen to God's plan. His plan—born in eternity—will withstand any attack of humanity. Atheists, antagonists, skeptics, scholars—they've slammed into the bridge, but it has never budged. Texas engineers are regretting their work, but God will never regret his. "The Glory of Israel will not lie or have regret," declared Samuel, "for he is not a man, that he should have regret" (1 Samuel 15:29 ESV).

HIS PLAN—BORN IN ETERNITY—WILL WITHSTAND ANY ATTACK OF HUMANITY.

God's plans will never change, because he makes his plans in complete knowledge. Forget hopeful forecasting. He declares "the end from the beginning" (Isaiah 46:10). Nothing takes him by surprise. "The plans of the LORD stand firm forever" (Psalm 33:11 NIV).

The cross will not lose its power. The blood of Christ will not fade in strength. Heaven will never announce the collapse of the bridge. God will never return to the drawing board. "What He does in time He planned from eternity. And all that He planned in eternity He carries out in time."[4]

"The LORD Almighty has spoken—who can change his plans? When his hand moves, who can stop him?" (Isaiah 14:27 NLT). God never changes. Everyone else does. Everything else will.

In the hours I prepared this message, the movers all but emptied the Lucado house. Christmas meals, dinner-table laughter, good-night hugs for my clan under that roof—all past tense. Yet another constant becomes a transient. What changes are you facing?

Cemeteries interrupt the finest families.

Retirement finds the best employees.

Age withers the strongest bodies.

With life comes change.

But with change comes the reassuring appreciation of heaven's permanence. His "firm foundation stands" (2 Timothy 2:19 ESV). His house will stand forever.

CHAPTER SEVEN

God's Great Love

7

Several hundred feet beneath my chair is a lake, an underground cavern of crystalline water known as the Edwards Aquifer. We South Texans know much about this aquifer. We know its length (175 miles). We know its layout (west to east except under San Antonio, where it runs north to south). We know the water is pure. Fresh. It irrigates farms and waters lawns and fills pools and quenches thirst. We know much about the aquifer.

But for all the facts we do know, there is an essential one we don't. We don't know its size. The depth of the cavern? A mystery. Number of gallons? Unmeasured. No one knows the amount of water the aquifer contains.

Watch the nightly weather report, and you'd think otherwise. Meteorologists give regular updates on the aquifer level. You get the impression that the amount of water is calculated. "The truth is," a friend told me, "no one knows how much water is down there."

Could this be? I decided to find out. I called a water conservationist. "That's right," he affirmed. "We estimate. We try to measure. But the exact quantity? No one knows." Remarkable. We use it, depend upon it, would perish without it . . . but measure it? We can't.

Bring to mind another unmeasured pool? It might. Not a pool of water but a pool of love. God's love. Aquifer fresh. Pure as April snow. One swallow slackens the thirsty throat and softens the crusty heart. Immerse a life in God's love, and watch it emerge cleansed and changed. We know the impact of God's love.

But the volume? No person has ever measured it.

Moral meteorologists, worried we might exhaust the supply, suggest otherwise. "Don't drink too deeply," they caution, recommending rationed portions. Some people, after all, drink more than their share. Terrorists and traitors and wife beaters—let such scoundrels start drinking, and they may take too much.

GOD'S LOVE . . . ONE SWALLOW SLACKENS THE THIRSTY THROAT AND SOFTENS THE CRUSTY HEART.

But who has plumbed the depths of God's love? Only God has. "Want to see the size of my love?" he invites. "Ascend the winding path outside of Jerusalem. Follow the dots of bloody dirt until you crest the hill. Before looking up, pause and hear me whisper, 'This is how much I love you.' "

Whip-ripped muscles drape his back. Blood rivulets over his face. His eyes and lips are swollen shut. Pain rages at wildfire intensity. As he sinks to relieve the agony of his legs, his airway closes. At the edge of suffocation, he shoves pierced muscles against the spike and inches up the cross. He does this for hours. Painfully up and down until his strength and our doubts are gone.

Does God love you? Behold the cross, and behold your answer.

God the Son died for you. Who could have imagined such a gift? At the time Martin Luther was having his Bible printed in Germany, a printer's daughter encountered God's love. No one had told her about Jesus. Toward God she felt no emotion but fear. One day she gathered pieces of fallen Scripture from the floor. On one paper she found the words "For God so loved the world, that he gave . . . " The rest of the verse had not yet been printed. Still, what she saw was enough to move her. The thought that God would give anything moved her from fear to joy. Her mother noticed the change of attitude. When asked the cause of her happiness, the daughter produced the crumpled piece of partial verse from her pocket. The mother read it and asked, "What did he give?" The child was perplexed for a moment and then answered, "I do not know. But if He loved us well enough to give us anything, we should not be afraid of Him."[1]

Had God given his children a great idea or a lyrical message or an endless song . . . but he gave himself. "[God the Son] loved us and gave himself up for us as a fragrant offering and sacrifice to God" (Ephesians 5:2 NIV). What species of devotion is this? Find the answer under the category "unfailing." The holiness of God demanded a sinless sacrifice, and the only sinless sacrifice was God the Son. And since God's love never fails to pay the price, he did. God loves you with an unfailing love.

England saw a glimpse of such love in 1878. The second daughter of Queen Victoria was Princess Alice. Her young son was infected with a horrible affliction known as black diphtheria. Doctors quarantined the boy and told the mother to stay away.

But she couldn't. One day she overheard him whisper to the nurse, "Why doesn't my mother kiss me anymore?" The words melted her heart. She ran to her son and smothered him with kisses. Within a few days, she was buried.[2]

What would drive a mother to do such a thing? What would lead God to do something greater? Love. Trace the greatest action of God to the greatest attribute of God—his love.

But how does God's love square with the theme of this book? After all, "It's not about me." If it's not about me, does God care about me? God's priority is his glory. He occupies center stage; I carry props. He's the message; I'm but a word. Is this love?

No doubt. Do you really want the world to revolve around you? If it's all about you, then it's all up to you. Your Father rescues you from such a burden. While you are valuable, you aren't essential. You're important but not indispensable.

If it's all about you, then it's all up to you.

Still don't think that's good news?

Perhaps a story would be helpful. My father, an oil-field mechanic, never met a car he couldn't fix. Forget golf clubs or tennis rackets, my dad's toys were sockets and wrenches. He relished a wrecked engine. Once, while he was driving us to visit his sister in New Mexico, the car blew a rod. Most men would have groaned all the way to the mechanic. Not Dad. He called a tow truck and grinned the rest of the ride to my aunt's house. To this day I suspect paternal sabotage. A week of family chitchat repulsed him. But a week under the hood? *Forget the coffee and cookies. Hand me the manifold.* Dad did with a V-8 engine what Patton did with a platoon—he made it work.

Oh, that the same could be said for his youngest son. It can't. My problem with mechanics begins with the ends of the car. I can't remember which one holds the engine. Anyone who confuses the spare tire with the fan belt is likely not gifted in car repair.

My ignorance left my dad in a precarious position. What does a skilled mechanic do with a son who is anything but? As you begin formulating an answer, may I ask this question: What does God do with us? Under his care the universe runs like a Rolex. But his children? Most of us have trouble balancing a checkbook. So what does he do?

I know what my dad did. Much to his credit, he let me help him. He gave me jobs to do—holding wrenches, scrubbing spark plugs. And he knew my limits. Never once did he say, "Max, tear apart that transmission, will you? One of the gears is broken." Never said it. For one thing, he liked his transmission. For another, he loved me. He loved me too much to give me too much.

So does God. He knows your limitations. He's well aware of your weaknesses. You can no more die for your own sins than you can solve world hunger. And, according to him, that's okay. The world doesn't rely on you. God loves you too much to say it's all about you. He keeps the cosmos humming. You and I sprinkle sawdust on oil spots and thank him for the privilege. We've peeked under the hood. We don't know what it takes to run the world, and wise are we who leave the work to his hands.

To say "It's not about you" is not to say you aren't loved; quite the contrary. It's because God loves you that it's not about you.

You can no more die for your own sins than you can solve world hunger.

And, oh, what a love this is. It's "too wonderful to be measured" (Ephesians 3:19 CEV). But though we cannot measure it, may I urge you to trust it? Some of you are so hungry for such love. Those who should have loved you didn't. Those who could have loved you wouldn't. You were left at the hospital. Left at the altar. Left with an empty bed. Left with a broken heart. Left with your question, "Does anybody love me?"

Please listen to heaven's answer. As you ponder him on the cross, hear God assure, "I do."

Someday someone will likely find the limits of the South Texas aquifer. A robotic submarine, even a diver, will descend through the water until it hits solid ground. "We've plumbed the depths," newspapers will announce. Will someone say the same of God's love? No. When it comes to water, we'll find the limit. But when it comes to his love, we never will.

PART TWO

GOD-PROMOTING

CHAPTER EIGHT

God's Mirrors

8

G. R. Tweed looked across the Pacific waters at the American ship on the horizon. Brushing the jungle sweat from his eyes, the young naval officer swallowed deeply and made his decision. This could be his only chance for escape.

Tweed had been hiding on Guam for nearly three years. When the Japanese occupied the island in 1941, he ducked into the thick tropical brush. Survival hadn't been easy, but he preferred the swamp to a POW camp.

Late in the day July 10, 1944, he spotted the friendly vessel. He scurried up a hill and positioned himself on a cliff. Reaching into his pack, he pulled out a small mirror. At 6:20 P.M., he began sending signals. Holding the edge of the mirror in his fingers, he tilted it back and forth, bouncing the sunrays in the direction of the boat. Three short flashes. Three long. Three short again. Dot-dot-dot. Dash-dash-dash. Dot-dot-dot. SOS.

The signal caught the eye of a sailor on board the USS *McCall*. A rescue party boarded a motorized dinghy and slipped into the cove past the coastal guns. Tweed was rescued.[1]

He was glad to have that mirror, glad he knew how to use it, and glad that the mirror cooperated. Suppose it hadn't. (Prepare yourself for a crazy thought.) Suppose the mirror had resisted, pushed its own agenda. Rather than reflect a message from the sun, suppose it had opted to send its own. After all, three years of isolation would leave one starved for attention. Rather than sending an SOS, the mirror could have sent an LAM. "Look at me."

An egotistical mirror?

The only crazier thought would be an insecure mirror. *What if I blow it? What if I send a dash when I'm supposed to send a dot? Besides, have you seen the blemishes on my surface?* Self-doubt could paralyze a mirror.

So could self-pity. *Been crammed down in that pack, lugged through jungles, and now, all of a sudden expected to face the bright sun and perform a crucial service. No way. Staying in the pack. Not getting any reflection out of me.*

Good thing Tweed's mirror didn't have a mind of its own.

But God's mirrors? Unfortunately we do.

We are his mirrors, you know. Tools of heaven's heliography. Reduce the human job description down to one phrase, and this is it: Reflect God's glory. As Paul wrote: "And we, with our unveiled faces reflecting like mirrors the brightness of the Lord, all grow brighter and brighter as we are turned into the image that we reflect; this is the work of the Lord who is Spirit" (2 Corinthians 3:18 JB).

REDUCE THE HUMAN JOB DESCRIPTION DOWN TO ONE PHRASE, AND THIS IS IT: REFLECT GOD'S GLORY.

Some reader just arched an eyebrow. *Wait a second,* you are thinking. *I've read that passage before, more than once. And it sounded different.* Indeed it may have. Perhaps it's because you are used to reading it in a different translation. "But we all, with unveiled face, *beholding as in a mirror* the glory of the Lord, are being transformed into the same image from glory to glory, just as from the Lord, the Spirit" (emphasis mine).

One translation says, "beholding as in a mirror;" another says, "reflecting like mirrors." One implies contemplation; the other implies refraction. Which is accurate?

Actually both. The verb *katoptrizo* can be translated either way. Translators are in both camps:

"with unveiled face, *beholding*" (RSV)

"*beholding* as in a glass" (KJV)

"*reflecting* like mirrors" (JB)

"be mirrors that brightly *reflect*" (TLB)

"we . . . all *reflect* the Lord's glory" (NIV)

But which meaning did Paul intend? In the context of the passage, Paul paralleled the Christian experience to the Mount Sinai experience of Moses. After the patriarch *beheld* the glory of God, his face *reflected* the glory of God. "The people of Israel could not bear to look at Moses' face. For his face shone with the glory of God" (2 Corinthians 3:7 NLT).

The face of Moses was so dazzling white that the "people of Israel could no more look right at him than stare into the sun" (2 Corinthians 3:7 MSG).

Upon beholding God, Moses could not help but reflect God. *The brightness he saw was the brightness he became.* Beholding led to becoming. Becoming led to reflecting. Perhaps the answer to the translation question, then, is "yes."

Did Paul mean "beholding as in a mirror"? Yes.

Did Paul mean "reflecting like a mirror"? Yes.

Could it be that the Holy Spirit intentionally selected a verb that would remind us to do both? To behold God so intently that we can't help but reflect him?

What does it mean to behold your face in a mirror? A quick glance? A casual look? No. To behold is to study, to stare, to contemplate. Beholding God's glory, then, is no side look or occasional glance; this beholding is a serious pondering.

Isn't that what we have done? We have camped at the foot of Mount Sinai and beheld the glory of God. Wisdom unsearchable. Purity unspotted. Years unending. Strength undaunted. Love immeasurable. Glimpses of the glory of God.

Beholding leads to becoming. Becoming leads to reflecting.

As we behold his glory, dare we pray that we, like Moses, will reflect it? Dare we hope to be mirrors in the hands of God, the reflection of the light of God? This is the call.

"Whatever you do, do all to the glory of God" (1 Corinthians 10:31 NKJV).

Whatever? Whatever.

Let your message reflect his glory. "Let your light shine before men, that they may see your good deeds and praise your Father in heaven" (Matthew 5:16 NIV).

Let your salvation reflect God's glory. "Having believed, you were marked in him with a seal, the promised Holy Spirit, who is a deposit guaranteeing our inheritance until the redemption of those who are God's possession—to the praise of his glory" (Ephesians 1:13–14 NIV).

Let your body reflect God's glory. "You are not your own.

. . . Glorify God in your body"(1 Corinthians 6:19–20).

Your struggles. "These sufferings of ours are for your benefit. And the more of you who are won to Christ, the more there are to thank him for his great kindness, and the more the Lord is glorified" (2 Corinthians 4:15 TLB; see also John 11:4).

Your success honors God. "Honor the LORD with your wealth" (Proverbs 3:9 NIV). "Riches and honor come from you" (1 Chronicles 29:12 NCV). "God . . . is giving you power to make wealth" (Deuteronomy 8:18).

Your message, your salvation, your body, your struggles, your success—all proclaim God's glory.

"Whatever you do in word or deed, do all in the name of the Lord Jesus, giving thanks through Him to God the Father" (Colossians 3:17).

HE SENDS THE MESSAGE;
WE MIRROR IT.

He's the source; we are the glass. He's the light; we are the mirrors. He sends the message; we mirror it. We rest in his pack awaiting his call. And when placed in his hands, we do his work. It's not about us; it's all about him.

Mr. Tweed's use of a mirror led to a rescue.

May God's use of us lead to millions more.

CHAPTER NINE

My Message Is About Him

9

Behind him, a trail of tracks.

Beneath him, a pounding stallion.

Before him, miles of trail to cover.

Within him, a flint-rock resolve.

Squinty eyed. Firm jawed. Rawboned. Pony Express riders had one assignment—deliver the message safely and quickly. They seized every advantage: the shortest route, the fastest horse, the lightest saddle. Even the lightest lunchbox.

Only the sturdy were hired. Could they handle the horses? The heat? Could they outrun robbers and outlast blizzards? The young and the orphans were preferred. Those selected were given $125 a month (a good salary in 1860), a Colt revolver, a lightweight rifle, a bright red shirt, blue trousers, and eight hours to cover eighty miles, six days a week.

Hard work and high pay. But the message was worth it.[1]

The apostle Paul would have loved the Pony Express. For he, like the riders, had been entrusted with a message.

"I have a duty to all people," Paul told the Roman church (Romans 1:14 NCV). He had something for them—a message. He'd been entrusted as a Pony Express courier with a divine message, the gospel. Nothing mattered more to Paul than the gospel. "I am not ashamed of the gospel," he wrote next, "because it is the power of God for the salvation of everyone who believes" (Romans 1:16 NIV).

Paul existed to deliver the message. How people remembered him was secondary. (Else why would he introduce himself as a slave? Romans 1:1). How people remembered Christ was primary. Paul's message was not about himself. His message was all about Christ.

How difficult for us to maintain this focus. Don't we tend to tinker with the message? Aren't we prone to insert lines of self-service?

A young guide in the art museum was. One sentence summarized his job: Lead people to the paintings, answer their questions, and step out of the way. Initially he succeeded. He walked the clients to the framed treasures, identified the artists, and stepped out of view.

"This is a Monet," he would say and move back as people oohed and aahed and asked a question or two. When they were ready, he would lead them to the next masterpiece and repeat the sequence. "This is the work of Rembrandt." He stepped back; they leaned in. He stood; they stared.

Simple job. Delightful job. He took great pride in his work.

Too much pride, one might say. For in a short time, he forgot his role. He began thinking the people had come to see him. Rather than step away from the work of art, he lingered near it. As they oohed and aahed, he smiled. "Glad you like it," he replied, chest lifting, face blushing. He even responded with an occasional "thank you," taking credit for work he didn't do.

Visitors disregarded his comments. But they couldn't dismiss his movements. Lingering near a painting was no longer sufficient for the guide. Little by little he inched toward it. Initially extending his arm over the frame, then his torso over part of the canvas. Finally his body blocked the entire piece. People could see him but not the art. The very work he was sent to reveal he began to conceal.

That's when his Superior intervened. "This job isn't about you, Max. Don't obscure my masterpieces."

How many times has he had to remind me? The very first time I was called to display a painting, I was tempted to eclipse it.

The request came when I was twenty. "Can you address our church youth group?" We aren't talking citywide crusade here. Think more in terms of a dozen kids around a West Texas campfire. I was new to the faith, hence new to the power of the faith. I told my story, and, lo and behold, they listened! One even approached me afterward and said something like, "That moved me, Max." My chest lifted, and my feet shifted just a step in the direction of the painting.

God has been nudging me back ever since.

I BELIEVE SATAN TRAINS BATTALIONS OF DEMONS TO WHISPER ONE QUESTION IN OUR EARS: "WHAT ARE PEOPLE THINKING OF YOU?"

Some of you don't relate. The limelight never woos you. You and John the Baptist sing the same tune: "He must become greater and greater, and I must become less and less" (John 3:30 NLT). God bless you. You might pray for the rest of us. We applause-aholics have done it all: dropped names, sung loudly, dressed up to look classy, dressed down to look cool, quoted authors we've never read, spouted Greek we've never studied. For the life of me, I believe Satan trains battalions of demons to whisper one question in our ears: "What are people thinking of you?"

A deadly query. What they think of us matters not. What they think of God matters all. God will not share his glory with another (Isaiah 42:8). Next time you need a nudge away from the spotlight, remember: *You are simply one link in a chain, an unimportant link at that.*

Don't agree? Take it up with the apostle. "So the one who plants *is not important*, and the one who waters *is not important.* Only God, who makes things grow, is important" (1 Corinthians 3:7 NCV, emphasis mine).

Remember the other messengers God has used?

A donkey to speak to Balaam (Numbers 22:28).

A staff-turned-snake to stir Pharaoh (Exodus 7:10).

He used stubborn oxen to make a point about reverence and a big fish to make a point about reluctant preachers (1 Samuel 6:1–12; Jonah 1:1–17).

God doesn't need you and me to do his work. We are expedient messengers, ambassadors by his kindness, not by our cleverness.

It's not about us, and it angers him when we think it is. Jesus has a stern warning for gallery guides who eclipse his work.

> When you do something for someone else, don't call attention to yourself. You've seen them in action, I'm sure—"playactors" I call them—treating prayer meeting and street corner alike as a stage, acting compassionate as

long as someone is watching, playing to the crowds. They get applause, true, but that's all they get. (Matthew 6:2 MSG)

Pony Express riders didn't take credit for kind letters.

Gallery guides don't deserve applause for great art.

And we entrusted with the gospel dare not seek applause but best deflect applause. For our message is about Someone else.

GOD DOESN'T NEED YOU AND ME TO DO HIS WORK. WE ARE EXPEDIENT MESSENGERS, AMBASSADORS BY HIS KINDNESS, NOT BY OUR CLEVERNESS.

A European village priest in medieval times once gathered his church for a special service. "Come tonight," he told them, "for a special sermon on Jesus." And they did. They came. To their surprise, however, no candles illuminated the sanctuary. They groped their way to the pews and took their seats. The priest was nowhere to be seen. But soon he was heard walking through the church toward the front. When he reached the crucifix that hung on the wall, he lit a candle. Saying nothing, he illuminated the pierced feet of Christ, then the side, then one hand, and then the other. Lifting the candle, he shed light on the blood-masked face and the crown of thorns. With a puff, he blew out the candle and dismissed the church.[2]

May we do nothing more.

May we do nothing less.

CHAPTER TEN

My Salvation Is About Him

10

A large American food company released the perfect cake mix. It required no additives. No eggs, no sugar. Just mix some water with the powder, pop the pan in the oven, and presto! Prepare yourself for a treat.

One problem surfaced. No one purchased the product! Puzzled, the manufacturer conducted surveys, identified the reason, and reissued the cake with a slight alteration. The instructions now called for the cook to add one egg. Sales skyrocketed.[1]

Why are we like that? What makes us want to add to what is already complete? Paul asked the same questions. People puzzled him by adding their work to a finished project. Not eggs to a recipe but requirements for salvation. Not much, just one small rule: You must be circumcised to be saved.

Such talk rankled the apostle. "We . . . put no confidence in the flesh," he declared (Philippians 3:3 NIV). "God's way of making us right with himself depends on faith—counting on

Christ alone" (3:9 TLB, emphasis mine). Paul proclaimed a pure grace: no mixtures, no additives, no alterations. The work of Christ is the bungee cord for the soul. Trust it and take the plunge.

We quickly side with Paul on the circumcision controversy. The whole discussion sounds odd to our Western ears. But is it so strange? We may not teach Jesus + circumcision, but how about:

Jesus + evangelism: *How many people have you led to Christ this year?* Or:

Jesus + contribution: *Are you giving all you can to the church?* Or:

Jesus + mysticism: *You do offer penance and pray to the Virgin Mary, don't you?* Or:

Jesus + heritage: *Were you raised in "the church"?* Or:

Jesus + doctrine: *When you were baptized, was the water running or still? Deep or shallow? Hot or cold?*

Legalism. The theology of "Jesus +." Legalists don't dismiss Christ. They trust in Christ a lot. But they don't trust in Christ alone.

We're tempted to dismiss legalism as harmless. After all, legalists look good. They act religious. They promote morality and decency and good living. Is there any harm to their teaching?

Paul responds with a resounding "yes!" He reserves a biting

tone for the legalist. "Watch out for those who do evil, who are like dogs, who demand to cut the body" (Philippians 3:2 NCV). Ouch! Can you hear the intolerance in those terms? "Evil." "Dogs." Those "who demand to cut the body" or, as one paraphrase renders it, "knife-happy circumcisers" (MSG).

LEGALISTS TRUST IN CHRIST A LOT. BUT THEY DON'T TRUST IN CHRIST ALONE.

Why the bared fangs? Why the hot ink? Paul didn't go barefisted with others this way. Though antiadultery, he didn't call two-timers names. He was intolerant of homosexuality, but he didn't blast the gay crowd with a verbal blowtorch. He preached against drunkenness, but did he ever call drunks "dogs"?

And if you think he's ticked off in this passage, read his wish for the legalists of Galatia. "I wish the people who are bothering you would castrate themselves" (Galatians 5:12 NCV).

Why the intensity? Why so strident against legalists? Simple. Self-salvation makes light of our problem.

On our own, we're spiritually sunk, my friend. As sunk as the *Kursk*. Remember the nuclear submarine *Kursk*, the pride of the Russian navy? August 12, 2000, was to be her banner day. Five high-ranking naval officers journeyed to sea to witness a demonstration of her strength. But then came two explosions, enormous thundering booms that registered 1.5 and 3.5 on the Richter scale. Something had gone dreadfully wrong.

The seven-ton vessel immediately took on water and plunged 350 feet to the seabed of the Arctic Ocean. Most of the 118 crew members died instantly. Others were left to spend their last hours in freezing, horrid conditions.[2]

Are we not like the sailors? Are we not equally helpless and hopeless? Like them, we are submerged—not in salt water but in sin. We need to be lifted up—not out of the ocean but out of our failures. "There is no one who always does what is right, not even one" (Romans 3:10 NCV). Like the sailors, we've hit bottom.

But suppose one of the submerged sailors thought of a solution. Suppose he declared to his fellow crewmen, "I know what to do. Let's all press our hands on the ceiling and push. We will shove the sub to the surface." Can you imagine the looks the crew would give him? *Push a seven-ton vessel up through 350 feet of water?* If they said anything, they would tell him to come to his senses. "You don't understand the gravity of the situation. We don't have what it takes to save our lives. We aren't strong enough. We aren't big enough. We don't need muscles; we need a miracle."

Paul's point precisely. Separating you and God is not 350

feet of ocean water but an insurmountable flood of imperfection and sin. Do you think that by virtue of your moral muscle you can push this vessel to the surface? Do you think your baptism and Sunday attendance will be enough to save you?

Legalists do. They miss the gravity of the problem. By offering to help, they not only make light of sin, they mock God.

LEGALISM IS JOYLESS BECAUSE LEGALISM IS ENDLESS.

Who would look at the cross of Christ and say, "Great work, Jesus. Sorry you couldn't finish it, but I'll take up the slack"?

Dare we question the crowning work of God? Dare we think heaven needs our help in saving us? We're stuck on the bottom of the ocean. We can't see the light of day! Legalism discounts God and in the process makes a mess out of us.

To anyone attempting to earn heaven, Paul asks, "How is it that you are turning back to those weak and miserable principles? Do you wish to be enslaved by them all over again? . . . What has happened to all your joy?" (Galatians 4:9, 15 NIV).

Legalism is joyless because legalism is endless. There is always another class to attend, person to teach, mouth to feed. Inmates incarcerated in self-salvation find work but never joy.

How could they? They never know when they are finished. Legalism leaches joy.

Grace, however, dispenses peace. The Christian trusts a finished work. "Gone are the exertions of law-keeping, gone the disciplines and asceticism of legalism, gone the anxiety that having done everything we might not have done enough. We reach the goal not by the stairs, but by the lift. . . . God pledges his promised righteousness to those who will stop trying to save themselves."[3]

Grace offers rest. Legalism never does. Then why do we embrace it? "Those who trust in themselves are foolish" (Proverbs 28:26 NCV). Why do we trust in ourselves? Why do we add to God's finished work? Might the answer include the verb *boast?*

Saving yourself is heady stuff. Even headier than a high school varsity football jacket. I still own mine. I wore it every day of my senior year. Who cared if the temperature was in the nineties? I wanted everyone to see what I had accomplished. If making a football team feels great, how much more would earning a spot on God's team?

But the truth is, we don't. If we think we do, we have missed the message. "What is left for us to brag about?" Paul wonders (Romans 3:27 CEV). What is there indeed? What have you contributed? Aside from your admission of utter decadence, I can't think of a thing. "By His doing you are in Christ Jesus" (1 Corinthians 1:30). Salvation glorifies the Savior, not the saved.

Your salvation showcases God's mercy. It makes nothing of your effort but everything of his. "I—yes, I alone—am the one who blots out your sins *for my own sake* and will never think of them again" (Isaiah 43:25 NLT, emphasis mine). He saves us for the same reason he saved the Jews:

> For my own sake and for the honor of my name I will hold back my anger and not wipe you out. I refined you in the furnace of affliction, but found no silver there. You are worthless, with nothing good in you at all. Yet for my own sake—yes, *for my own sake*—I will save you from my anger and not destroy you lest the heathen say their gods have conquered me. I will not let them have my glory (Isaiah 48:9–11 TLB).

YOUR SALVATION SHOWCASES GOD'S MERCY. IT MAKES NOTHING OF YOUR EFFORT BUT EVERYTHING OF HIS.

Can you add anything to this salvation? No. The work is finished.

Can you earn this salvation? No. Don't dishonor God by trying.

Dare we boast about this salvation? By no means. The giver of bread, not the beggar, deserves praise. "Let him who boasts, boast in the Lord" (1 Corinthians 1:31).

It's not about what we do; it's all about what he does.

CHAPTER ELEVEN

My Body Is About Him

11

You're acquainted with house-sitters. You've possibly used one. Not wanting to leave your house vacant, you ask someone to stay in your home until you return. Let me describe two of your nightmares.

The house-sitter redecorates your house. White paint is changed to pink. Berber carpet to shag. An abstract plastic chair sits in the place of your cozy love seat. His justification? "The house didn't express me accurately. I needed a house that communicated who I am."

Your response? "It's not yours! My residence does not exist to reflect you! I asked you to take care of the house, not take over the house!" Would you want a sitter like this?

You might choose him over nightmare number two. She didn't redecorate; she neglected. Never washed a dish, made a bed, or took out the trash. "My time here was temporary. I knew you wouldn't mind," she explains.

Of course you'd mind! Does she know what this abode cost you?

Both house-sitters made the same mistake. They acted as if the dwelling were theirs. How could they?

Or, better asked, how could we? When it comes to our bodies, the Bible declares that we don't own them. "You are no longer your own. God paid a great price for you. So use your body to honor God" (1 Corinthians 6:19–20 CEV).

Use your body to indulge your passions? To grab attention? To express your opinions? No. Use your body to honor God. "Use your whole body as a tool to do what is right for the glory of God" (Romans 6:13 NLT). Your body is God's instrument, intended for his work and for his glory.

The Corinthian Christians had serious trouble with this. When it came to the body, they insisted, "We can do anything we want to" (1 Corinthians 6:12 CEV). Their philosophy conveniently separated flesh from spirit. Have fun with the flesh. Honor God with the spirit. Wild Saturdays. Worshipful Sundays. You can have it all.

Paul disagreed. He dismissed the dichotomy. He reminded his readers that God interwove body with soul, elevating them to equal status. Your body is no toy. Quite the contrary. Your body is a tool. "Do you not know that your bodies are members of Christ himself?" (1 Corinthians 6:15 NIV).

I remember seeing a sign on a mechanic's toolbox that read: "Don't ask to borrow my tools. I use them to feed my family." Understandable request. To do his work, the mechanic needed his instruments. He needed them present and functional. When he looked for his wrench, he wanted to find it. When he pulled out a screwdriver, he wanted it to be clean. His work was important; hence his tools were important.

What work is more important than God's? Doesn't it stand to reason that God's tools should be maintained?

Hold on there. I heard that sigh. *Maintain my body? I don't want to talk about my body.*

We've heard it all, haven't we? Eat balanced meals. Exercise regularly. Avoid fat. Eat protein. Get rest. We've heard it all. And we've blown it all. Each of us has. To one degree or another we have mismanaged our bodies. You're thinking, *Lucado is reaching for the guilt hammer.* I'm not. You don't need a reprimand. A reminder maybe, but a reprimand? No. Yes, your belly may be a bit soft, but so is your heart. Soft for Christ. Soft for others. Otherwise you wouldn't be reading this book. Stay that way. "Workouts

YOUR BODY IS GOD'S INSTRUMENT, INTENDED FOR HIS WORK AND FOR HIS GLORY.

in the gymnasium are useful, but a disciplined life in God is far more so, making you fit both today and forever" (1 Timothy 4:8 MSG). If forced to choose, take the soft heart over the hard body.

But I don't think a choice is required. Maintain God's instrument. Feed it. Rest it. When he needs a sturdy implement—a servant who is rested enough to serve, fueled enough to work, alert enough to think—let him find one in you. He uses you.

Greater still, he lives in you. "Don't you know that your body is the temple of the Holy Spirit, who lives in you?" (1 Corinthians 6:19 NLT). Paul wrote these words to counter the Corinthian sex obsession. "Run away from sexual sin!" reads the prior sentence. "No other sin so clearly affects the body as this one does. For sexual immorality is a sin against your own body" (v. 18 NLT).

What a salmon scripture! No message swims more upstream than this one. You know the sexual anthem of our day: "I'll do what I want. It's my body." God's firm response? "No, it's not. It's mine."

Be quick to understand, God is not antisex. Dismiss any notion that God is antiaffection and anti-intercourse. After all, he developed the whole package. Sex was his idea. From his perspective, sex is nothing short of holy.

He views sexual intimacy the way I view our family Bible. Passed down from my father's side, the volume is one hundred years old and twelve inches thick. Replete with lithographs, scribblings, and a family tree, it is, in my estimation, beyond value. Hence, I use it carefully.

When I need a stepstool, I don't reach for the Bible. If the foot of my bed breaks, I don't use the family Bible as a prop. When we need old paper for wrapping, we don't rip a sheet out of this book. We reserve the heirloom for special times and keep it in a chosen place.

Regard sex the same way—as a holy gift to be opened in a special place at special times. The special place is marriage, and the time is with your spouse.

Casual sex, intimacy outside of marriage, pulls the Corinthian ploy. It pretends we can give the body and not affect the soul. We can't. We humans are so intricately psychosomatic that whatever touches the *soma* impacts the *psyche* as well. The me-centered phrase "as long as no one gets hurt" sounds noble, but the truth is, we don't know who gets hurt. God-centered thinking rescues us from the sex we thought would make us happy. You may think your dalliances are harmless, and years may pass before the x-rays reveal the internal damage, but don't be fooled. Casual sex is a diet of chocolate—it tastes good for a while, but the imbalance can ruin you. Sex apart from God's plan wounds the soul.

Sex according to God's plan nourishes the soul. Consider his plan. Two children of God make a covenant with each other. They disable the ejection seats. They burn the bridge back to Momma's house. They fall into each other's arms beneath the canopy of God's blessing, encircled by the tall fence of fidelity. Both know the other will be there in the morning. Both know the other will stay even as skin wrinkles and vigor fades. Each gives the other exclusive for-your-eyes-only privileges. Gone is the guilt. Gone the undisciplined lust. What remains is a celebration of permanence, a tender moment in which the body continues what the mind and the soul have already begun. A time in which "the man and his wife were both naked and were not ashamed" (Genesis 2:25).

Sex is a celebration of permanence, a tender moment in which the body continues what the mind and the soul have already begun.

Such sex honors God. And such sex satisfies God's children. Several years ago *USA Today* ran an article with this lead:

Aha, call it the revenge of the church ladies. Sigmund Freud said they suffer from an "obsessional neurosis" accompanied by guilt, suppressed emotions and repressed sexuality. Former *Saturday Night Live* comedian Dana Carvey satirized them as uptight prudes who believe sex is downright dirty. But several major research studies show that church ladies (and the men who sleep with them) are among the most sexually satisfied people on the face of the earth. Researchers at the University of Chicago seem to think so. Several years ago when they released the results of the most "comprehensive and methodologically sound" sex survey ever conducted, they reported that religious women experienced significantly higher levels of sexual satisfaction than non-religious women.[1]

(I'm thinking this article would be an effective evangelism tool.)

Your body, God's tool. Maintain it.

Your body, God's temple. Respect it.

"God owns the whole works. So let people see God in and through your body" (1 Corinthians 6:20 MSG).

Manage God's house in such a way that passersby stop and notice. "Who lives in that house?" they will ask. And when they hear the answer, God will be honored.

CHAPTER TWELVE

My Struggles Are About Him

12

Martin and Gracia Burnham married with mission work in their hearts.[1] For seventeen years they served God in the Philippines. With three children born on the mission field and valuable skills in the ministry's aviation program, they were acclimated and essential to the work. He, single-minded. She, gracious and convicted.

Then why didn't God block the bullets? Why did he let her get shot? And why did God let him die?

On May 27, 2001, while celebrating their eighteenth wedding anniversary at a beachside resort, Martin and Gracia were taken hostage by a militant terrorist organization with ties to Osama bin Laden. Captors chained the couple to guards, marched them through jungles, and rationed their food. They endured seventeen firefights and for over four hundred days were either running for their lives or bored. Their health deteriorated, but their faith remained sturdy. "We might not leave this jungle alive," said Martin, "but at least we can leave this world serving the Lord with gladness." A premonition led Martin to write a farewell letter to his children.

The premonition proved accurate. On June 7, 2002, Philippine Rangers attacked the terrorist camp, catching Martin and Gracia in the cross-fire. One bullet entered her leg. Another took his life. She was left a widow, and we are left to wonder why. Is this how God honors his chosen? How do you explain such a tragedy?

And as you're thinking of theirs, how do you explain yours? The tension at home. The demands at work. The bills on your desk or the tumor in your body. You aren't taken hostage, but aren't you occasionally taken aback by God's silence? He knows what you are facing. How do we explain this?

Maybe God messed up. Cancer cells crept into your DNA when he wasn't looking. He was so occupied with the tornado in Kansas that he forgot the famine in Uganda. He tried to change the stubborn streak in your spouse but just couldn't get him to budge. Honestly. A bumbling Creator? An absent-minded Maker? What evidence does Scripture provide to support such a view? What evidence does creation offer? Can't the Maker of heaven and earth handle bad traffic and prevent bad marriages? Of course he can. Then why doesn't he?

Perhaps he is mad. Have we so exhausted the mercy of God's bank account that every prayer bounces like a bad check? Did humanity cross the line millenniums ago, and now we're getting what we deserve? Such an argument carries a dash of merit. God does leave us to the consequences of our stupid decisions. Think Egyptian soldiers in Red Sea, Hebrews in Babylon, Peter weeping with the sound of a crowing rooster in his ears. Bang your head against the wall, and expect a headache. God lets us endure the fruit of sin. But to label him peeved and impatient? To do so you need to scissor from your Bible some tender passages such as:

> God is sheer mercy and grace;
> not easily angered, he's rich in love.
> He doesn't endlessly nag and scold,
> nor hold grudges forever.
> He doesn't treat us as our sins deserve,
> nor pay us back in full for our wrongs.
> As high as heaven is over the earth,
> so strong is his love to those who fear him.
> (Psalm 103:8–11 MSG)

Don't blame suffering in the world on the anger of God. He's not mad; he didn't mess up. Follow our troubles to their headwaters, and you won't find an angry or befuddled God. But you will find a sovereign God.

Your pain has a purpose. Your problems, struggles, heartaches, and hassles cooperate toward one end—the glory of God. "Trust me in your times of trouble, and I will rescue you, and you will give me glory" (Psalm 50:15 NLT).

Not an easy assignment to swallow. Not for you. Not for me. Not for the blind man on the side of the road. When Jesus and his followers passed him, the disciples had a question.

> As He [Jesus] passed by, He saw a man blind from birth. And His disciples asked Him, "Rabbi, who sinned, this man or his parents, that he would be born blind?" Jesus answered, "It was neither that this man sinned, nor his parents; but it was so that the works of God might be displayed in him." (John 9:1–3)

Your pain has a purpose. Your problems, struggles, heartaches, and hassles cooperate toward one end—the glory of God.

Born blind. A lifetime of darkness. Never saw a mother smile or a sunset fade. *Who did this?* the disciples wondered, anxious to blame someone. Such a bad plight can be traced back to a bad deed. Right?

Wrong, Jesus replied. Don't search the family tree. Don't

request a copy of the man's rap sheet. Blame this blindness on a call from God. Why was the man sightless? So "the works of God might be displayed in him."

Odds are, he would have preferred another role in the human drama. Compared to others, his assignment held little glamour.

"Mary, be a mother to my son."

"Peter, you'll be my first preacher."

"Matthew, the first gospel? It's all yours."

Then God turns to this man, "And you?"

"Yes, Lord?"

"You'll be blind for my glory."

"I'll be blind?"

"Yes."

"For your glory?"

"Yes."

"But I don't understand."

"You'll see."

The blind man wasn't the only candidate for a complaint. Consider the case of Martha and Mary. Personal friends of Jesus. Confidantes. He stayed at their house and ate at their table. And when their brother, Lazarus, became ill, the sisters blitzed a message to Jesus. If the Nazarene would heal anyone, it would be Lazarus.

Wrong again. "But when Jesus heard this, He said, 'This sickness is not to end in death, but for the glory of God, so that the Son of God may be glorified by it'" (John 11:4).

Feverish, clammy, knocking on the door of death—why? Because he ate the wrong food? Didn't guard his health? Drank too much? None of these. He was sick for the sake of God. Call it the assignment of sickness. How else do you explain the puzzle of the next two verses?

"Now Jesus loved Martha and her sister and Lazarus. So when He heard that he was sick, He then stayed two days longer in the place where He was" (John 11:5–6).

Talk about a left turn. You'd expect the verse to read: "Jesus loved Martha and her sister and Lazarus . . . so he made a fast dash to their house to heal Lazarus." Just the opposite occurred. Because Jesus loved the trio, he lingered until Lazarus died.

Blindness displays the works of Christ? Death glorifies the power of Christ? How can this be?

I'm looking around my office for an answer. A frame displays my favorite picture of Denalyn. A metal stand displays an antique pot. My brother gave me a stained-glass window from a country church. It is displayed by virtue of two wires and two hooks. Picture frames and metal stands, wires and hooks—different tools, same job. They display treasures.

What these do for artifacts, the blind man did for Christ.

He was the frame in which Jesus' power was seen, the stand upon which Jesus' miracle was placed. Born sightless to display heaven's strength. Do you suppose the sight of his sight showcased the work of Christ?

Is there any chance, any possibility, that you have been selected to struggle for God's glory?

And the fading pulse and final breath of Lazarus? You think the news of a three-days-dead man walking out of a tomb amplified God's power?

And you? Now it gets a bit sticky. What about your struggles? Is there any chance, any possibility, that you have been selected to struggle for God's glory? Have you "been granted for Christ's sake, not only to believe in Him, but also to suffer for His sake" (Philippians 1:29)?

Here is a clue. Do your prayers seem to be unanswered? What you request and what you receive aren't matching up? Don't think God is not listening. Indeed he is. He may have higher plans.

Here is another. Are people strengthened by your struggles? A friend of mine can answer yes. His cancer was consuming more than his body; it was eating away at his faith. Unanswered petitions perplexed him. Well-meaning Christians confused him. "If you have faith," they said, "you will be healed."

No healing came. Just more chemo, nausea, and questions. He assumed the fault was a small faith. I suggested another answer. "It's not about you," I told him. "Your hospital room is a showcase for your Maker. Your faith in the face of suffering cranks up the volume of God's song."

Oh, that you could have seen the relief on his face. To know that he hadn't failed God and God hadn't failed him—this made all the difference. Seeing his sickness in the scope of God's sovereign plan gave his condition a sense of dignity. He accepted his cancer as an assignment from heaven: a missionary to the cancer ward. A week later I saw him again. "I reflected God," he said, smiling through a thin face, "to the nurses, the doctors, my friends. Who knows who needed to see God, but I did my best to make him seen."

Bingo. His cancer paraded the power of Jesus down the Main Street of his world. He, the blind man, Lazarus, and millions of others form a unique society: selected to suffer for God's glory. His light prisms through their aching lives and spills forth in a cascade of colors. God-glimpses.

God will use whatever he wants to display his glory. Heavens and stars. History and nations. People and problems. A kidnapped couple in the Philippines. My dying dad in West Texas.

The last three years of his life were scarred by ALS. The disease took him from a healthy mechanic to a bedbound paralytic. He lost his voice and his muscles, but he never lost his faith. Visitors noticed. Not so much in what he said but more in what he didn't say. Never outwardly angry or bitter, Jack Lucado suffered stately.

Your faith in the face of suffering cranks up the volume of God's song.

His faith led one man to seek a like faith. After the funeral this man sought me out and told me. Because of my dad's example, he became a Jesus follower.

Did God orchestrate my father's illness for that very reason? Knowing the value he places on one soul, I wouldn't be surprised. And imagining the splendor of heaven, I know my father's not complaining.

A season of suffering is a small assignment when compared to the reward.

Rather than begrudge your problem, explore it. Ponder it. And most of all, use it. Use it to the glory of God.

Martin and Gracia did.

During their captivity, they not only spoke of Jesus, they

lived Jesus. Didn't complain. Did their work and volunteered for more. Chained every night to a guard, Martin always wished his captors a good night and told them about Jesus. The Burnhams allowed God to use their suffering for his glory.

Because of Martin's death, nations around the world heard the name of Christ. I heard the report on a London, England, news channel. Millions saw the forbearing figure of his wife and heard a moving interview with his father, who said God would get them through this. Every major network gave priceless minutes to the story of a man who loved Christ more than life.

Through the Burnhams' struggle, God was seen.

Through Martin's death, God was seen.

Through your problems and mine, may he be seen as well.

CHAPTER THIRTEEN

My Success Is About Him

13

How well do you know the following people and organizations?

Jack Tinker and Partners

Doyle Dane Bernbach

BBDO

Foote, Cone and Belding

J. Walter Thompson

How did you do? Not too good? If not, then the ones on the list are pleased. Advertising agencies don't exist to make a name for themselves. They exist to make a name for others. While you may not be acquainted with the companies, aren't you familiar with their work?

"Plop, plop, fizz, fizz, oh what a relief it is." The work of Jack Tinker and Partners for Alka-Seltzer in 1976.

"We try harder." Doyle Dane Bernbach created the slogan for Avis Rent A Car in 1962.

"M'm! M'm! Good! M'm! M'm! Good!" Credit BBDO with the catch-phrase Campbell's Soup has used since 1935.

While you've never heard of Foote, Cone and Belding, have you ever heard this motto: "When you care enough to send the very best"? Hallmark began using the line in 1934.

You don't hum the name of J. Walter Thompson, but have you hummed the jingle his agency wrote for Kellogg's "Snap! Crackle! Pop!" Rice Krispies?[1]

We could learn a lesson from these companies. What they do for clients, we exist to do for Christ. To live "reflecting like mirrors the brightness of the Lord" (2 Corinthians 3:18 JB).

As heaven's advertising agency, we promote God in every area of life, including success.

That's right—even your success is intended to reflect God. Listen to the reminder Moses gave the children of Israel: "Always remember that it is the LORD your God who gives you power to become rich, and he does it to fulfill the covenant he made with your ancestors" (Deuteronomy 8:18 NLT).

From where does success come? God. "It is the LORD your God who gives you power to become rich."

And why does he give it? For his reputation. "To fulfill the covenant he made with your ancestors."

God blessed Israel in order to billboard his faithfulness. When foreigners saw the fruitful farms of the Promised Land, God did not want them to think about the farmer but the farmer's Maker. Their success advertised God.

Nothing has changed. God lets you excel so you can make him known. And you can be sure of one thing: God will make you good at something. This is his principle: "True humility and fear of the LORD lead to riches, honor, and long life" (Proverbs 22:4 NLT).

Would we expect any less? A godly life often results in success. Consider a construction worker, for example. Imagine a trouble-making, hard-drinking fellow. Before he knows Christ, he's not much of an employee. Frequent hangovers, padded expense accounts. Sneaks out early on Friday afternoons . . . He does it all. And he pays the price—overdue bills, bail-bond debts, a resumé that reads like a rap sheet.

GOD LETS YOU EXCEL SO YOU CAN MAKE HIM KNOWN.

But then Christ finds him. Not only does God save his soul, he straightens out the man's work habits. The guy shows up on time. He does his job. He stops complaining and starts volunteering. Everything improves—attitude, productivity, cooperation.

And guess who notices? His boss. And guess what happens? Promotions. Pay increases. The company truck and credit card. Success. But with the success comes a problem.

Just ask Nadab, Elah, and Omri. Or interview Ahab, Ahaziah, or Jehoram. Ask these men to describe the problem of success. *I would*, you might be thinking, *if I knew who they were*. My point exactly. These are men we should know. They were kings of Israel. They ascended to the throne . . . but something about the throne brought them down. Their legacies are stained with blood spilling and idol worship. They failed at success. They forgot both the source and purpose of their success. King Nadab symbolized them all: "He did evil in the sight of the LORD, and walked in the way of his father and in his sin which he made Israel sin" (1 Kings 15:26).

You won't be offered a throne, but you might be offered a corner office, a scholarship, an award, a new contract, a pay raise. You won't be given a kingdom to oversee, but you might be given a home or employees or students or money or resources. You will, to one degree or another, succeed.

And when you do, you might be tempted to forget who helped you do so. Success sabotages the memories of the successful. Kings of the mountain forget who carried them up the trail.

The flea did. An old fable tells of an elephant lumbering across a wooden bridge suspended over a ravine. As the big animal crossed over the worn-out structure, it creaked and groaned under the elephant's weight. When he reached the other side, a flea that had nestled itself in the elephant's ear proclaimed, "Boy, did we shake that bridge!"[2]

The flea had done nothing! The elephant had done all the work.

What a fleabrained declaration! But don't we do the same? The man who begged for help in medical school ten years ago is too busy to worship today. Back when the family struggled to make ends meet, they leaned on God for daily bread. Now that there is an extra car in the garage and a jingle in the pocket, they haven't spoken to him in a while. In the early days of the church, the founding members spent hours in prayer. Today the church is large, well attended, well funded. Who needs to pray?

SUCCESS SABOTAGES THE MEMORIES OF THE SUCCESSFUL. KINGS OF THE MOUNTAIN FORGET WHO CARRIED THEM UP THE TRAIL.

Success begets amnesia. Doesn't have to, however. God offers spiritual ginseng to help your memory. His prescription is simply "Know the purpose of success." Why did God help you succeed? So you can make him known.

David Robinson knows this. Speaking of someone who God made good, this seven-foot-tall basketball player for the

San Antonio Spurs was good. For fourteen seasons he dominated the league: MVP, All-Star, two championship rings, two Olympic gold medals. But it was his character that caught the attention of the public. These words appeared in the *Washington Times* the day after Robinson's departing championship victory.

> Robinson showed that a player did not have to be cheap or dirty to be effective. He did not have to clutter his body with tattoos or litter the NBA cities with illegitimate children. Robinson never felt a need to bring attention to himself, to shimmy after a good play or point to the crowd, as if to say, "Look at me. Aren't I something special?"
>
> The good guys won. Robinson won. Decency won. We all won.[3]

Minutes after hoisting the trophy overhead, David was interviewed by a national network. "People in San Antonio know what I'm going to say," he told the reporter. And we did. We did because we had heard him say it and seen him live it for so long. "All the glory goes to God," he announced.

Three thousand years ago another David declared the same truth. "Riches and honor come from you alone, for you rule over everything. Power and might are in your hand, and it is at your discretion that people are made great and given strength" (1 Chronicles 29:12 NLT).

"They did not conquer the land with their swords; it was not their own strength that gave them victory. It was by your mighty power that they succeeded; it was because you favored them and smiled on them" (Psalm 44:3 NLT).

I know a frog who needed those verses. He had a real problem. His home pond was drying up. If he didn't find water soon, he would do the same. Word reached him of a vibrant stream over the adjacent hill. If only he could live there. But how could he? The short legs of a frog were not made for long journeys.

It's all about him—his present and future glory.

But then he had an idea. Convincing two birds to carry either end of a stick, he bit the center and held on as they flew. As they winged toward the new water, his jaws clamped tightly. It was quite a sight! Two birds, one stick, and a frog in the middle. Down below, a cow in a pasture saw them passing overhead. Impressed, he wondered aloud, "Now who came up with that idea?"

The frog overheard his question and couldn't resist a reply. "I diiiiiiii . . ."

Don't make the same mistake. "Pride goes before destruction, and haughtiness before a fall" (Proverbs 16:18 NLT). Why are you good at what you do? For your comfort? For your retirement? For your self-esteem? No. Deem these as bonuses, not as the reason. Why are you good at what you do? For God's sake. Your success is not about what you do. It's all about him—his present and future glory.

CHAPTER FOURTEEN

Upward Thinking

14

"So, you like Jewish authors?"

The fellow asking the question sat on the aisle seat. I had the window, which meant I had a view of the runway. The mechanical crew was repairing a bird dent on the wing. While they worked, I read. As I read my Bible, the rabbi interrupted.

"So, you like Jewish authors?"

The twinkle in his eye betrayed his pleasure in the question. His chest-length mop of a beard couldn't hide his smile. I had spotted him earlier in the waiting area. The tassels from his shirttail and hair-clipped yarmulke led me to peg him as the pious, silent type.

Pious. Yes. But silent? He loved to talk. He loved to talk Torah. I was in for a lesson. Tucked away in the ceremonies and laws of Moses, he explained, are pictures of God. Who could offer a sacrifice and not weep for God's grace? Who could read about servants redeeming their kinsmen and not think about

God redeeming us? And who could read the third commandment without remembering to live for God's glory?

I signaled a time-out, opened to Exodus, and read the third command: "You shall not take the name of the Lord your God in vain" (20:7). My puzzled expression was enough to request an explanation.

"Don't think language; think lifestyle," he instructed. "The command calls us to elevate the name or reputation of God to the highest place. We exist to give honor to his name. May I illustrate?"

We exist to give honor to his name.

By now the damaged wing was fixed (the plane's; can't speak for the bird). And as we gained altitude, so did the rabbi. I took notes. He proceeded to create a story involving a Manhattan skyscraper. Everyone in the building works for the CEO, who offices on the top floor. Most have not seen him, but they have seen his daughter. She works in the building for her father. She exploits her family position to her benefit.

One morning she approaches Bert, the guard. "I'm hungry, Bert. Go down the street and buy me a Danish."

The demand places Bert in a quandary. He's on duty.

Leaving his post puts the building at risk. But his boss's daughter insists, "Come on, now; hurry up."

What option does he have? As he leaves, he says nothing but thinks something like, *If the daughter is so bossy, what does that say about her father?*

She's only getting started. Munching on her muffin, she bumps into a paper-laden secretary. "Where are you going with all those papers?"

"To have them bound for an afternoon meeting."

"Forget the meeting. Come to my office and vacuum the carpet."

"But I was told . . . "

"And I am telling you something else."

The woman has no choice. After all, this is the boss's daughter speaking. Which causes the secretary to question the wisdom of the boss.

And on the daughter goes. Making demands. Calling shots. Interrupting schedules. Never invoking the name of her dad. Never leveraging her comments with, "My dad said . . . "

No need to.

Isn't she the boss's child? Doesn't the child speak for the father? And so Bert abandons his post. An assistant fails to finish a task. And more than one employee questions the wisdom of the man upstairs. *Does he really know what he is doing?* they wonder.

The rabbi paused here. We both felt the plane nosing downward. His remaining time was short. But his point was clear. The girl dishonored the name of her father, not with vulgar language, but with insensitive living. Keep this up and the whole building will be second-guessing the CEO.

But my traveling partner wasn't finished. He scratched his bearded chin and lifted both eyebrows as he proposed, "But what if the daughter acted differently?" and then proceeded to recast the story.

Rather than demand a muffin from Bert, she brings a muffin to Bert. "I thought of you this morning," she explains. "You arrive so early. Do you have time to eat?" And she hands him the gift.

En route to the elevator she bumps into a woman with an armful of documents. "My, I'm sorry. Can I help?" the daughter offers. The assistant smiles, and the two carry the stacks down the hallway.

And so the daughter engages the people. She asks about their families, offers to bring them coffee. New workers are welcomed, and hard workers are applauded. She, through kindness and concern, raises the happiness level of the entire company.

She does so not even mentioning her father's name. Never does she declare, "My father says . . . " There is no need to. Is she not his child? Does she not speak on his behalf? Reflect his heart? When she speaks, they assume she speaks for him. And because they think highly of her, they think highly of her father.

They've not seen him.

They've not met him.

But they know his child, so they know his heart.

MAY WE HAVE NO HIGHER GOAL THAN TO SEE SOMEONE THINK MORE HIGHLY OF OUR FATHER, OUR KING.

By now the flight was ending, and so was my Hebrew lesson. Thanks to the rabbi, the third command shouldered new meaning.[1] Paul, another rabbi, would have appreciated the point. He wrote: "We are ambassadors for Christ, as though God were making an appeal through us" (2 Corinthians 5:20). The ambassador has a singular aim—to represent his king. He promotes the king's agenda, protects the king's reputation, and presents the king's will. The ambassador elevates the name of the king.

May I close this book with a prayer that we do the same? May God rescue us from self-centered thinking. May we have no higher goal than to see someone think more highly of our Father, our King. After all, it's not about . . . well, you can finish the sentence.

"You know how the story ends?" the rabbi asked as we were taxiing to a stop. Apparently he had a punch line.

"No, I don't. How?"

"The daughter takes the elevator to the top floor to see her father. When she arrives, he is waiting in the doorway. He's aware of her good works and has seen her kind acts. People think more highly of him because of her. And he knows it. As she approaches, he greets her with six words."

The rabbi paused and smiled.

"What are they?" I urged, never expecting to hear an orthodox Jew quote Jesus.

"Well done, good and faithful servant."

May God sustain you until you hear the same.

Notes

Chapter 3: Divine Self-Promotion

1. Exodus 33:18; 1 Kings 8:10–11; Ezekiel 3:23; Luke 2:9; Hebrews 1:3; John 1:14; Mark 9:1–13; 2 Peter 1:16–18; Matthew 16:27; Revelation 21:23.

Chapter 4: Holy Different

1. Darren Brown, ed., *The Greatest Exploration Stories Ever Told: True Tales of Search and Discovery* (Guilford, Conn.: Lyons Press, 2003), 207–219.
2. Brown, *Greatest Exploration Stories,* 223.
3. Jerry Bridges, *The Pursuit of Holiness* (Colorado Springs, Colo.: NavPress, 1978), 64.
4. Edward W. Goodrick and John R. Kohlenberger, *Zondervan NIV Exhaustive Concordance,* 2d ed., ed. James A. Swanson (Grand Rapids, Mich.: Zondervan Publishing House, 1999), 1487.

Chapter 5: Just a Moment

1. Frederick Buechner, *The Sacred Journey* (San Francisco: Harper and Row, 1982), 9, 37, 76.

Chapter 6: His Unchanging Hand

1. Rick Reilly, "Sportsman of the Year: Lance Armstrong," *Sports Illustrated,* 16 December 2002, 56.
2. Rick Reilly, "The Life of Reilly: Pool Shark," *Sports Illustrated,* 24 March 2003, 126.
3. "Barge Accident Cuts South Padre Island Off from Mainland Texas," http://www.thetimesharebeat.com/archives/2001/ts/ttsept50.htm; "South Padre Island Bridge Collapse," www.bridgepros.com/projects/queenisabellacauseway.
4. J. I. Packer, *Knowing God* (Downers Grove, Ill.: InterVarsity Press, 1973), 71.

Chapter 7: God's Great Love

1. John Bishop, *1041 Sermon Illustrations, Ideas and Expositions,* ed. A. Gordon Nasby (Grand Rapids: Baker Book House, 1952), 213.
2. Rubel Shelly, *The ABCs of the Christian Faith* (Nashville: Wineskins, 1998), 21–22.

Chapter 8: God's Mirrors

1. Dictionary of American Naval Fighting Ships, Office of the Chief of Naval Operations, Naval History

Division, Washington, http://www.ibiblio.org/hyperwar/USN/ships/dafs/DD/dd400.html.

Chapter 9: My Message Is About Him

1. Mike Flanagan et al., *The Complete Idiot's Guide to the Old West* (New York: Alpha Books, 1999), 171–73.
2. Rick Atchley, *God's Love Does Not Change,* audiocassette of a sermon, Richland Hills Church of Christ, Fort Worth, Texas, 28 July 1996.

Chapter 10: My Salvation Is About Him

1. Alvin Toffler, *Future Shock* (New York: Bantam Books, 1970), 222.
2. James O. Jackson, "The Fatal Dive," *Time,* 28 August 2000, 30.
3. J. Alec Motyer et al., *The Message of Philippians* (Downers Grove, Ill.: InterVarsity Press, 1984), 166.

Chapter 11: My Body Is About Him

1. William R. Mattox Jr., "Aha! Call It the Revenge of the Church Ladies," *USA Today,* 11 February 1999, 15A.

Chapter 12: My Struggles Are About Him

1. Read a full account of Martin and Gracia's story in Gracia Burnham with Dean Merrill, *In the Presence of My Enemies* (Wheaton, Ill.: Tyndale House, 2003).

Chapter 13: My Success Is About Him

1. Ad Slogans Unlimited, http://www.adslogans.co.uk/hof/hofindx1.html.
2. Anthony de Mello, *Taking Flight: A Book of Story Meditations* (New York: Doubleday, 1988), 99.
3. Tom Knott, "Admiral Deserves a Salute from All," *Washington Times,* 17 June 2003.

Chapter 14: Upward Thinking

1. With appreciation to Rabbi Daniel Thomson for sharing this story.

IT'S NOT ABOUT ME

Study Guide

WRITTEN BY STEVE HALLIDAY

CHAPTER ONE

BUMPING LIFE OFF SELF-CENTER

Beholding

1. What Copernicus did for the earth, God does for our souls. Tapping the collective shoulder of humanity, he points to the Son—his Son—and says, "Behold the center of it all."
    - A. Why do you think we naturally look to ourselves as the center of the universe?
    - B. How does God reveal his Son as the center of everything?
2. What would happen if we accepted our place as Son reflectors?
    - A. What does it mean to be a "Son reflector"?
    - B. What do you find most difficult in your role as a "Son reflector"? Why?
3. Life makes sense when we accept our place. The God-centered life works. And it rescues us from a life that doesn't.
    - A. How does life make sense when we accept our place? What would you say is your place?
    - B. How does a God-centered life rescue us from a life that doesn't work?

Reflecting

1. Read Ephesians 1:18–23.
    - A. For what does Paul pray in verse 18? What reason does he give for his prayer in verses 18–19?

B. List the many ways Paul describes Christ in verses 20–23. How does it affect you, personally, that Christ is described in each of these ways?

2. Read 2 Corinthians 3:17–18.

A. How do believers "reflect" the Lord's glory? In what way do they reflect it?

B. What happens as they increasingly reflect God's glory (v. 18)? Who is responsible for this?

CHAPTER TWO

SHOW ME YOUR GLORY

Beholding

1. When our deepest desire is not the things of God, or a favor from God, but God himself, we cross a threshold. Less self-focus, more God-focus. Less about me, more about him.

A. What is your deepest desire? How is this desire reflected in the way you live?

B. Have you crossed the threshold just described? Explain.

2. You and I need what Moses needed—a glimpse of God's glory. Such a sighting can change you forever.

A. Have you ever caught a glimpse of God's glory? If so, describe how and when you made the sighting.

B. Why should a glimpse of God's glory change someone forever?

Reflecting

1. Read Exodus 33:12—34:10.
   A. What instructions does God give Moses in 34:1–4? How do these instructions heighten Moses' anticipation of what is about to happen?
   B. How does God describe himself in 34:5–7? How do the attributes he names contribute to his glory?
   C. How does Moses respond to the revelation of God's glory in 34:8–9? How is this significant for us?
   D. How does God reply to Moses' final request (34:10)? Should this fill us with hope or dread? Why?
2. Read 2 Corinthians 3:7–11.
   A. How does Paul compare and contrast the ministry of Moses with "the ministry of the Spirit"?
   B. In what way was Moses' ministry one "that condemns men" (v. 9 NIV)? If it condemned men, how could it be "glorious"?
   C. Why does the ministry of the Spirit outshine the ministry of Moses (vv. 9–11)?

CHAPTER THREE

DIVINE SELF-PROMOTION

Beholding

1. When you think "God's glory," think "preeminence." And, when you think "preeminence," think "priority." For God's glory is God's priority.

A. How do you display God's preeminence in your own life?

B. Why is God's glory God's priority?

C. Why should God's glory be our priority? When it isn't, why isn't it?

2. God has no ego problem. He does not reveal his glory for his good. We need to witness it for ours.

A. How would you answer someone who complained, "God must be very vain if he's so concerned with everybody seeing his glory"?

B. Why do we need to witness God's glory? How does this help us?

3. Why does the earth spin? For him. Why do you have talents and abilities? For him. Why do you have money or poverty? For him. Strength or struggles? For him. Everything and everyone exists to reveal his glory. Including you.

A. In what ways do you reveal God's glory?

B. In what ways do you think you could better reveal God's glory?

Reflecting

1. Read Exodus 15:11–13.

A. How would you answer the question in verse 11?

B. What does it mean to be "majestic in holiness"?

C. What does it mean to be "awesome in glory" (NIV)?

D. How do God's love and strength comfort and encourage God's people (v. 13)?

2. Read John 12:23–33.

A. How did Jesus expect to be "glorified" (vv. 23–24)?

B. In what way did Jesus expect his followers to mimic his example (vv. 25–26)?

C. Did Jesus look forward with great pleasure to what lay ahead for him (v. 27)? In what did he take ultimate pleasure?

D. How did God put his stamp of approval on Jesus and his mission (v. 29)?

E. How did Jesus picture his mission (vv. 30–33)? In what way was it for the benefit of his followers that he described events like this?

CHAPTER FOUR

HOLY DIFFERENT

Beholding

1. The first and final songs of the Bible magnify the holiness of God.

A. What does "holiness" mean to you? How would you describe it to someone who knew nothing about the Bible?

B. Why do you think the first and final songs of the Bible magnify the holiness of God? What's so important about his holiness?

2. God's holiness silences human boasting.
    A. When are you most tempted to boast?
    B. How does God's holiness silence human boasting?
3. God, who is quick to pardon and full of mercy, purges Isaiah of his sin and redirects his life.
    A. When was the last time you experienced God's quick pardon and fullness of mercy? Describe what happened.
    B. How has God redirected your own life?

Reflecting

1. Read Exodus 15:1–18 and Revelation 15:3–4.
    A. If you were to rewrite the Exodus song to reflect an event in your own life, what would it say?
    B. What is the relationship in the Revelation song between fear and glory and holiness? How does your own life reflect this relationship?
2. Read Isaiah 6:1–8.
    A. How does Isaiah react to this revelation of God's glory (v. 5)? How do you think you would have reacted? Explain.
    B. What resulted from Isaiah's cleansing (v. 8)? How do you think God wants to use Isaiah's experience in your own life?

CHAPTER FIVE

JUST A MOMENT

Beholding

1. God doesn't view history as a progression of centuries but as a single photo. He captures your life, your entire life, in one glance.
   - A. How does it make you feel to know that God knows all about you and all about everything that will ever happen to you?
   - B. If God really can capture your entire life in a single glance, then what sense does it make to disregard his commands and directions? Why do we often disregard them anyway?
2. Your world extends beyond the barnyard of time. A foreverness woos you.
   - A. How does it make you feel to know that you were created as an eternal being?
   - B. Describe a time when you felt "foreverness" wooing you.
3. The heavy becomes light when weighed against eternity.
   - A. What things feel especially heavy to you right now? How can remembering eternity help to lighten the load?
   - B. When you think of eternity, what comes to mind?

Reflecting

1. Read 2 Corinthians 4:13–18.
   - A. What hope keeps Paul going (v. 14)?
   - B. How does Paul keep from losing heart (v. 16)?

C. What important comparison does Paul make in verse 17?

D. What important life instruction does Paul give in verse 18? How can you follow this instruction in practice?

2. Read Romans 8:18–21.

A. What comparison does Paul make in verse 18? How does this knowledge help him to carry on his work? How can it help you to carry on your work?

B. Who is ultimately behind the story of Planet Earth (v. 20)?

C. To what hope does Paul point us in verse 21?

Chapter Six

His Unchanging Hand

Beholding

1. If you're looking for a place with no change, try a soda machine. With life comes change.

A. How has your life changed in the past year? In the past five years? In the past ten years?

B. How do you expect your life will change in the next year? In the next five years? The next ten years?

C. How do you usually deal with change? Do you generally celebrate it or resist it? Explain.

2. Set your bearings on the one and only North Star in the universe —God. For though life changes, he never does.

A. Are you glad that God doesn't change? Explain.

B. Why is it a good thing that God doesn't change?

3. With change comes the reassuring appreciation of heaven's permanence. God's house will stand forever.
   A. What hope does it give you that God's house will stand forever?

Reflecting

1. Read Malachi 3:6.
   A. What blanket statement does God make in this verse?
   B. What application does God make in light of this truth?
   C. How does God's unchanging nature affect you?
2. Read Hebrews 13:8.
   A. What blanket statement does the writer make in this verse?
   B. How would you describe Jesus as he was "yesterday"?
   C. How is Jesus treating you today as he treated his disciples in the Gospels?
   D. How do you expect Jesus to treat you in the future? Explain.

CHAPTER SEVEN

GOD'S GREAT LOVE

Beholding

1. Does God love you? Behold the cross, and behold your answer.
   A. How does the cross demonstrate God's love for you?
   B. How do difficult times sometimes obscure God's love from our eyes?

2. While you are valuable, you aren't essential. You're important but not indispensable.
   - A. Why is it good to know that you're valuable and important? Why is it just as good to know that you're not indispensable?
   - B. What would it imply about God if you were both essential and indispensable?
3. To say "It's not about you" is not to say you aren't loved; quite the contrary. It's because God loves you that it's not about you.
   - A. How does the fact that "it's not about you" show you God's love?
   - B. In what way does the sentiment "It's all about me" demonstrate the essence of sin?

Reflecting

1. Read John 3:13–15.
   - A. Why is it important to know where Jesus came from (v. 13)?
   - B. What picture does Jesus use to illustrate his own ministry (v. 14; see also Numbers 21:4–9)? What strikes you most about this picture?
   - C. How does someone gain eternal life, according to verse 15?
2. Read Ephesians 3:16–19.
   - A. What did Paul most want his readers to grasp, according to verse 18?
   - B. In what way does God's love surpass knowledge (v. 19)? Have you experienced this to be true? Explain.

C. What was Paul's ultimate prayer for his believing friends (v. 19)? How much of this ultimate desire have you experienced? Explain.

CHAPTER EIGHT

GOD'S MIRRORS

Beholding

1. Reduce the human job description down to one phrase, and this is it: Reflect God's glory.
   A. What does it mean to reflect God's glory?
   B. Describe a time when you knew you provided an excellent reflection of God's glory. What happened?
2. Could it be that the Holy Spirit intentionally selected a verb that would remind us to behold God so intently that we can't help but reflect him?
   A. In what ways do you best behold God?
   B. How does your beholding God enable you to reflect God?
3. He's the source; we are the glass. He's the light; we are the mirrors. He sends the message; we mirror it.
   A. Think of the last time you saw someone forget that God is the source and we are the glass. What happened?
   B. What most stands in the way of you effectively mirroring God's message to others?

Reflecting

1. Read Romans 2:17–24.
   - A. What advantages does Paul list for his fellow Jews in verses 17–20? Do you recognize any of these advantages in your own life? Explain.
   - B. What challenge does Paul give in verses 21–23? Why does he give this challenge?
   - C. What warning does Paul issue in verse 24? How is this warning relevant to us today? What does it have to do with reflecting God?
2. Read 1 Corinthians 10:31.
   - A. How does someone drink to the glory of God?
   - B. How does someone eat to the glory of God?
   - C. How can doing everything to the glory of God change not only what you do, but how you do it?

Chapter Nine

My Message Is About Him

Beholding

1. Paul existed to deliver the message. How people remembered him was secondary. (Else why would he introduce himself as a slave?)
   - A. Why do you think Paul so often introduced himself as a slave? Whose slave was he?
   - B. Would you describe yourself as a slave? Explain.

2. I believe Satan trains battalions of demons to whisper one question in our ears: "What are people thinking of you?"
   - A. Why do we care so much what people might be thinking of us?
   - B. How can we train ourselves not to listen to Satan's battalions of demons?

3. God doesn't need you and me to do his work. We are expedient messengers, ambassadors by his kindness, not by our cleverness.
   - A. What does it mean to be an ambassador by his kindness?
   - B. What kind of an ambassador for God are you? Do most people know who you represent? And if so, what do they generally think of him?

Reflecting

1. Read Matthew 6:1–4.
   - A. What temptation do we often face when we do a kind thing for someone else, according to verse 1? What instruction does Jesus give us? What warning?
   - B. How do we sometimes announce our charitable acts with "trumpets" (vv. 2–4)? How does Jesus instruct us to proceed instead? What promise does he give for those who heed his words?
   - C. What do all of these verses have to do with God's glory and God's message?

2. Read 1 Corinthians 1:18–31.
   A. What groups does Paul contrast throughout this passage? Why does he build such a contrast?
   B. Why do any of us receive God's mercy and grace, according to verse 30?
   C. Who alone is fit to boast, according to verse 31? About what should these individuals boast? Why?

CHAPTER TEN

MY SALVATION IS ABOUT HIM

Beholding

1. The work of Christ is the bungee cord for the soul. Trust it and take the plunge.
   A. In what way is the work of Christ the bungee cord for the soul?
   B. How do you trust the work of Christ and take the plunge?
2. Legalism discounts God and in the process makes a mess out of us.
   A. How does legalism discount God?
   B. How does legalism make a mess out of us?
3. Your salvation showcases God's mercy. It makes nothing of your effort but everything of his.
   A. How does your salvation make "nothing" of your effort? How does it make "everything" of God's effort?
   B. How do some of us try to add other things to the work of Christ?

Reflecting

1. Read Isaiah 48:10–11.
    - A. How does God describe his care of his people in verse 10? Can you identify with this? Explain.
    - B. What reason does God give in verse 11 for his actions? Why does he go to such great lengths to purify a people for his own?
2. Read Philippians 3:7–11.
    - A. How much did Paul lose because of his connection to Christ (v. 8)? How did he feel about this loss?
    - B. How does Paul describe his righteousness in verse 9? Where does this new standing come from?
    - C. How does Paul describe his greatest hope in verses 10–11? Does this describe your own greatest hope? Explain.

CHAPTER ELEVEN

MY BODY IS ABOUT HIM

Beholding

1. The me-centered phrase "as long as no one gets hurt" sounds noble, but the truth is, we don't know who gets hurt.
    - A. Why is the phrase "as long as no one gets hurt" described as "me-centered"?
    - B. Why don't we know who gets hurt?
2. Casual sex is a diet of chocolate—it tastes good for a while, but

the imbalance can ruin you. Sex apart from God's plan wounds the soul.

   A. How can casual sex ruin a person? What "imbalance" is meant here?
   B. Why does sex apart from God's plan wound the soul?

3. Manage God's house in such a way that passersby stop and notice. "Who lives in that house?" they will ask. And when they hear the answer, God will be honored.
   A. When was the last time anyone asked you the equivalent of "Who lives in your house"? Explain.
   B. How is God honored when we are asked such a question?

Reflecting

1. Read 1 Corinthians 6:12–13.
   A. What guideline does Paul use to manage his freedom in Christ (v. 12)?
   B. How does verse 13 point to a future event that ought to shape how we live today?
   C. For what is the body meant, according to verse 13? What does this mean?
   D. How can you honor God with your own body?
2. Read Romans 6:12–14.
   A. How can you refuse to "let" sin reign in your body?
   B. How do we sometimes offer the parts of our body to sin?

C. In what way can sin become our master? How can we depend on God's grace to make sure this doesn't happen?

CHAPTER TWELVE

MY STRUGGLES ARE ABOUT HIM

Beholding

1. Can't the Maker of heaven and earth handle bad traffic and prevent bad marriages? Of course he can. Then why doesn't he?
   A. Describe the last time you wondered why God didn't intervene to stop some sad event. What answer did you come up with?
   B. How would you answer someone who asked the question above?
2. Don't blame suffering in the world on the anger of God. He's not mad; he didn't mess up. Follow our troubles to their headwaters, and you won't find an angry or befuddled God. But you will find a sovereign God.
   A. What does it mean to you that God is sovereign?
   B. If God is sovereign, then why shouldn't we blame him for the suffering in the world?
3. Rather than begrudge your problem, explore it. Ponder it. And most of all, use it. Use it to the glory of God.
   A. What does it mean to explore your problem rather than begrudge it?

B. What problem do you have right now that you could use to the glory of God? How could it be so used?

Reflecting

1. Read John 9:1–38.
   A. How is the question asked in verse 2 very much like some questions still asked today?
   B. How does Jesus answer the question? In what way must his answer have greatly surprised the crowd?
   C. How does the man respond to Jesus (v. 38)? In what way did this glorify God?
2. Read John 11:1–45.
   A. How does Jesus respond to the message about Lazarus (vv. 4–6)? Why does he respond like this?
   B. Did Mary and Martha understand Jesus' words in verse 23? How about in verses 38–40?
   C. In what way is the crowd's question in verse 37 still being asked today about all kinds of tragedies?
   D. How did Jesus' disciples, friends, and others see God's glory, as Jesus promised in verses 4 and 40?
   E. What was the result of seeing God's glory (v. 45)?

CHAPTER THIRTEEN

MY SUCCESS IS ABOUT HIM

Be[illegible]g

1. [illegible]en foreigners saw the fruitful farms of the Promised Land, [illegible]d did not want them to think about the farmer but the [illegible]mer's Maker. Their success advertised God.
   A. Does your own success advertise God? Explain.
   B. Who in your acquaintance best advertises God? How does he or she do this?

They failed at success. They forgot both the source and purpose of their success.
   A. How is it possible to fail at success? Have you ever done so? Explain.
   B. How do you remind yourself of the source and purpose of your success?

3. Why are you good at what you do? For God's sake. Your success is not about what you do. It's all about him—his present and future glory.
   A. What are you good at? How do you use what you're good at for God's sake?
   B. How does what you do advertise God's glory? How can it advertise God's future glory?

Reflecting

1. Read Deuteronomy 8:6–18.
   - A. How did God instruct his people to respond to th
     fortune (v. 10)? Is this still a good idea? Why?
   - B. What warning did God give his people (vv. 11–14)
     it still apply today? Why or why not?
   - C. What forecast does God give in verse 17? Why does
     give it?
2. Read Psalm 44:1–3.
   - A. What does the psalmist remember in the first two verses? Why is it important to remember such things?
   - B. What lesson does the psalmist teach in verse 3? Why is this lesson always important to keep in mind?
   - C. Why did God give his people victory, according to verse 3? Can this same truth give us victory today? Explain.

CHAPTER FOURTEEN

UPWARD THINKING

Beholding

1. The girl dishonored the name of her father, not with vulgar language, but with insensitive living. Keep this up and the whole building will be second-guessing the CEO.
   - A. How does insensitive living on the part of God's children cause people to second-guess God?

   B. What issues of insensitive living do you struggle with the most? How can you best deal with these issues?

2. May God rescue us from self-centered thinking. May we have no higher goal than to see someone think more highly of our Father, our King.

   A. In what areas of life is it easiest for you to slip into self-centered thinking?

   B. What practical steps can you take today to help others think more highly of your God than they do of you?

Reflecting

1. Read Exodus 20:7.

   A. How have you normally interpreted this commandment?

   B. Why is God so concerned with the use of his name?

2. Read Matthew 25:14–23.

   A. Why is it important to know that the master was gone "a long time" (v. 19)?

   B. How does the master respond to the first two servants (vv. 20–23)?

   C. How can you be like either of the first two servants? Do you expect one day to hear words similar to those they heard? Explain.

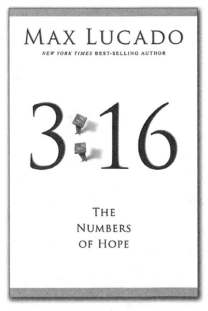

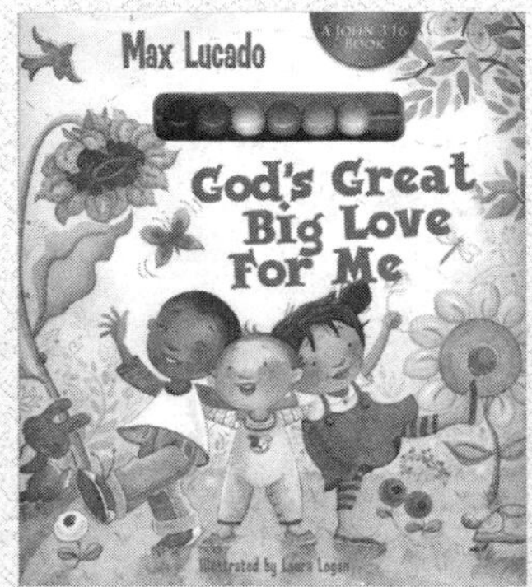

God's Great Big Love for Me

With colored beads built right in, this board book is the perfect book to teach the verse and meaning behind John 3:16 to preschool children.

Available February 2008

3:16 – The Numbers of Hope Teen Edition

Max offers his unique and simple storytelling for this important message while Tricia Goyer writes teen responses to Max's message, guiding teens to fully understand how this verse can impact their lives. From confession to praise, these responses are sure to bring an insightful look into the personal faith of teens.

Available February 2008

A DVD for Small Group Study

This is a kit designed and priced specifically for small groups. It will include a copy of the study guide for small groups, an evangelism booklet, the Indelible DVD, and a CD-ROM with facilitator's guide information and promotional material.

3:16 Songs of Hope CD

Featuring songs and artists inspired by the book *3:16*. The two disc set will also include DVD-Rom featuring digital Bible study material.

3:16 Stories of Hope DVD

This DVD product will feature 12 compelling moments of hope with Max Lucado. It will include a short, evangelistic film conveying through drama and metaphor the 3:16 promise. It will also provide musical elements and interviews with artists.

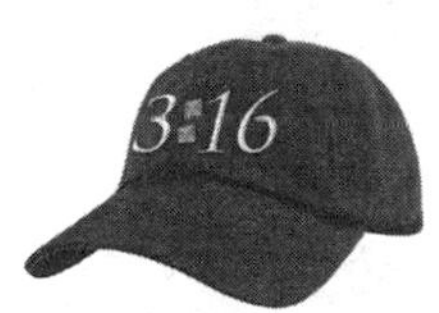

Share the message of *3:16* with t-shirts and ball caps.

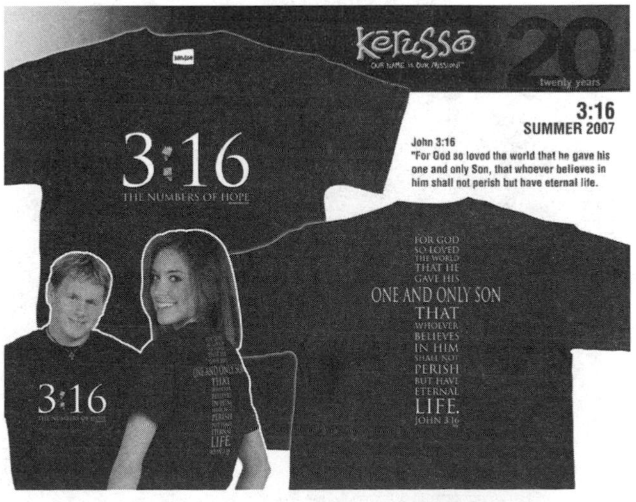

A complementary jewelry line will be available from Bob Siemon Designs.

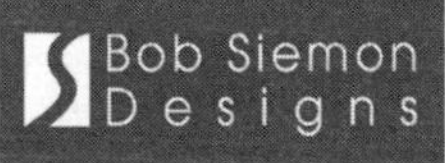